Frommer's

# AMERICA'S
## BEST - LOVED
# DRIVING
# TOURS

Simon & Schuster Macmillan

Written by Eric Inglefield

Revised second edition 1995, published in this format 1997
First published January 1991
Reprinted December 1997

Edited, designed and produced by AA Publishing.

Published by AA Publishing

Published in the United States by Macmillan Travel
A Simon & Schuster Macmillan Company
1633 Broadway, New York, NY 10019

Macmillan is a registered trademark of Macmillan, Inc

ISBN 0-02861568-9

Cataloging-in-Publication Data is available from the Library of
Congress.

Color separation: Daylight Colour Art,
Singapore

Printed and bound by G. Canale. & C. S.P.A.,
Torino, Italy

Opposite: *Statue of Liberty, New York*

# CONTENTS

# ABOUT THIS BOOK

This book is not only a practical touring guide for the independent traveler, but is also invaluable for those who would like to know more about the country.

It is divided into 10 regions, each containing between 2 and 5 tours which start and finish in major cities considered to be the best centers for exploration.

Each tour has details of the most interesting places to visit en route, some of which may be open only in summer. Panels catering for special interests follow some of the main entries – for those whose interest is in history, wildlife or walking, and those who have children. There are also panels which highlight scenic stretches of road and which give details of special events, crafts and customs.

The simple route directions are accompanied by an easy-to-use tour map at the beginning of each tour, along with a chart showing how far it is from one town to the next in miles and kilometers. This can help you to decide where to take a break and stop overnight, for example. (All distances quoted are approximate.)

Before setting off it is advisable to check with the information center at the start of the tour for recommendations on where to break your journey and for additional information on what to see and do, and when best to visit.

For detailed information on motoring, camping and caravanning in the USA see pages 158–65.

## PRACTICAL INFORMATION FOR VISITORS
### Banks
Banks are open from 9am to 3pm Monday to Friday and closed on weekends and public holidays (except at international airports), although in some major towns and tourist areas hours may be longer.

### Camping and Caravanning
For information on camping and caravanning see pages 159–65.

### Credit Cards
All the major credit cards are widely used and accepted, and one is essential when renting a car.

### Currency
The American monetary unit is the dollar ($), which is divided into 100 cents (¢). Coins are issued in cent denominations of 1 (penny), 5 (nickel), 10 (dime), 25 (quarter), 50 (half-dollar) and 1 dollar. Notes (bills) are issued in denominations of 1, 2, 5, 10, 20, 50 and 100 dollars. All bills are the same size and color. The amount of the bill is clearly shown in all corners and each bill has its own US statesman pictured in the center. Always carry US dollar travelers' checks since they can be used as cash.

### Customs Regulations
Customs regulations are currently under review so check before departure. They stand as follows: adults may bring into the US, duty free, any items meant for personal use, including cameras and tape recorders, up to one liter of alcohol, 200 cigarettes, 100 cigars or 3lb (1.4kg) of tobacco, or proportionate amounts of each. There is no limit on the amount of money, US or otherwise, brought into the country, although you must file a report with Customs if the amount exceeds $10,000. Drugs (other than prescribed) are banned, and fresh meat, fruit, vegetables and plants are either prohibited from entering the US, or restricted.

### Electricity
The standard electricity supply in the US is 110 volts (60 cycles). You may have to bring an adaptor to convert. Sockets take plugs with two flat pins.

### Emergency Telephone Numbers
There is no nationwide emergency system in the US. There are emergency numbers you can call, sometimes indicated on pay phones, but they vary from place to place. There is one all-America helpline: 1–800–336–HELP. The best thing to do is call the operator by dialing '0' to connect you.

### Entry Regulations
British visitors (and visitors from EU countries) need to hold a valid passport (not the visitors' kind) but in most cases do not now require a visa, providing they are staying in the US for less than 90 days, are holding a return or onward ticket, and are traveling with a carrier who has agreed to participate in the no-visa program. To ensure you will not be turned back at the port of entry, confirm with your airline prior to departure that no visa is required. However, rules at city gateways vary about transit stops and visitors may not be able to re-enter the US after a visit outside the country without a visa.

Other nationals (except for Canadians and Mexicans) will require a valid passport and visa.

### Health Matters
Health care in the US is of a very high standard but it is also very expensive. International visitors

should be covered by adequate health insurance before they set out and, if they are on prescribed medicines, should take a sufficient amount with them plus the actual prescription.

## Motoring

For information on all aspects of motoring in the USA, including accidents, breakdowns and speed limits, see pages 158–9.

## Post Offices

Some main post offices stay open 24 hours a day, but they usually open between 8am and 6pm Monday to Friday and 8am to noon Saturdays. Stamps are available from drug stores, hotels, motels and transport terminals.

## Public Holidays

1 January – New Year's Day
3rd Monday in January – Martin Luther King Day
3rd Monday in February – Washington's Birthday
March/April – Easter
last Monday in May – Memorial Day
4 July – Independence Day

1st Monday in September – Labor Day
2nd Monday in October – Columbus Day
11 November – Veterans' Day
4th Thursday in November – Thanksgiving
25 December – Christmas Day
You may encounter regional holidays not listed such as Lincoln's Birthday (12 February) and Election Day (November – Tuesday after 1st Monday). Traditional Day (30 May) is still observed by some states.

## Route Directions

Throughout this book the following abbreviations are used for US roads:
I – Interstate Highway
US – US Highway
SR – State Route.

## Telephones

Exact change in 5, 10 or 25 cent pieces is required to place a call. Phone cards are increasingly being used.

In the case of an emergency dial '0' for the operator if there is no obvious emergency number. To make a call, lift the receiver,

listen for a tone, then deposit coin or card. If you want to make a reverse-charge call, dial the operator and ask for a 'collect' call, in which case your initial coin (25 cents) is refunded.

Country codes for international calls:
Australia 61;
Canada 1;
Ireland 353;
New Zealand 64;
UK 44.

## Time

The US has four major time zones. Eastern Standard Time is three hours ahead of Pacific Standard Time, two hours ahead of Mountain Time and one hour ahead of Central Time. In April clocks are put forward one hour to take advantage of extra daylight, and they are put back again in late October.

Eastern Standard Time is five hours behind Greenwich Mean Time (GMT), 17 hours behind Sydney and 19 hours behind New Zealand for most of the year.

Tenaya Lake, Yosemite National Park, in California

# NEW ENGLAND & THE EMPIRE STATE

White clapboard churches with sharp-pointed spires, ripe yellow pumpkins piled against a red-painted barn, forested hillsides ablaze with fall foliage, quaint old whaling ports bobbing with sailboats – the old, time-worn images of beautiful New England are still valid. Despite the ubiquitous automobile and tourist bus, the rural charm of this part of America – Maine, New Hampshire, Vermont, Massachusetts, Connecticut and Rhode Island – and of neighboring New York State has so far survived.

A third of the 30 million people who live in this Northeast region are concentrated in Boston and New York City. The land dips into the Atlantic Ocean along a deeply indented shoreline of rocky inlets, sandy bays, craggy headlands and offshore islands, with the long arm of Cape Cod jutting into the sea from Massachusetts' South Shore. Inland, the forest-clad ranges of the Appalachians – the Catskills, White Mountains, Green Mountains, and Berkshires among them – form the region's rugged backbone.

The Northeast's stony soil is not easy to cultivate, nor is it fertile, so farming is accompanied by forestry and fishing. Industry developed early along the region's coastal belt, where Boston, New York and other cities emerged as the power-houses of economic activity. Although the cities are major centers of tourism, visitors also flock to such regional attractions as Niagara Falls, the Adirondacks, Newport, Cape Cod and the fall foliage display.

The first overseas visitors – the Vikings – appeared along the coast in the 10th century AD. Others followed later – Cabot in the 1490s, da Verrazano in 1524 and Hudson in 1609. An English settlement was eventually established in 1620, when the Pilgrim Fathers landed at Plymouth, Massachusetts. Less than 50 years later, the English ousted the Dutch from their colony of New Netherland, which included the Connecticut and Hudson valleys. A prize capture was the settlement of New Amsterdam on Manhattan Island, which the Dutch had acquired from local Indians for just a few trinkets in 1626. The English renamed it New York. A century later, Boston became a hotbed of protest in the dispute with Britain over trade and taxation, which finally led to revolution and independence.

The Romanesque-style Trinity Church (1877) in Boston

## Boston

The events and personalities of the Revolutionary War still figure prominently in the consciousness of this historic port city, founded in 1630. If you follow the marked 1½-mile (2.5km) Freedom Trail on foot, you will find, tucked away among the modern glass skyscrapers, many of the historic buildings and sites associated with them.

Boston is New England's largest city and a major business center. Known as the 'Athens of America', it is a very civilized city, with fine shops, restaurants, entertainment and nightlife, a lively performing arts scene, and museums – like the renowned Museum of Fine Arts – with its international reputation. Boston is essentially a walking city and suffers from frequent traffic congestion. But there is a good subway system.

Observation decks in the Prudential Tower and John Hancock Tower offer spectacular views of the city and harbor and, across the Charles River, the neighboring city of Cambridge, home of prestigious Harvard University and the Massachusetts Institute of Technology (MIT).

## New York

Many of the immigrants who came to America around the turn of the century sailed into New York's great harbor past the Statue of Liberty. She now gazes across the water at one of the most spectacular skylines in the world, the skyscrapers of Manhattan Island.

From the rooftop observation decks of the 110-story World Trade Center and the old Empire State Building, there are stunning panoramas of this 12½-mile (20km) finger of land lying between the Hudson and East rivers. Manhattan is one of the five boroughs – together with the Bronx, Queens, Brooklyn and Staten Island – that make up this magnetic city, a pulsating maelstrom of people and traffic. Here are the shops of Fifth Avenue, the theaters of Broadway, the bright lights of Times Square, elegant hotels and restaurants, world-famous museums, and the green space of Central Park. Here, too, are the colorful neighborhoods of Greenwich Village, SoHo, Chinatown and Little Italy, streets of brownstone houses, architectural gems side by side with demoralizing slums.

New York's Chrysler Building, pinnacle of success

# New England's
## Heritage

This tour takes you back through nearly four centuries of American history to the landing of the first Pilgrims. On the way you will see the first battlegrounds of the Revolutionary War, a rural village as it was in the 1800s, an old whaling port straight out of *Moby Dick*, and the opulent summer mansions of America's super-rich. You will also experience the cultural and historic heritage of cities like Worcester and Providence, taste the unique tangy flavor of Cape Cod and enjoy a kaleidoscope of changing scenery.

**3 DAYS • 324 MILES • 519KM**

| ITINERARY | | |
|---|---|---|
| **BOSTON** | ▶ | **Lexington (14m-22km)** |
| LEXINGTON | ▶ | **Concord (7m-11km)** |
| CONCORD | ▶ | **Worcester (33m-53km)** |
| WORCESTER | ▶ | **Sturbridge (18m-29km)** |
| STURBRIDGE | ▶ | **Providence (49m-78km)** |
| PROVIDENCE | ▶ | **Newport (30m-49km)** |
| NEWPORT | ▶ | **New Bedford (31m-50km)** |
| NEW BEDFORD | ▶ | **Hyannis (69m-110km)** |
| HYANNIS | ▶ | **Plymouth (33m-53km)** |
| PLYMOUTH | ▶ | **Boston (40m-64km)** |

Henry Kitson's statue of Captain John Parker, the Minute Man statue, stands on Lexington Green

[i] 147 Tremont Street, Boston

▶ *From downtown Boston follow Storrow Drive along the Charles River and pick up* **SR 2** *northbound for about 10 miles (16km) through Cambridge. Turn north on to* **SR 4/225** *for another 4 miles (6km) to Lexington.*

**❶Lexington,** Massachusetts
In this small village just outside Boston, America's Revolutionary War against Britain began on April 19, 1775. The first clash took place on Lexington's grassy common, now called Battle Green, when someone – no one knows who – fired the first shot in a confrontation between local militiamen, or Minute Men, and British Redcoats.

You can watch a dramatic re-enactment of the battle if you visit Lexington in mid-April. In any case, make your way to the Visitor Center by the Green for information and then take a walk to see the Minute Man Statue and other memorials on the Green, the Buckman Tavern, the Monroe Tavern, Hancock-Clarke House and other historic buildings in the surrounding area.

[i] 1875 Massachusetts Avenue, Lexington Green

▶ *Drive along* **SR 2A** *(the Battle Road) for 7 miles (11km) to Concord.*

**❷ Concord,** Massachusetts
The Battle Road was the route used by the British to march to Concord. It is now part of the Minute Man National Historical Park, which also includes the site of the second clash on that fateful day. This occurred in Concord when 'the shot heard round the world' was fired on 19 April 1775, at the Old North Bridge over the Concord River. It is a moving experience to walk down the quiet, tree-lined path to the reconstructed bridge and the Minute Man Monument that now commemorates the battle.

---

**BACK TO NATURE**

Nature is at its most spectacular in this region in early October, when the forested landscapes are ablaze with the reds, browns and yellows of the fall foliage. A favorite place for bird-watchers is the Great Meadows National Wildlife Refuge near Concord, while seabirds and shorebirds of all kinds can be seen anywhere along the coastal sections of the itinerary.

---

Concord also has other memories. Around the downtown area are the homes of such well-known writers as Louisa May Alcott, Ralph Waldo Emerson and Nathaniel Hawthorne, which you can visit. On the way out of town there is the tranquil beauty of Walden Pond, where Henry David Thoreau built his solitary cabin.

[i] Visitors Kiosk, Heywood Street

▶ *From Concord follow* **SR 126** *(Concord Road) south for about 8 miles (13km) to Wayland. Turn west on to* **US 20** *and continue for 18 miles (29km) to Shrewsbury, then 7 miles (11km) on* **SR 9** *to Worcester.*

Sturbridge town center, a pleasant place to wander

which Providence guards with pride, is the historic district centered on Benefit Street, the city's 'Mile of History'. Among the old buildings that line the streets here, there really is a house where George Washington once slept – the Stephen Hopkins House. Wander around and enjoy the atmosphere, then walk down to South Main Street for a browse among the boutiques and galleries that are now bringing life back to old waterfront buildings. And finally, hop into your car for a drive up Federal Hill to explore the evocative neighborhood of Little Italy.

*i* *30 Exchange Terrace*

▶ *For the 30-mile (48km) drive from Providence to Newport take I–95 south to Exit 9, SR 4 south to Allenton, and SR 138 over the Verrazano and Newport bridges across Narragansett Bay.*

**❸ Worcester,** Massachusetts
Worcester is New England's second largest city, a major industrial and commercial center with strong educational and cultural traditions. The city is known for its fine museums, the pick of which are the Worcester Art Museum, whose exhibits include pre-Columbian, Asiatic and ancient Greek and Roman art, and the Higgins Armory Museum, with outstanding collections of historic weapons and armor. For an evening out, there are the old Victorian-style Mechanics Hall, an arena for concerts, and The Centrum.

*i* *33 Waldo Street*

▶ *Leave downtown Worcester via I–290 southbound and after about 6 miles (10km) pick up I–90 (Massachusetts Pike: toll) westbound for another 12 miles (19km) to Sturbridge.*

**❹ Sturbridge,** Massachusetts
If you would like to see what life was like in rural New England in the early 1800s, a tour of Old Sturbridge Village, in Sturbridge, will turn back the clock for you. Here an entire village community of the 1830s has been re-created in a 200-acre (80-hectare) area, with restored houses, craft workshops, meeting houses, a working farm,

gardens and woodlands. First go to the Visitor Center, then wander around and watch costumed performers demonstrating everyday tasks of the time. Be sure to see the Freeman Farm and to sample the New England fare served at the Bullard Tavern before you leave. And don't forget to see Sturbridge itself. In addition to the old Publick House and restaurant, there are two fascinating museums, one displaying cars, the other one dolls.

*i* *Old Sturbridge Village, 1 Old Sturbridge Village Road*

▶ *Take US 20 east for 16 miles (25km) through Auburn, then turn south on to SR 146 for the 33-mile (53km) drive along the Blackstone River valley to Providence.*

**❺ Providence,** Rhode Island
Little Rhody's busy modern capital has come a long way since it was founded by religious dissenters in 1636 and named in gratitude for 'God's merciful Providence'. But its downtown area is still small enough to explore on foot – and there is plenty to see. Apart from the majestic State Capitol and City Hall, you will admire, as you wander along the streets, the old Union Station building and the Greek-style Arcade shopping center.
But its greatest treasure,

**❻ Newport,** Rhode Island
When you catch your first glimpse of the bustling activity in the harbor at Newport, you will find it hard to imagine that the 'East Coast's Yachting Capital' dates back to 1639. When you have had your fill of state-of-the-art boutiques on the waterfront and enjoyed a one-hour cruise around the harbor, take a stroll through the charming back streets. Buildings dating from the Colonial era still stand here, like the famed Hunter House and the White Horse Tavern. But stealing the limelight in Newport are the extravagantly opulent mansions which the super-rich of the last century – the Vanderbilts, the Astors and others – built around the town as their summer 'cottages'. You will see most of them if you drive down Bellevue Avenue, but if you have time to visit only one, make it The Breakers, Cornelius Vanderbilt's Renaissance-style palace of 1895, or Hammersmith Farm, Jacqueline Kennedy's 1887 family home.

*i* 10 Americas Cup Avenue

## RECOMMENDED WALK

Although it can be a little dangerous in places, the 3½-mile (6km) Cliff Walk at Newport, Rhode Island, is one of the finest trails on this tour. It follows the rugged east shoreline between Memorial Boulevard and Bailey's Beach and offers fine views of the sea and glimpses of Newport's great mansions along the way.

## SCENIC ROUTES

If you can't manage the Cliff Walk around Newport's rugged peninsula, stay in your car and follow the 9½-mile (15km) Ocean Drive for an even more spectacular trip with ocean views and a sight of those great mansions.
For a scenic drive back to Boston, take the alternative route via SR 3A along Massachusetts' South Shore through picturesque historic towns like Duxbury and Scituate.

▶ *From Newport take SR 114 and SR 24 north for 19 miles (30km) to Fall River, then I–195 east for 12 miles (19km) to New Bedford.*

### 7 New Bedford,
Massachusetts

Now the home port for a large fishing fleet, New Bedford has a long seafaring history that goes back to its days as a whaling port. Here you can follow in the footsteps of Herman Melville, author of the whaling saga *Moby Dick*, as you walk down the gaslit cobblestone streets of Johnny Cake Hill to join in the excitement of the morning fish auction on the old waterfront. The Seamen's Bethel, with its pulpit like a ship's prow, is where Melville once worshiped, and, across the street, the marvelous Whaling Museum has a half-size replica of the kind of whaler he once knew. Walk on through the town and you will find other places of interest, including the wonderful Glass Museum housed in a Federal-style mansion on North Second Street dating from 1821.

*i* 70 North Second Street

▶ *Continue east from New Bedford on I–195 for 16 miles (26km) to Exit 22. Then follow SR 25 east for 9 miles (14km) over the Cape Cod Canal to Bourne and Cape Cod. For the 50-mile (80km) tour of Cape Cod follow SR 28 south to Falmouth and Woods Hole, then east through Mashpee to Hyannis. Return from Hyannis on SR 132 and US 6 to Sandwich.*

### 8 Hyannis and Cape Cod,
Massachusetts

Once you cross the Bourne Bridge into Cape Cod, you are in a year-round vacation playground that provides for every 20th-century need, and in summer it is very crowded. With its long sandy beaches, oceans of sea grass, wildlife preserves, fishing villages, yacht harbors, seafood restaurants and many other attractions, you can make it as busy or as quiet as you wish. This itinerary covers only the Upper Cape as far as Hyannis. Amid the rampant commercialism, especially on Highway 28, there are sightseeing attractions you should not miss.

Near Highway 28 are the replica Aptuxcet Trading Post at Bourne; the historic houses and Historical Society Museum around Falmouth's Village Green; the aquarium at the ferry port of Woods Hole; and the sea views from Nobska Point. At Mashpee you will see the Old Indian Meeting House of 1684 and the burial ground. And at the popular yachting port of Hyannis, the home of the Kennedy family, there is a one-hour harbor cruise to view the Kennedy compound from the sea and, in town, the John F Kennedy Museum and Memorial, which are popular places of pilgrimage. On the

## FOR CHILDREN

Cape Cod has many attractions of special interest to children. Sandwich, for example, has the Yesteryears Doll and Miniature Museum, with its collection of antique dolls and miniature shops and houses, and the Thornton W Burgess Museum, containing mementos of the children's author best known for his *Peter Rabbit* and *Briar Patch* stories.

One of the many fine old houses that abound in the historic town of Newport

return journey along US 6, make a stop at Sandwich, the Cape's oldest town. It has many attractions, especially the Glass Museum and the lovely gardens at the fascinating Heritage Plantation, which portrays aspects of early American life.

▶ *Cross the Sagamore Bridge from Sandwich for the 17-mile (27km) drive along SR 3 to Plymouth.*

**❷ Plymouth,** Massachusetts
One of the best-known stories in American history tells of the storm-tossed voyage of the Protestant Pilgrims across the Atlantic Ocean on the *Mayflower* in 1620 and of their survival in the New World with the help of local Indians.

If you turn off Highway 3 just south of Plymouth, you can roll back the centuries at a convincing re-creation of the Pilgrims' Plimoth Plantation, as it was in 1627, and a Wampanoag Indian campsite. If you speak to the costumed 'villagers' as they go about their typical chores, don't be surprised if you hear strange 17th-century English dialects.

You will have a similar experience when you drive down to Plymouth's harbor and board the full-size replica of the *Mayflower II* at the pier. As you leave, don't miss Plymouth Rock, the boulder on the nearby beach where the Pilgrims are said to have landed.

In the streets around the harbor area you will find other points of interest, including several 17th-century houses and a burial ground, and museums with exhibits related to the Pilgrims, especially Pilgrim Hall and Plymouth National Wax Museum. But don't leave town without visiting the unique Cranberry World Visitors Center on the waterfront, a fascinating museum dedicated to Massachusetts' foremost agricultural crop, cranberries.

☐ *130 Water Street*

---

### FOR HISTORY BUFFS

On a hill overlooking Plymouth, you will see an imposing 81-foot (25m) tribute to the Pilgrim settlers, the Forefathers' Monument. Built between 1859 and 1889, the solid granite structure was a prototype for the Statue of Liberty in New York City.

Just south of Boston take Exit 8 from I–93 into Quincy, the 'City of Presidents'. Here you can take guided tours of the birthplaces of John Adams, the second president, and his son John Quincy Adams, the sixth president, at 133 and 141 Franklin Street.

You can also visit the Adams family home and garden, now the Adams National Historic Site, at 135 Adams Street.

---

### SPECIAL TO...

Plymouth County, Massachusetts, offers two memorable adventures if you have time. From Plymouth you can take an exciting whale-watching cruise to the waters off Cape Cod.

---

▶ *From Plymouth continue north on SR 3 and I–93 for about 40 miles (64km) to Boston. Alternatively, take the longer shoreline route on SR 3A if you have time.*

The Mayflower Society House, where Ralph Waldo Emerson married Lydia Jackson in 1835

# The
# Majestic
## Hudson
## Valley

Ever since Henry Hudson explored it in 1609, the Hudson River Valley has been admired for its spectacular scenic beauty. As a major waterway it was keenly fought for in the Revolutionary War, and many historic sites commemorate the old battles. Scattered among the wooded hillsides are historic riverfront towns, mansions built by the rich and famous, old inns, orchards and meadows and vineyards producing fine wines. 'America's Rhine' cuts through a land rich in folklore, alive with festivals and craft fairs and brimming with opportunities for outdoor recreation.

**3/4 DAYS • 252 MILES • 403KM**

| ITINERARY | |
|---|---|
| **NEW YORK CITY** | ▶ **Yonkers (15m-24km)** |
| YONKERS | ▶ **Croton-on-Hudson (20m-32km)** |
| CROTON-ON-HUDSON | ▶ **Garrison (20m-32km)** |
| GARRISON | ▶ **Poughkeepsie (27m-43km)** |
| POUGHKEEPSIE | ▶ **Hyde Park (6m-10km)** |
| HYDE PARK | ▶ **Hudson (30m-48km)** |
| HUDSON | ▶ **Catskill (6m-10km)** |
| CATSKILL | ▶ **Kingston (35m-56km)** |
| KINGSTON | ▶ **Newburgh (31m-50km)** |
| NEWBURGH | ▶ **West Point (11m-18km)** |
| WEST POINT | ▶ **New York City (51m-82km)** |

☐ *2 Columbus Circle, Manhattan*

▶ *Leaving from West Side Manhattan follow the Henry Hudson Parkway (SR 9A) northbound for about 12 miles (19km) to Exit 23. Take US 9 (Broadway), still heading north, to Yonkers.*

### ❶ Yonkers, New York

You will barely have time to get settled in the car before you reach the first sightseeing attraction on the tour. It is Philipse Manor Hall, in Yonkers, now an art and history museum with fine paintings of US Presidents. 'Yonkers' comes from the Dutch word *jonkheer*, which means young nobility. Down the road, at Irvington, is Sunnyside, the pretty cottage of early 19th-century writer Washington Irving. At Tarrytown, further along Route 9, are Lyndhurst, an impressive 19th-century mansion in the flamboyant 'Hudson Gothic' style which was once the home of financier Jay Gould, and stone-built Philipsburg Manor, an 18th-century farm estate and trading center with a water-powered grist mill still working.

▶ *Continue north on US 9 for Croton-on-Hudson.*

### ❷ Croton-on-Hudson, New York

Van Cortlandt Manor, with its 20 acres (8 hectares) of period gardens, a tavern and other buildings, is a restored 18th-century Dutch-English manor, the home of Pierre Van Cortlandt, the first lieutenant governor of New York State.

Further along, at Peekskill, the extraordinary Dick's Hilltop Castle is the nearest thing you will ever see to a replica of Spain's Alhambra Palace, but it remains unfinished because former owner Evans Dick lost his fortune in the stock market crash of 1911.

▶ *Continue north on US 9, SR 403 and SR 9D to Garrison.*

### ❸ Garrison, New York

By this point on the tour you will be aware of the spectacular scenery, so if you want a panoramic view of the Hudson Valley, a good place to stop is Garrison, perched high above the river. You can enjoy marvelous views (and perhaps a summer concert) at the lovely gardens of luxurious Boscobel mansion before driving on to explore the antique shops of the nearby towns of Cold Spring and Nelsonville.

The Hudson River Valley, Peekskill, north of Croton-on-Hudson

▶ *Follow SR 9D for another 27 miles (43km) to Poughkeepsie.*

### ❹ Poughkeepsie, New York

The town of Poughkeepsie, among its other claims to fame, is the place where Smith's cough drops come from. It is also the location of Vassar, the top women's college, which you can visit.

The town has some fine old buildings, including Clinton House, which was the governor's home in 1777 when Poughkeepsie served briefly as state capital, and the 1853 Italian-style villa of Samuel F B Morse, who invented the telegraph. The house contains period furnishings, art, china and original telegraph equipment.

▶ *Continue driving north on US 9 for 6 miles (10km) to Hyde Park, then another 10 miles (16km) to Rhinebeck.*

### ❺ Hyde Park, New York

At Hyde Park, the best place to eat well is unquestionably one of the gourmet restaurants at the Culinary Institute of America, the training school for great chefs. People generally come here, however, to tour the riverfront home of President Franklin D Roosevelt, its library and museum, his wife Eleanor's private retreat, called Val-Kill, and the elegant Vanderbilt Mansion nearby. All are National Historic Sites.

If you are still in the mood for house-visiting as you drive away, stop at Staatsburg to tour the opulent Mills Mansion and State Park. Otherwise, drive on to Rhinebeck, where a unique experience awaits you at the Old Aerodrome – a weekend air show, with a mock aerial battle and rides in vintage planes. Take a walk around the lovely old town and don't miss the historic Beekman Arms Hotel.

▶ *Continue north through the orchard country along SR 9G for 25 miles (40km) to Hudson.*

### 6 Hudson, New York

Along the highway to Hudson are two more impressive historic mansions that are worth a stop: first Clermont, the Livingston family home at Germantown, then Olana, the 'Oriental Gothic' home of landscape painter Frederic Edwin Church, just south of Hudson. In Hudson, take a walking tour of the Warren Street Historic Restoration Area and see the old fire engines at the American Museum of Fire Fighting.

*i* 141 Union Street

---

### RECOMMENDED WALKS

If you are not worn out by touring all those mansions, gardens and historic sites, then visit the Hudson Valley's state parks, such as Hudson Highlands, near Beacon; Mills-Norrie, at Staatsburg; and Bear Mountain, where you can enjoy spectacular views from the Appalachian Trail on Bear Mountain Bridge. There are also pleasant nature trails in the woods at Montgomery Place, Annandale-on-Hudson.

---

▶ *Cross the Rip Van Winkle Bridge on SR 23 to Catskill.*

### 7 Catskill, New York

Catskill is a pleasant river town at the northern gateway to the scenic Catskill Mountains. When you have toured its marinas, antique shops and Court House, take a drive out of town for a delightful encounter with animals from around the world at the Catskill Game Farm, just 12 miles (19km) west, off SR 32.

▶ *Follow SR 32 south from Catskill Game Farm for about 13 miles (21km) to pick up the New York State Thruway (I–87) at southbound Entry 20 (Saugerties). Continue south for 10 miles (16km) and take Exit 19 for Kingston.*

---

### FOR CHILDREN

There is plenty for children to enjoy on this tour, but for a real bonanza of fun and excitement take them down Highway 32 west of Catskill. In addition to the Catskill Game Farm, adventures on offer here include the Wild West town of Carson City, Junior Speedway and the fascinating Reptile Institute.

---

### BACK TO NATURE

Slide Mountain (4,204 feet/1,281m) is the highest peak in the Catskill Mountains and one of the best for wildlife. The forested slopes – a mixture of conifers and hardwoods – harbor small mammals including white-tailed deer, squirrels, cottontail rabbits and raccoons. Birds include wild turkeys, ruffed grouse, pileated woodpeckers, yellow-bellied sapsuckers (a species of woodpecker), several species of thrushes and at least 12 species of warblers.

---

### 8 Kingston, New York

The old river port of Kingston was founded in 1652 as a Dutch trading settlement and became New York State's first capital in 1777. Many of its early buildings still survive, including the Old Dutch Church of 1659, the Senate House and the Ulster County Court House. Costumed guides will take you on a walking tour of the original stockade area.

On the historic waterfront you can ride an old trolley car, take a pleasant cruise to the lighthouse and learn about the town's heyday as a boat-building and river trade center at the Hudson River Maritime Center. For evening entertainment, you can choose a sailboat ride with food

Halloween preparations in the Catskill Mountains

and music, or perhaps take in a show at the historic Ulster Performing Arts Center, on Broadway.

*i* *7 Albany Avenue*

### FOR HISTORY BUFFS

Leave the New York State Thruway (I–87) from Kingston at Exit 18 to visit historic New Paltz, a French Huguenot settlement of 1678. Here you will see six of the original stone houses and a reconstructed church on Huguenot Street, one of the oldest streets in America and a National Historic Landmark (tours available).
Then drive west out of town to visit the historic Mohonk Mountain House resort, which has panoramic views of Lake Mohonk, the Shawangunk Mountains and the Hudson Valley.

▶ *Continue south on I–87 for 31 miles (50km) to Newburgh (Exit 17).*

West Point Military Academy's monument. Here, visitors can stroll in the footsteps of many famous Americans

TO THE AMERICAN SOLDIER

### ⑨ Newburgh, New York

Newburgh is another old river port with surviving 18th- and 19th-century buildings open to visitors in its downtown area. Among them is the Hasbrouck House of 1750, which was George Washington's headquarters in the final days of the Revolutionary War. The order to end the Revolutionary War was given by Washington from this site. Its adjoining museum contains exhibits relating the role of the Continental Army in the area.

South of town, in the Vails Gate area, you can tour the house used by General Knox and his staff and watch enactments of military life at that time at the New Windsor Cantonment, the final campsite of Washington's Continental Army when hostilities ended. Exhibits include a blacksmith shop and military demonstrations.

If you like modern art, drive south on SR 32 to the Storm King Art Center in Mountainville. This sculpture park and museum has a permanent collection of more than 130 sculptures by over 90 contemporary artists, and you can also enjoy marvelous views of the Hudson River.

*i* *72 Broadway*

### SPECIAL TO...

The Hudson Valley has more than 30 operating wineries that are open for tours and tastings, many of them concentrated south of Kingston on US 9W.
A popular stop for visitors on Route 94 southwest of town is the famous old Brotherhood Winery at Washingtonville.

▶ *Take US 9W and SR 218 south for a 23-mile (37km) drive that takes in West Point, Bear Mountain State Park and Stony Point.*

### ⑩ West Point, New York

The country between Newburgh and Stony Point encompasses some of the finest mountain and river scenery on the tour. At West Point you can admire superb river vistas from historic Fort Putnam and Trophy Point and watch the cadets parade in spring and fall at the US Military Academy.

A few miles south you will see the spectacular Bear Mountain Bridge, which carries the Appalachian Trail over the Hudson River into Bear Mountain State Park. In the park you will find many facilities for outdoor recreation (including swimming, boating and skating), the charming Bear Mountain Inn, a trailside museum, and a mountain-top observation tower offering spectacular views of the Hudson River below and even Manhattan on a clear day.

At Stony Point you can tour the battle site where General 'Mad Anthony' Wayne's army proved more than a match for the Redcoats in 1779. In mid-July you can see a rousing re-enactment of the fight.

*i* *Building 618, Thayer Gate (South Gate), US Military Academy, West Point (Academy only)*

▶ *Continue south on US 9W through Nyack and Tappan for 51 miles (82km) to the George Washington Bridge and Manhattan.*

### SCENIC ROUTES

Every bend on this itinerary seems to open up marvelous new views of the Hudson Valley's scenic splendor. But there are extra-special sections of highway, including the drives between Peekskill and Beacon and between Newburgh and Stony Point, and the side-trips on SR 32 to Mountainville and on the Perkins Memorial Drive up Bear Mountain.

# Around
## Long Island

If you need to wind down for a while after New York's frenetic pace, do what many New Yorkers do and take off for a change of scene amid the peace of Long Island. Leave behind the seething conurbation at the west end of the island and head east to sandy beaches, sheltered bays, rolling dunes, quaint fishing villages, farms, even a few windmills, and wildlife refuges, silent but for the breeze and the shrill call of seabirds. It is a place for enjoying outdoor activities, eating rich seafood, hunting for antiques and touring historic places, millionaires' estates, museums and wineries.

**3/4 DAYS • 292 MILES • 467KM**

| ITINERARY | |
|---|---|
| **NEW YORK CITY** | ▶ **Old Bethpage** (36m-58km) |
| OLD BETHPAGE | ▶ **Jones Beach** (16m-26km) |
| JONES BEACH | ▶ **Fire Island** (16m-26km) |
| FIRE ISLAND | ▶ **Westhampton** (38m-61km) |
| WESTHAMPTON | ▶ **Montauk** (43m-70km) |
| MONTAUK | ▶ **Sag Harbor** (22m-35km) |
| SAG HARBOR | ▶ **Greenport** (8m-13km) |
| GREENPORT | ▶ **Riverhead** (22m-35km) |
| RIVERHEAD | ▶ **Stony Brook** (29m-46km) |
| STONY BROOK | ▶ **Centerport** (19m-30km) |
| CENTERPORT | ▶ **New York City** (43m-69km) |

*i* *2 Columbus Circle, Manhattan*

▶ *Take the Midtown Tunnel from Manhattan under the East River and follow the Long Island Expressway (I–495) east for about 32 miles (51km). At **Exit 48** follow Round Swamp Road to Old Bethpage.*

**❶ Old Bethpage,** New York
Old Bethpage Village, one of Long Island's top visitor attractions, reminds you that this vacationer's paradise has a history. It is a re-created farm village of the pre-Civil War era, with buildings gathered here from other parts of the island, including a church, tavern and general store. The costumed 'villagers' will show you how to churn butter, bake bread, shear sheep and do many other everyday chores of bygone days.

▶ *From Old Bethpage take **SR 110** south for 6 miles (10km). Turn west on Sunrise Highway (**SR 27**) for 4 miles (6km), then south for 6 miles (10km) on Wantagh State Parkway (**SR 105**) to reach Jones Beach.*

**❷ Jones Beach,** New York
Thousands of sun worshippers flock to Jones Beach every summer to bake on the sparkling white sand that stretches for miles along this offshore barrier island.

The many recreational and entertainment facilities include an outdoor roller-skating rink, court games and a pitch-and-putt golf course. There are also nightly concerts in the Jones Beach Theatre in summer. If the scene here is too busy for you, try Gilgo or Captree Beach further east.

Long Island's Robert Moses Causeway

▶ *Follow Ocean Drive east along the island for 16 miles (26km) to Captree Beach for Fire Island.*

**❸ Fire Island,** New York
Drive across the sea inlet from Captree to Fire Island. You can go only as far as Robert Moses State Park, so if you want a closer look at this roadless wilderness island, a long slip of sand where pirates once buried their treasure, you will have to take a ferry from Sayville, Bay Shore or Patchogue, off SR 27. With its opportunities for walking, swimming, boating, wildlife-watching and other outdoor activities in unspoiled surroundings, this National Seashore island is a popular destination for New Yorkers.

*i* 120 Laurel Street, Patchogue

▶ Head north on the Robert
Moses Causeway and turn
right on to **SR 27**. Continue
east past Sayville and the
other ferry ports for Fire Island
through the five towns known
as 'The Hamptons'.

### FOR CHILDREN

If you wish to add to all the
exciting things for children on
this tour, take Exit 60 north
from SR 27 before you reach
The Hamptons and see
the animals and sealion
shows at Long Island Game
Farm and Zoological Park,
Manorville.

## 4 Westhampton and The Hamptons, New York

Westhampton, Hampton Bays,
Southampton, Bridgehampton
and East Hampton – The
Hamptons in the order in which
you reach them – have long been
a favorite haven for writers,
artists and other celebrities. With
their marvelous beaches, smart
boutiques and fine restaurants,
they are also a popular destination for summer visitors. Each
has its own individual attractions.

At Southampton, the Parrish
Art Museum has displays of
Renaissance and 19th-century
American art, while the old
Halsey Homestead is of interest
for its Colonial herb garden.
There are automobile and
motorcycle racing at
Bridgehampton; and the
boyhood home of theater man
John Howard Payne, composer
of *Home Sweet Home*, is at East
Hampton.

*i* 76 Main Street, Southampton

▶ Follow **SR 27** east along the
South Fork Peninsula east to
Montauk.

The sleepy waterside community
of Sag Harbor was once a busy
whaling port

## 5 Monktauk, New York

You will be tempted to visit the
Town Marine Museum at
Amagansett, with its exhibits of
shipwrecks and life on and
under the sea. But eventually
you will arrive at Montauk, a
popular deep-sea-fishing port
and whale-watching center lying
amid the rocky bluffs, woodlands and sand dunes at the end
of the peninsula. There is an
excellent golf course here, but
don't miss the 5-mile (8km)
drive to Montauk Point to enjoy
the sea views from the famous
lighthouse built here in 1795 by
order of George Washington.

▶ From Montauk return to East
Hampton on **SR 27**, then

follow **SR 114** north for 7
miles (11km) to Sag Harbor.

### SPECIAL TO...

Long Island's abundant opportunities for saltwater fishing –
whether surf casting, open
boat fishing or deep-sea
charter fishing – make it a
paradise for sports fishermen.
Montauk is a popular starting
point for the big-fish hunters.

## 6 Sag Harbor, New York

This little community, lying in a
sheltered bay on the north shore
of the South Fork, was a thriving
whaling port in the 19th century,

as you will discover if you visit its Whaling Museum. But its history goes back to 1707, and the town center has been declared a National Historic District. You will see the historic Custom House and the Fire Department Museum as you walk around.

▷ *Continue north on **SR 114** from Sag Harbor for the 8-mile (13km) journey to Greenport, on the North Fork which includes two ferry crossings and a drive across Shelter Island.*

**7 Greenport,** New York
There is plenty to see and do at Greenport, a lively, bustling old seaside town and fishing port which harvests especially good oysters. A well-known attraction is the Museum of Childhood, a special delight for children with its collection of antique dolls and other toys.

At Cutchogue, southwest on SR 25, you can tour one of the area's many wineries and see the historic buildings on the village green.

▷ *From Cutchogue follow **SR 25** west along the North Fork to Riverhead.*

---

### FOR CHILDREN

Children might be interested, too, in the armored vehicles and artillery displayed at the American Armored Foundation Inc Tank Museum, at Mattituck on the North Fork.

---

**8 Riverhead,** New York
Riverhead is known for its potatoes, annual Polish Street Fair and Festival, and Suffolk County Historical Museum, which has whaling and local Indian exhibits in its collections. Strawberries, peaches and cauliflowers are also a major industry. Legend has it that Captain Kidd landed on this part of the island to bury his treasure here.

▷ *From Riverhead continue west on **SR 25**, then take **SR 25A** for 29 miles (46km) to Stony Brook.*

**9 Stony Brook,** New York
Past Port Jefferson, stop to see the 18th-century Thompson House in Setauket and the restored historic buildings and museum complex along Stony Brook's Main Street. Here you will enjoy the varied collections of the Carriage Museum, Art Museum and History Museum and see several period structures, including a grist mill and blacksmith's shop. On the state university campus you might also catch a show at one of the five theaters in the Fine Arts Center.

▷ *Follow **SR 25A** west from Stony Brook for about 19 miles (30km) (including a short stretch on **SR 25** at The Branch) to Centerport and the Gold Coast.*

---

### FOR HISTORY BUFFS

A must-see along the itinerary involves a short detour off SR 25A between Centerport and Huntington. A few miles south along SR 110 you can see manuscripts, pictures, changing exhibits and other memorabilia of the poet Walt Whitman at his boyhood home at 246 Walt Whitman Road, Huntington Station, a farmhouse furnished in period (circa 1810).

---

**10 Centerport,** New York
At the turn of the century, anyone who was anyone had a luxurious mansion and estate on the fabled Gold Coast, Long Island's north shore. As you tour these houses today you can imagine the elegant lifestyle of their owners. Not to be missed is the estate of William K Vanderbilt, with its impressive planetarium and museum, at Centerport. More than 2,000 wildlife and marine specimens are on display in the mansion

rooms and the Marine Museum, and the planetarium features exhibits on astronomy and a sky theater with a 60-foot-diameter (18m) dome. Wonderful Sagamore Hill, Theodore Roosevelt's summer home is just outside Oyster Bay; and Old Westbury Gardens, the mansion and estate of John S Phipps, is further south near the Long Island Expressway. In the north shore towns you will stumble across many other places of

---

### SPECIAL TO...

If oysters are your pleasure, come to Oyster Bay in mid-October, when you can join in the orgy of eating, cooking demonstrations and shucking (shelling) contests at the Annual Oyster Festival.

---

interest. Huntington, for example, has superb art collections in its Heckscher Museum; Cold Spring Harbor boasts its excellent Whaling Museum; and in Oyster Bay there are fine botanical displays in the Planting Fields Arboretum, site of the Coe Mansion.

▶ *From Oyster Bay follow **SR 106** south), then take the Long Island Expressway heading west into Manhattan.*

The Vanderbilt family spent part of their fortune on this elaborate rural retreat near Centerport

### RECOMMENDED WALKS

Apart from the beaches, good places for stretching your legs and whetting your appetite are Long Island's many state parks. You will find pleasant trails in Heckscher State Park, near Bay Shore; Hither Hills State Park, near Montauk; and Sunken Meadow State Park, east of Centerport; not forgetting the nature trails on Fire Island.

### SCENIC ROUTES

Except for the spectacular Ocean Drive along the south shore from Jones Beach, the most scenically attractive highways are generally concentrated at the eastern end of Long Island.
Especially enjoyable are the drive through rolling hills, woodlands and dunes from The Hamptons to Montauk on SR 27; the island-hopping trip from Sag Harbor to Greenport on SR 114; and the stretch of SR 25 along the North Fork.

### BACK TO NATURE

Long Island is renowned as a location for observing bird migration, especially in the autumn. Robert Moses State Park on Fire Island is good for land birds. 'Falls' occur in September and October. The Montauk Peninsula is excellent for seabirds, with Montauk Point State Park also being a 'hotspot' for landbirds. Shorebirds can be found almost anywhere around the Long Island coast, but Orient Beach State Park (near Montauk) and Jones Beach State Park (near Jones Inlet) are especially good.

# THE MID-ATLANTIC STATES

George Washington Country roughly corresponds to the Mid-Atlantic region of America's east coast and encompasses the states of New Jersey, Pennsylvania, Maryland, Virginia and Delaware, with the District of Columbia. It is a region in which momentous events forged the birth and destiny of the nation. Its territory saw the founding of Swedish, Dutch and English colonies in the 1600s, the long struggle for independence from Britain in the Revolutionary War (1776–83) and the Civil War, which raged from 1861 to 1865. The epic story echoes with the names of the great – Thomas Jefferson, Benjamin Franklin, Abraham Lincoln and Robert E Lee to mention but a few – but it is the memory of George Washington (1732–99) that gives this part of America its historic identity.

Philadelphia's Liberty Bell, America's symbol of freedom

Today, nearly 34 million people live in this region, many of them in the industrial cities of Newark and Pittsburgh, historic Philadelphia and Richmond, the port of Baltimore, and Washington DC. Washington, Richmond and several other regional cities took root at the point where rivers, like the Potomac, plunge down falls or rapids at the head of navigation.

To the east of this fall line stretches the densely populated coastal plain, deeply indented by the river estuaries known as Delaware and Chesapeake bays. Beyond the farmlands the tidewater marshes are the home of large numbers of waterfowl and shorebirds, while the bays yield blue crabs, oysters and clams. Testimony to this coastline's diversity are the natural wilderness of New Jersey's Pine Barrens, the casinos and boardwalk of Atlantic City, the Colonial settlements and plantation homes along the James River, and the great naval base at Norfolk.

West of the fall line an irregular patchwork of fields, pastures, orchards and woodlands extends across the rolling country of the Piedmont region, scattered with historic towns such as York, Frederick, Alexandria and Fredericksburg. Further west lie the beautiful forested ridges of the Appalachian Mountains, nowhere lovelier than in Shenandoah National Park. These hills and valleys are the home of hardy mountain folk, mostly of Scots-Irish stock, whose lifestyle is colored by country music, yarn-telling, shooting matches and simple traditional crafts.

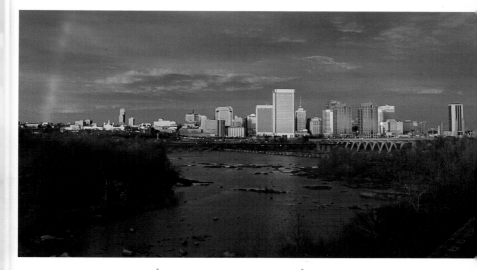

## Washington DC

With its tree-lined boulevards, imposing public buildings, cultural institutions, monuments and parklands, the nation's capital reflects the wish of its original designer, the French-born Pierre Charles L'Enfant, to create a city 'magnificent enough to grace a great nation'. Nearly 3½ million people now inhabit the metropolitan area, which occupies the 69-square-mile (179sq km) District of Columbia beside the Potomac River.

The city's focal point is the grassy expanse extending around the 555-foot (169m) Washington Monument to the Capitol Building, White House, Lincoln Memorial and Jefferson Memorial. Here are world-famous cultural institutions, such as the National Gallery of Art and several museums that form part of the Smithsonian Institution.

Near by, the downtown business district contains the Pavilion at the Old Post Office-Pavilion shopping center and historic Ford's Theater where President Abraham Lincoln was assassinated in 1865.

In the northwestern districts are the elegant shops of Connecticut Avenue, the for-eign missions along 'Embassy Row', and the lovely old town-houses, boutiques, restaurants and nightspots of historic Georgetown. And across the Potomac, Arlington Cemetery guards the last resting place of many great national figures.

## Philadelphia

The historic port city of Philadelphia, founded on the Delaware River in 1682 by the English Quaker William Penn, played a leading role in America's struggle for independence. Preserved in the heart of the city are some of the nation's most revered historic treasures, including Independence Hall, where the Declaration of Independence and the Constitution were agreed, and the hallowed Liberty Bell, protected inside a glass pavilion.

Near by are the historic riverfront area of Penn's Landing and the Old City district, containing Elfreth's Alley and the house of Betsy Ross, who reputedly sewed together the first Stars and Stripes. Several of the city's major cultural institutions, including the Philadelphia Museum of Art, the Rodin Museum, and the Franklin Institute Science Museum, line Benjamin

Sunset over Richmond, Virginia's state capital

Franklin Parkway on the way to magnificent Fairmount Park.

## Richmond

The City Hall skydeck, on Broad Street, affords striking views of Virginia's state capital, an old Colonial tobacco port laid out by the James River in 1737. Buildings and monuments reflecting nearly three centuries of history are scattered around its old streets. Among them are the State Capitol, designed by Thomas Jefferson in 1785, the Old Stone House of 1737, and St John's Church of 1741, where patriot Patrick Henry made his famous 'Give me liberty or give me death' speech. Echoes of the Civil War, when the city was the Confederate capital, remain at old St Paul's Church, the Museum and White House of the Confederacy, and Richmond National Battle-field Park. Fine 19th-century homes still grace the historic Fan district, Monument Avenue and Jackson Ward, while busy shops, restaurants and night spots brighten the old commercial Shockoe Slip district by the river.

# Shenandoah &
## Historic Virginia

War and peace are the themes of this tour. You can follow George Washington's footsteps in Fredericksburg and Alexandria and at his Mount Vernon estate. You can relive the pain and the glory of the Civil War at the battlefields of Manassas and Fredericksburg. And all around you is the breathtaking beauty of the Virginia countryside, nowhere more captivating than in the mountains of Shenandoah National Park.

**3/4 DAYS • 288 MILES • 461KM**

ITINERARY

| | | |
|---|---|---|
| **WASHINGTON DC** | ▶ | **Manassas** (30m-48km) |
| MANASSAS | ▶ | **Front Royal** (45m-72km) |
| FRONT ROYAL | ▶ | **Chancellorsville** |
| | | (148m-237km) |
| CHANCELLORSVILLE | ▶ | **Fredericksburg** |
| | | (8m-13km) |
| FREDERICKSBURG | ▶ | **Mount Vernon** |
| | | (41m-66km) |
| MOUNT VERNON | ▶ | **Alexandria** (9m-14km) |
| ALEXANDRIA | ▶ | **Washington DC** |
| | | (7m-11km) |

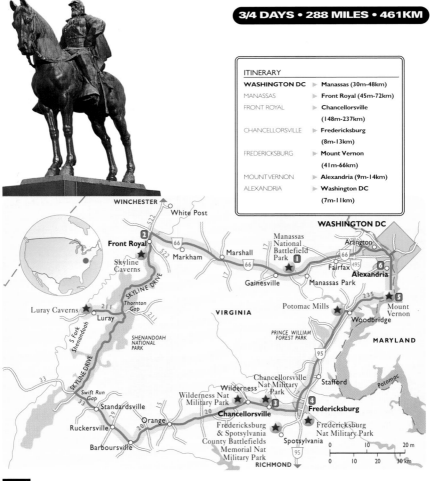

Above: the Shenandoah Valley
Opposite: monument to Ulysees S Grant, Manassas

ℹ️ *1455 Pennsylvania Avenue, Washington DC*

▶ *From downtown Washington DC cross the Potomac River to Arlington and drive 30 miles (48km) along I–66 to Manassas National Battlefield Park.*

## **❶ Manassas National Battlefield Park,** Virginia

Two major Civil War battles were fought along the creek known as Bull Run, in July 1861 and in August a year later. Both were Confederate victories. Start your tour of the site at the Visitor Center and see the audio-visual presentation explaining the battle maneuvers. Then take the 1½-hour driving tour of the main scenes of the fighting. Don't miss a walk up Henry Hill, a key position in both battles, where you will have a panoramic view of the whole battle area. It was here that Confederate General Thomas J Jackson's calm courage earned him the nickname 'Stonewall', and an equestrian statue now stands in his memory.

ℹ️ *Park Visitor Center on SR 234, between I–66 and US 29*

▶ *Continue west on I–66 for 45 miles (72km) to Front Royal and Shenandoah National Park.*

## **❷ Front Royal and Shenandoah,** Virginia

Just south of Front Royal is the start of the famed Skyline Drive, the scenic highway that meanders for 105 miles (169km) through Shenandoah National Park and along the forested crests of the Blue Ridge Mountains – a land the Indians poetically called 'Daughter of the Stars'. Unless you want to explore the underground sights of the Skyline Caverns at the start of the drive, go straight to the Dickey Ridge Visitor Center and arm yourself with useful maps and information about the park. Along the highway from here, you will find many overlooks that offer outstanding views of the legendary Shenandoah Valley to the west and the rolling hills to the east.

There are also many picnic spots, campsites and walking trails to let you enjoy the forest scenery and see the abundant wildlife. You can join guided hikes conducted to the main points of interest in the summer, or just take off on your own along the recommended trails. This is an invigorating place, so do get out of your car and enjoy

the tangy fresh air of the woods.

When you reach Thornton Gap, turn right on to US 211 for a 25-mile (40km) round trip to Luray Caverns, where you can marvel at the fantastic underground rock formations and listen to 'music' made on the famed 'stalactite organ'. While here, you can also take a look at the old vehicles exhibited at the Car and Carriage Caravan. Complete your drive along Skyline Drive at Swift Run Gap, exiting east on to US 33.

### FOR HISTORY BUFFS

In addition to the battlefields, another interesting source of information about the Civil War is the Warren Rifles Confederate Museum at Front Royal. Here you will see military uniforms, weapons, battle flags and various other relics of the conflict.
About 4 miles (6km) west of Orange on SR 20, look out for Montpelier, the stately mansion built by the father of America's fourth president, James Madison, between 1755 and 1765. You can tour the house and garden before going on to visit the James Madison Museum in Orange, which is dedicated to his memory.

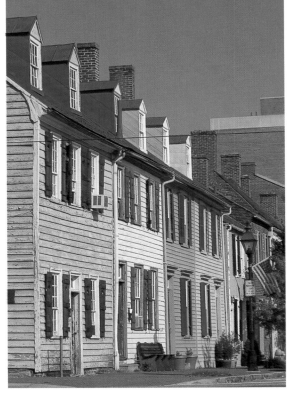

## FOR CHILDREN

If the children have had enough of the scenery, George Washington and the Civil War, you might arouse some enthusiasm with a tour of Dinosaur Land at White Post, just 9 miles (14km) north of Front Royal on US 522. Here they will see the monsters displayed realistically in a replica prehistoric forest.

## BACK TO NATURE

Highlight of the tour for nature lovers is Shenandoah National Park. Along the trails you might see black bear, deer, raccoon, skunk, gray fox, chipmunk and many other animals, and catch a glimpse of all kinds of birds, including ravens, hawks, turkey vultures and wild turkeys. Wildflowers abound in the meadows in spring, but later in the year the great deciduous trees steal the limelight with their spectacular displays of fall foliage.

▶ Follow **US 33** for 21 miles (34km) to Barboursville. Turn left (north) on to **SR 20** and continue through Orange for 34 miles (56km) to Wilderness. Turn right (east) on to **SR 3** for 5 miles (8km) to Chancellorsville.

**❸ Chancellorsville,** Viginia
At Chancellorsville's Visitor Center you can get information and see an audio-visual presentation before touring the countryside where more than 100,000 soldiers fell during four tremendous Civil War battles. At Fredericksburg in December 1862 and Chancellorsville in May 1863, the Confederacy won the day, but at the Wilderness and Spotsylvania Court House in May 1864, Grant's Yankees came out on top.
Before driving into Fredericksburg you can, if you wish, tour one, two or all three, of the battlefields outside the city, either by car or on foot along the trails to the main landmarks of the fighting.

▶ Continue into Fredericksburg.

**❹ Fredericksburg,** Virginia
Even without its reminders of the Civil War – 'that terrible stone wall' on Marye's Heights in particular – it is easy to see why Fredericksburg is often called 'America's most historic city'. When you tour its picturesque streets, you will find buildings that were once lived in or frequented by members of George Washington's family or by other notables of Colonial times. You will see the Masonic Lodge where, in 1752, Washington was initiated; the charming 'in-town' cottage he bought for his mother, Mary; his sister Betty's stately Kenmore mansion, where you should sample the gingerbread made to Mary's recipe; and the cele-

Fredericksburg, a prosperous river port that grew from a 1676 fort

brated Rising Sun Tavern built by his youngest brother, Charles (you will get only colonial spiced tea here now, as this fine old hostelry lost its liquor license back in 1827). Also in the town you can visit the quaint apothecary shop run by Washington's friend Hugh Mercer, and the law office and library of America's fifth president, James Monroe. In the Historic Fredericksburg Museum, a treasure trove of colonial and Civil War exhibits, you can recapture the atmosphere of the city's early days.

ℹ️ *706 Caroline Street*

▶ Leave Fredericksburg on **I–95** and drive north through Woodbridge to **Exit 54**. Continue north on **US 1** for about 5 miles (8km), turn right (east) at the **SR 235** intersection and continue for 2 miles (3km) to Mount Vernon.

**5 Mount Vernon,** Virginia
Overlooking the Potomac River, this beautiful mansion – the home of George and Martha Washington – is the most visited historic estate in America. When Washington acquired the family property in 1754, he enlarged the smaller house built by his father and developed the estate as a working plantation. The house has since been authentically restored and still contains many of the original furnishings. After touring the buildings, take a stroll through the grounds and visit George and Martha's tomb at the foot of the hill.

▶ Follow the Mount Vernon Memorial Highway north along the Potomac River for 9 miles (14km) to Alexandria.

**6 Alexandria,** Virginia
Less than 7 miles (11km) from the White House, Alexandria has all the trappings of a prosperous suburb of Washington DC, with the usual modern buildings, fine shops, fashionable restaurants and art and antique galleries. But it is, in fact, much older than the capital and has considerable historic charm and interest. Once a thriving tobacco port, it has a walkable 7-by-11 block downtown area called the Old Town which has gaslit, cobble-stoned streets and buildings that were known to George Washington and Robert E Lee. After stopping for information at the Ramsay House Visitor Center, wander around adjacent Market Square. Here you will see the historic City Hall; the elegant Carlyle House of 1752; the Stabler-Leadbeater Apothecary Shop of 1792, where Martha Washington bought her medicines; and Gadsby's Tavern, where George met with other revolutionaries and danced with Martha during his birth-night celebrations (now an annual city event). A few blocks away is Christ Church, where the Washingtons and, later, the Lees worshipped. The Lee family home (the Lee-Fendall House) and Robert's boyhood home are some blocks north, on Oronoco Street.

Don't miss a tour of the artist's studios in the unattractive Torpedo Factory Art Center, a former munitions manufacturing plant where you can watch artists and craftsmen painting, sculpting and making pottery, stained glass and jewelry. Take a Potomac River cruise or stroll through Waterfront Park to see the schooner *Alexandria*.

☐ *221 King Street*

▶ *Leave Alexandria via North Washington Street for the 7-mile (11km) drive to downtown Washington DC.*

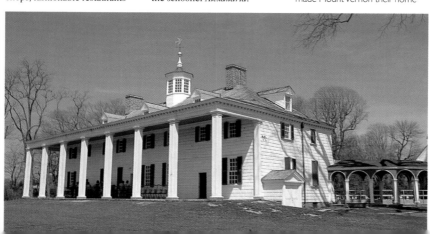

George and Martha Washington made Mount Vernon their home

# Four States
## Historic Tour

This tour offers a taste of the scenic beauty and historic heritage of Virginia, West Virginia, Pennsylvania and Maryland. Less than an hour's drive takes you from the bustle of the nation's capital to the tranquility

**3 DAYS • 210 MILES • 336KM** of Virginia's 'Hunt Country'.

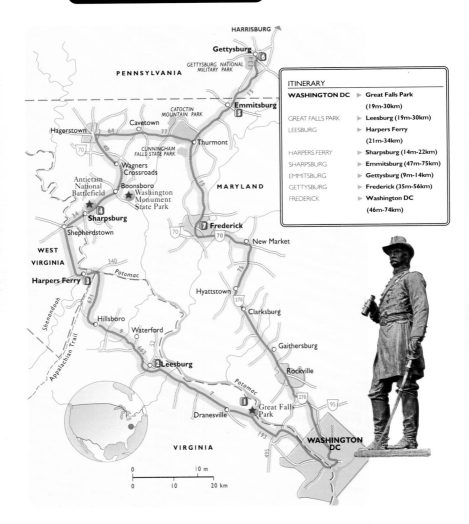

ITINERARY

| | | |
|---|---|---|
| **WASHINGTON DC** | ▶ | **Great Falls Park** (19m-30km) |
| GREAT FALLS PARK | ▶ | **Leesburg** (19m-30km) |
| LEESBURG | ▶ | **Harpers Ferry** (21m-34km) |
| HARPERS FERRY | ▶ | **Sharpsburg** (14m-22km) |
| SHARPSBURG | ▶ | **Emmitsburg** (47m-75km) |
| EMMITSBURG | ▶ | **Gettysburg** (9m-14km) |
| GETTYSBURG | ▶ | **Frederick** (35m-56km) |
| FREDERICK | ▶ | **Washington DC** (46m-74km) |

ⓘ *1455 Pennsylvania Avenue, Washington DC*

▶ *From downtown Washington cross the Potomac River and drive north on George Washington Parkway to enter southbound Capital Beltway (I–495). At **Exit 13** take the Georgetown Pike (**SR 193**) west for about 4½ miles (7km), then turn on to **SR 738** to Great Falls Park.*

## ❶ Great Falls Park, Virginia

This pleasant wooded park, 15 miles (24km) from Washington, offers spectacular views of the falls and rocky gorge where the Potomac River tumbles over the

Leesburg is an attractive old town with a Historic District packed with lovely colonial homes, fine antique shops and restaurants. Stop by the Loudoun Museum and Visitor Center for brochures and a slide presentation before taking a walking tour around its streets. Then drive out into the surrounding country, where you will find quaint old villages, like Waterford on SR 662, charming country inns, horse farms, wineries and perhaps even a craft fair or a meet of the local hunt. Foxhunting and other equestrian activities are a strong tradition here, for this is Virginia's 'Hunt Country'. Horses feature promi-

## ❸ Harpers Ferry, West Virginia

This historic town lies at the junction of the Potomac and the Shenandoah rivers amid the wooded slopes of the Blue Ridge, a spectacular setting best viewed from the hillside overlook at Jefferson Rock. With its strategic position, the town changed hands several times in the Civil War. It was here that, in 1859, just before the war, the antislavery campaigner John Brown made his ill-fated raid on the Federal Arsenal and became a folk hero through the old battle song '*John Brown's Body Lies Amoldering in the Grave*'. You will see the fort where he was

edge of the Piedmont Plateau. A favorite escape for city dwellers, it has good walking trails and picnic sites, but stay on the trails and observe the signs as there are some hazardous spots.

▶ *Continue along **SR 193** for about 5 miles (7km) through the town of Great Falls and join **SR 7** northbound at Dranesville. Continue for about 14 miles (23km) to Leesburg.*

## ❷ Leesburg and Hunt Country, Virginia

With a history that goes back more than two centuries,

nently at two of the area's leading visitor attractions. Oatlands Plantation, south of Leesburg, hosts equestrian events throughout the year, while Morven Park, to the north, has a fox-hunting museum and a marvelous carriage collection. Both are beautiful places to visit, even if you have never been on a saddle.

ⓘ *108 South Street SE*

▶ *From Leesburg follow **SR 9** and **SR 671** north for 21 miles (34km) to Harpers Ferry.*

The Potomac cascades in a series of rugged falls and turbulent rapids

### BACK TO NATURE

Although it is difficult to single out any one location for wildlife, the Appalachian Trail provides the best opportunities for seeing the birds and mammals of upland forest. Look for deer, squirrels and raccoons and birds such as black-capped chickadees, ravens, ruffed grouse and chestnut-sided warblers.

captured, on a tour of the
National Historical Park which
encompasses the town.

⃞ *Shenandoah Street*

### RECOMMENDED WALKS

Opportunities for walking
abound on this tour, but there
are some places where
stretching your legs is especially enjoyable. They include the
towpath of the historic
Chesapeake and Ohio Canal at
Harpers Ferry and the
Appalachian Trail near Harpers
Ferry and Boonsboro.

▶ *Follow **US 340** west for 2
miles (3km), then **SR 230**
north for 8 miles (13km) to
Shepherdstown. Cross the
Potomac into Maryland and
follow **SR 34** for 4 miles (6km)
to Sharpsburg.*

### ❹ Sharpsburg, Maryland
John Brown's activities took him
to Sharpsburg, and you can
follow in his footsteps to the
Kennedy Farmhouse, which was
used by his band before the
Harpers Ferry raid. Most people
come here, however, to visit the
site of the battle of Antietam (or
Sharpsburg). At Antietam Creek,
just north of the town, more than
23,000 men fell on September
17, 1862. It was the Civil War's
bloodiest single day of fighting.
The battle ended in a stalemate,
but it halted the Confederate
invasion of Maryland. After stopping at the Visitor Center you
can take a self-guided auto tour
of the main landmarks in the
battle.

▶ *Take **SR 34** from Sharpsburg
for 7 miles (11km) to
Boonsboro, then **SR 66** north
for 4 miles (6km) to Wagners
Crossroads. Continue north on
**US 40** for 8 miles (13km) to
Hagerstown. From here follow
**SR 64** and **SR 77** east for 19
miles (31km) to Thurmont,
then turn north on **US 15** for*

*the 9-mile (14km) drive to
Emmitsburg.*

### FOR HISTORY BUFFS

Just south of Thurmont, the
Catoctin Furnace Historic
District contains the ruins of a
17th-century iron-making village including the workers'
stone cottages. The furnace,
which continued operating
until 1905, made iron for the
Civil War battleship *Monitor*.

### FOR CHILDREN

Near Thurmont, kids can get
close to animals in the petting
area at the Catoctin Mountain
Zoological Park.

### ❺ Emmitsburg and the Blue Ridge Mountains, Maryland
If you enjoy mountain scenery
with thick forests, crystal-clear
streams and green valleys, you
will love Maryland's scenic Blue
Ridge region. Among the
wooded ridges of South
Mountain, once the scene of
Civil War conflict, and the
Catoctin Mountains further east,
you will find opportunities for
fishing, hunting, boating, canoeing, cross-country skiing and
hiking or just strolling along

Statue of Union commander
General Meade, Gettysburg

stretches of the Appalachian
Trail and other designated path-
ways. Places of interest abound
along the route. Boonsboro has
its Museum of History, and
nearby are the Crystal Grottoes,
Old South Mountain Inn and
Washington Monument State
Park. Hagerstown's attractions
include historic buildings like
the Jonathan Hager House and
Miller House. But for beautiful
mountain scenery take a walk in
Cunningham Falls Park and
adjoining Catoctin Mountain
Park, the location not only of the
presidential retreat at Camp
David but also of the historic
Blue Blazes Whiskey Still. If you

Mabry Mill, Blue Ridge Parkway, is
America's most photographed mill

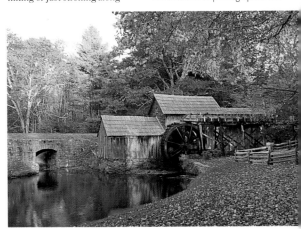

**FOR CHILDREN**

At Frederick, they can explore the log cabin, blacksmith shop, carriages and other farm objects at the Rose Hill Manor Children's Museum, with its interesting hands-on displays.

► *From Frederick follow I–70 east for 7 miles (11km) for a brief tour of New Market, then take **SR 75** south and join I–270 southbound at Hyattstown for the 46-mile (74km) drive through Rockville back to Washington DC.*

**SPECIAL TO...**

The town of New Market, east of Frederick, is the place to go for bargains in bric-à-brac and special antique treasures. The 'Antiques Capital of Maryland' is packed with more than 50 stores.

**FOR HISTORY BUFFS**

Rockville's West Montgomery Avenue Historic District contains more than 100 old buildings of architectural and historic interest. In the Beall-Dawson House, you can pore over a collection of gruesome 19th-century medical instruments. Also in the town are the graves of writer F Scott Fitzgerald and his wife, Zelda.

**SCENIC ROUTES**

In addition to the pleasant drive to Great Falls at the start of the tour, the most scenic stretches of highway are in the Blue Ridge region; SR 671, Hillsboro to Harpers Ferry; SR 66, Boonsboro to Wagners Crossroads; SR 77, Cavetown to Thurmont; and US 15 Thurmont to Emmitsburg.

want to learn how to make liquor, this is the place. Other places of interest await you along the lovely drive to Emmitsburg. Among them are the Roddy Road covered bridge; Our Lady of Lourdes Grotto, the beautiful replica of the Grotto of Lourdes in southern France; and the Shrine of Elizabeth Ann Seton, the first American-born saint.

ℹ️ *US 15 Southbound, Emmitsburg*

**BACK TO NATURE**

The First Monument to George Washington in Washington Monument State Park is the best spot for observing migrating birds of prey in October and September.

► *From Emmitsburg drive north for 9 miles (14km) on **US 15** and **SR 134** across the Mason-Dixon Line to Gettysburg.*

**6** **Gettysburg,** Pennsylvania
Although the Gettysburg area has plenty of interesting things to see and do, people come here mainly to visit the Gettysburg National Military Park, where the bloodiest and most crucial battle of the Civil War was fought between July 1 and 3, 1863, resulting in 51,000 casualties and defeat for the Confederate army under General Lee, turning the tide

against the South. Before touring the battlefield, stop at the Visitor Center and ride up the National Tower for a panoramic view of the area. Then take the shuttle bus for a tour of President Dwight D Eisenhower's home (a National Historic Site) and stroll around the downtown Historic District.

ℹ️ *35 Carlisle Street*

► *From Gettysburg follow the same route back to Thurmont, Maryland, then continue south on **US 15** for another 17 miles (27km) to Frederick.*

**7** **Frederick,** Maryland
This charming old colonial town lies in rolling farmland and orchard country in the shadow of the Catoctin Mountains. Known as the 'City of Clustered Spires', Frederick boasts many historic buildings in its downtown National Historic District. Every visitor wants to see the house of Barbara Fritchie, that redoubtable old lady who reputedly confronted Confederate General Stonewall Jackson with a Union flag as he rode by. You can see her grave in Mount Olivet Cemetery, the last resting place also of Francis Scott Key, author of *The Star Spangled Banner*, who lived in Frederick for a time.

Also worth a visit is the old German farmhouse called Schifferstadt.

ℹ️ *19 East Church Street*

# Pennsylvania
## Dutch Country

There is much to enjoy on this tour of Pennsylvania's southeastern counties. You will experience the unique way of life of the Pennsylvania Dutch people who pioneered this land, see traces of Delaware's Scandinavian heritage, feel the birth pangs of American nationhood at famous Revolutionary War sites and tour Pennsylvania's state capital and other cities of differing personalities, as well as the estates of the du Ponts and enjoy the fun – and the chocolate – at Hershey.

**3 DAYS • 287 MILES • 459KM**

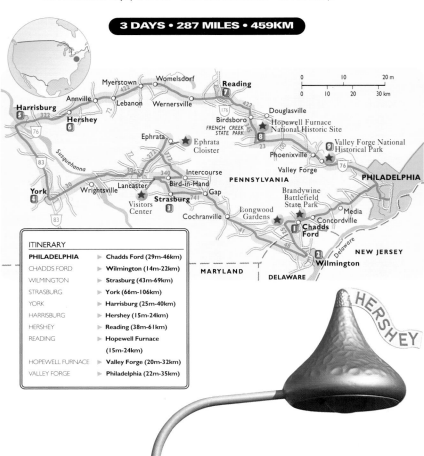

**ITINERARY**

| | |
|---|---|
| **PHILADELPHIA** | ▶ **Chadds Ford (29m-46km)** |
| CHADDS FORD | ▶ **Wilmington (14m-22km)** |
| WILMINGTON | ▶ **Strasburg (43m-69km)** |
| STRASBURG | ▶ **York (66m-106km)** |
| YORK | ▶ **Harrisburg (25m-40km)** |
| HARRISBURG | ▶ **Hershey (15m-24km)** |
| HERSHEY | ▶ **Reading (38m-61km)** |
| READING | ▶ **Hopewell Furnace (15m-24km)** |
| HOPEWELL FURNACE | ▶ **Valley Forge (20m-32km)** |
| VALLEY FORGE | ▶ **Philadelphia (22m-35km)** |

*1525 John F Kennedy Boulevard, Philadelphia*

▶ *Cross the Schuylkill River from Downtown Philadelphia and pick up the northbound Schuylkill Expressway. After about 4 miles (6km) take Exit 33 west on to US 1 and continue for about 25 miles (40km) to Chadds Ford. West of town follow SR 52 south down the Brandywine Valley.*

## ❶ Chadds Ford and the Brandywine Valley,
Pennsylvania and Delaware
At Chadds Ford US 1 crosses Brandywine Creek as it flows south down its beautiful valley to Wilmington, Delaware. The Chadds Ford area boasts several early 18th-century houses; a winery; the Brandywine Battlefield Park, site of a 1777 British victory in the Revolutionary War; and the attractive Brandywine River Museum, which has paintings by the Wyeths and other American artists.

Not to be missed to the west of town are the beautiful landscaped grounds and conservatories of Longwood Gardens, the country estate of industrialist Pierre S du Pont. Down the Brandywine Valley on Route 52 are more impressive du Pont mansions and fine museums, highlighted by the magnificent Winterthur Museum and Gardens, which contains Henry Francis du Pont's world-famous collection of antique furniture, paintings and other art treasures.

*Longwood Gardens, Route 1, Kennett Square*

▶ *Continue driving south on US 52 into Wilmington.*

## ❷ Wilmington, Delaware
Delaware's largest city is a major center of the chemical industry and the headquarters of many US companies and banks. At the foot of 7th Street are historic reminders of the city's first Scandinavian settlers of 1638, including the Old Swedes Church, the Hendrickson House and the site of Fort Christina. Among the shops along Market Street are other sightseeing treasures, such as the Old Town Hall, the Grand Opera House and the restored 18th-century houses at Willingtown Square. At the foot of King Street you can tour the 1934 cutter

The Marquis de Lafayette's headquarters at the Brandywine Battlefield Park

*Mohawk* and take a cruise on the Christina River.

Don't miss the Delaware Art Museum, in the north part of the city, where you can see fine American works as well as English pre-Raphaelite paintings among the collections.

*1300 Market Street*

### FOR HISTORY BUFFS

Of historic interest on this tour are the industrial exhibits at Hagley Museum. It is situated 3 miles (5km) north of Wilmington on SR 141 in 230 acres (110 hectares) of the original Du Pont Mills site along the Brandywine River.
Many of the mills have been restored to full working order, and there are exhibits and demonstrations, including an operating steam engine, a wooden water wheel and a restored machine shop from the 1870s.

▶ *From Wilmington drive north-west on Lancaster Avenue (SR 48) and SR 41 for about 34 miles (55km), then take SR 741 west for about 9 miles (14km) to Strasburg and Lancaster County.*

## ❸ Strasburg and Lancaster County, Pennsylvania

The rich, rolling farmlands of Lancaster County are the heartland of Pennsylvania Dutch Country. The plain, simple lifestyle of the local Amish and Mennonite people, traditionally averse to modern gadgets and

Amish father and son. Some Amish farms and homesteads are available for tours

attitudes (including visitors' cameras), has ironically become a tourist attraction. So you can tour farms and historic homes, sample excellent home cooking, ride in a horse-drawn buggy and buy fine, locally handmade crafts. You will get advice on places to visit at the Visitor Center on Greenfield Road just outside Lancaster.

Quaint Strasburg is the site of the famed Railroad Museum,

which traces the history of railroads in Pennsylvania through memorabilia and restored locomotives, and many other attractions.

On the road from Strasburg to Lancaster you can detour on to Route 340 to the varied attractions of Bird-in-Hand and Intercourse, where you can visit the craft shops of Kitchen Kettle Village and see beautiful quilts at the Quilt Museum; northwards on Routes 772 and 272 to the historic Ephrata Cloister religious community site; then south on Route 272 to the city of Lancaster, with a stop just north of town to learn something of the state's German rural heritage at the excellent Landis Valley Museum.

In Lancaster City take a walking tour of downtown to see the colorful old Central Market; the Heritage Center; Museum of Lancaster County; and the Demuth Tobacco Shop of 1770, the oldest in America.

And further out of town, visit the 1792 Rock Ford Plantation and James Buchanan's elegant Federal-style Wheatland Mansion of 1828. He was the only Pennsylvanian to become president of the United States.

ⓘ *501 Greenfield Road, Lancaster*

---

### SPECIAL TO...

Special experiences at various points along the tour include the fun-packed Renaissance Faire at the Mount Hope Estate on Route 72 north of Lancaster. It takes place at weekends from July to mid-October, including Mondays up to August, and is a fantasy re-creation of a 16th-century English Tudor village with costumed performers juggling, jousting, conjuring and dragon-slaying.

---

▶ *From Lancaster take US 30 west for 24 miles (39km) across the Susquehanna River to York.*

---

### FOR CHILDREN

The exciting Toy Train Museum and Choo Choo Barn, in Strasburg, is a 1,700-square-foot (160sq m) miniature display of Lancaster County and Pennsylvania Dutch Country. It has 13 operating toy trains with over 135 animated and automated figures and vehicles, and there are miniatures of many of the area's landmarks.

---

## ❹ York, Pennsylvania

The manufacturing city of York is known today for its motorcycles, shopping outlets and markets, cultural activities and events like the York Interstate Fair and Halloween Parade, and historic buildings. But for several months in 1777 to 1778 it was, in effect, America's first capital, after the Continental Congress fled here following the British occupation of Philadelphia.

While touring the Historic District around Market Street, be sure to visit the reconstruction of the original 1755 York County Colonial Courthouse where the Congress met, and hear dramatic sound-and-light re-enactments of the delegates' debates.

ⓘ *One Market Way East*

▶ *From York follow I–83 north for 25 miles (40km) to Harrisburg.*

## ❺ Harrisburg, Pennsylvania

It was in the late 1700s that John Harris Jr laid out the town that was to become Pennsylvania's state capital, and you can still see the mansion he built by the Susquehanna River in 1766 as you tour the historic district along South Front Street. Be sure to visit also the imposing domed Capitol, in the complex of public buildings in the Midtown district; the State Museum of Pennsylvania nearby, with its historic and other collections; the fine Governor's Mansion; and Strawberry Square, a shopping and restaurant showplace. Walk, too, along 5-mile (8km) River Park, site of summer events, and take a leisurely riverboat cruise from City Island.

_i_ | *114 Walnut Street*

▶ *Head east on I–83, US 322/422 and Hershey Park Drive (SR 39 north) to Hershey.*

**❻ Hershey,** Pennsylvania
A short distance from Harrisburg is 'Chocolate Town USA', a paradise for children. The town of Hershey, founded in 1903 by Milton S Hershey, is one of the largest chocolate and cocoa plants in the world.

Stop first at the Chocolate World Visitors Center and take the short simulated tour of the chocolate-making process. You will then have to choose from the many other attractions on offer. For fun-seekers, old and

young, there are 87 acres (35 hectares) of exciting rides, roller-coasters, water attractions and shows on the Hersheypark complex. The less energetic might prefer a quiet tour of the Hershey Museum of American Life, to see native wild animals and plants at the ZooAmerica North American Wildlife Park, or to stroll around the superb seasonal flower displays in the 23-acre (9-hectare) Hershey Gardens.

_i_ | *See Harrisburg*

▶ *Continue east on US 422 for 38 miles (61km) through the Lebanon Valley to Reading.*

**❼ Reading,** Pennsylvania
While in Reading, don't miss a drive up to the oriental Pagoda that overlooks the city from its perch on top of nearby Mount Penn, where you can enjoy magnificent panoramic views of the surrounding area. Down in the city, take a walk around the Callowhill Historical District to

see the fine 19th-century buildings in the Penn Square and 5th Street areas. Then go and hunt for bargains in Reading's numerous shopping outlets, many of them housed in the city's six major complexes.

> **BACK TO NATURE**
>
> Nature takes second place to other sightseeing attractions on this tour. But if you have time, drive 20 miles (32km) on Route 61 north of Reading to see migrating hawks and eagles – best in September and October – and resident birds and mammals at the famed Hawk Mountain Sanctuary.

▶ *Follow **US 422** east from Reading to Birdsboro, then take **SR 345** south for 5 miles (8km) to Hopewell Furnace.*

Hopewell Furnace National Historic Site

### 8 Hopewell Furnace,
Pennsylvania

Nestled in the quiet countryside around French Creek State Park is the Hopewell Furnace National Historic Site, a restored village that operated between 1771 and 1883 and one of the finest examples of an early American iron-making community. On a tour of the buildings you will see demonstrations of iron-molding, blacksmithing, and open-hearth cooking and metal casting as well as re-enactments of village life by interpreters in period costumes.

*i* *Visitor Center, Hopewell Furnace National Historical Site*

▶ *About 2 miles (3km) south of Hopewell take SR 23 east for about 18 miles (29km) to the village of Valley Forge.*

### 9 Valley Forge, Pennsylvania
The 3,000-acre (1,214-hectare) Valley Forge National Historical Park commemorates one of the most moving episodes of America's Revolution. Following defeat by the British at Brandywine in September 1777, George Washington's dispirited Continental Army encamped here and heroically recuperated during a winter of terrible privation. Call at the Visitor Center and take a self-guided tour of the fortifications and other park landmarks.

### BACK TO NATURE

Be sure to visit Mill Grove, naturalist John James Audubon's home near Valley Forge, and walk through the wildlife sanctuary there.

*i* *Visitor Center, Valley Forge National Historical Park*

▶ *Pick up I–76 (Schuylkill Expressway) eastbound from Valley Forge at Interchange 24 and continue for about 22 miles (35km) to downtown Philadelphia.*

Valley Forge National Historical Park, site of the Continental Army's 6-month winter encampment

### SCENIC ROUTES

The most pleasant stretches of road include Route 52 down the Brandywine Valley; Routes 772 and 272 through Lancaster County's farmlands between Intercourse and Ephrata; and the 3-mile (5km) Skyline Drive to the mountaintop Pagoda at Reading.

### RECOMMENDED WALKS

When you have seen the pictures at the Brandywine River Museum, enjoy a pleasant stroll down the trails through the woodland nearby. There are more enjoyable walks at Longwood Gardens (near Chadds Ford); along the Union Canal towpath west of Reading; and at French Creek State Park, near Hopewell Furnace, where you can follow part of the lengthy Horse Shoe Traill.

# Birthplace of
## Colonial Virginia

From Richmond around Virginia's Tidewater region, the natural scenery, lush, green and pleasant though it is, takes a back seat to the places of historic importance, especially those along the Virginia Peninsula. At the forefront are Civil War battlefields around Confederate Richmond; plantations along the James River; and major Colonial sites in the 'Historic Triangle' of Jamestown, Williamsburg and Yorktown.

**3/4 DAYS • 272 MILES • 435KM**

| ITINERARY | |
|---|---|
| **RICHMOND** | ▶ **Battlefield Park** (14m-22km) |
| BATTLEFIELD PARK | ▶ **Shirley Plantation** (7m-11km) |
| SHIRLEY PLANTATION | ▶ **Jamestown (44m-70km)** |
| JAMESTOWN | ▶ **Williamsburg** (9m-14km) |
| WILLIAMSBURG | ▶ **Newport News** (23m-37km) |
| NEWPORT NEWS | ▶ **Yorktown (15m-24km)** |
| YORKTOWN | ▶ **Stratford Hall** (83m-134km) |
| STRATFORD HALL | ▶ **Paramount's King's Dominion (55m-88km)** |
| PARAMOUNT'S KING'S DOMINION | ▶ **Richmond (22m-35km)** |

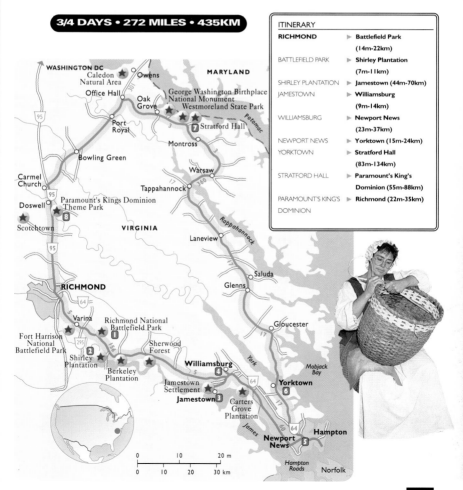

ⓘ *1710 Robin Hood Road, Richmond*

▶ *From downtown Richmond follow East Broad Street to Richmond National Battlefield Park headquarters in Chimborazo Park. Retrace Broad Street to 25th Street and drive south to New Market Road (SR 5). Continue east to either the Fort Harrison or Malvern Hill battle site.*

## ❶ Richmond National Battlefied Park, Virginia

As capital of the Confederacy, Richmond was the Union forces' prime objective throughout the Civil War, and several major battles were fought east and south of the city in 1862 and 1864. These battle sites are now encompassed in the Richmond National Battlefield Park. Get information and see the audio-visual presentation at the Chimborazo Park Visitor Center. Then visit one of the battle-fields, off Route 5; either Fort Harrison, which fell to Grant's Union forces in 1864, or Malvern

Replica of one of the three ships that brought settlers to Virginia

Hill, where the Confederates stopped the first advance on Richmond in 1862.

ⓘ *3215 East Broad Street*

▶ *Continue southeast on SR 5 to Shirley Plantation.*

## ❷ Shirley Plantation and the James River Plantations, Virginia

The Virginia Peninsula, east of Richmond, is probably the most historic stretch of real estate in all America. Along the north shore of the James River, Route 5 links a string of old plantation homes and stately mansions whose owners include several early US presidents and signers of the Declaration of Independence. Some are open only by prior appointment, but you should try to visit at least one.

In the order in which you will reach them after leaving Richmond, they are: Shirley Plantation (circa 1613), Edgewood (1849), Berkeley (1726), Westover (grounds only, 1730), Evelynton (1930s), Belle Air (circa 1670) and Sherwood Forest (circa 1730).

▶ *Continue driving along SR 5 to Jamestown.*

## ❸ Jamestown, Virginia

Now part of the Colonial National Historical Park, Jamestown, beside the James River, was the first permanent English settlement in America, established in 1607. You can still see the ruins of the original site as you drive around what is now Jamestown Island (it was then connected by an isthmus). But to get an idea of what that first community was really like, spend some time soaking up the atmosphere at the nearby re-created Jamestown Settlement. Here costumed interpreters re-enacting the life of the early settlers take you back centuries as you tour the reconstructed James Fort stockade, the Indian Village, the Glasshouse used for making glass objects, and one of the three ships which are repli-cas of the ones that brought the first settlers to Virginia in 1607.

ⓘ *Visitor Center, Jamestown*

▶ *Take the Colonial Parkway north for 9 miles (14km) to Williamsburg.*

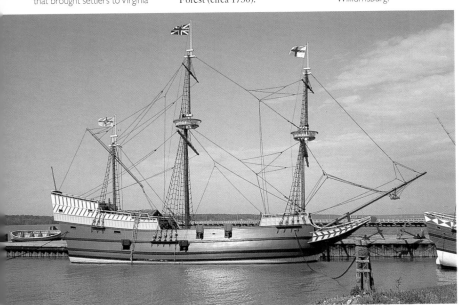

**4 Williamsburg,** Virginia
Though some might regard it as
a stage set, the restoration of
Williamsburg's 18th-century
Historic Area – Colonial
Williamsburg – is quite remarkable, not only for the colossal
scale of the enterprise but also
for its historic authenticity. As
you stroll around the streets and
mingle with the 'citizens' in
period dress who are re-enacting
the life of those early days, you
can almost believe you have
entered a time warp. Take a
special look at the Governor's
Palace, the Capitol, the College
of William and Mary, and two of
the town's lively old hostelries,
both conveniently on Duke of
Gloucester Street – the famous
Raleigh Tavern and
Wetherburn's Tavern.

In the Williamsburg area are
two popular entertainment parks
– Water Country USA and Busch
Gardens/The Old Country –
where you can have a little relaxing fun.

i Visitor Center, Route 132Y

**FOR HISTORY BUFFS**

If you enjoy touring stately
homes and plantations, there
are two more important
historic houses which are conveniently close to the route
for a visit.
Lovely Carter's Grove
Plantation, off US 60 near
Williamsburg, was built in the
1750s, and in its grounds are
reconstructions of slave cabins,
and the archeological site of
17th-century Wolstenholme
Towne.

▶ Take either I–64 or US 60
for the 23-mile (37km) drive
to Newport News and
Hampton.

**5 Newport News and
Hampton,** Virginia
These two adjoining cities overlook the immense natural harbor
of Hampton Roads from the tip
of the Virginia Peninsula. To
get a good look at this great port
area and the ships anchored at

Williamsburg: the Governor's
Palace (above) and re-enacting
the early days (below)

Norfolk Naval Base across the
water, take an exhilarating boat
cruise from the Newport News

waterfront. With its long tradition of shipbuilding, Newport News is the location of the world-famous Mariners' Museum, which tells the story of mankind's eventful relationship with the sea.

Not far away the excellent War Memorial Museum portrays American military history since independence, complete with marvelous war posters. At Hampton are the Virginia Air and Space Center/Hampton Roads History Center, with displays on flight and space exploration, and the Casemate Museum, at historic Fort Monroe, which traces American history since independence.

ⓘ *3560 Jefferson Avenue, Newport News*

▶ *Take I–64 north from Hampton to Exit 258B, then US 17 north to Yorktown, a journey of about 15 miles (24km).*

---

**FOR CHILDREN**

Youngsters are well provided for on this tour, but two additional places that should prove fun for animal lovers are: Bluebird Gap Farm, at Hampton, a sort of combined farm, park and zoo with native Virginia wild animals and farm animals; and Virginia Living Museum, at Newport News, which is even better known for its exciting exhibits of native Virginia wild creatures.

---

**6 Yorktown,** Virginia
In colonial times, Yorktown was a thriving tobacco port on the York River which, on October 19, 1781, saw the dramatic surrender of British forces under General Cornwallis that brought the Revolutionary War to an end. You can relive the momentous events at the Colonial National Historical Park, which contains the battle site. Watch a stirring film about the battle at the

Yorktown Victory Center, then tour the battlefield landmarks and the Moore House, where the surrender terms were negotiated.

ⓘ *Visitor Center, Yorktown*

▶ *Follow US 17 across the York River through Gloucester for 59 miles (95km) to Tappahannock. Take US 360 for 7 miles (11km) to Warsaw, then SR 3 north for 17 miles (28km) to Stratford Hall and George Washington's Birthplace.*

**7 Stratford Hall,** Virginia
Stratford Hall, the ancestral home of the Lee family, was built between 1729 and 1730 on the southern shore of the Potomac River, in Virginia's lovely Northern Neck region. It was here that the most illustrious member of the family, General Robert E Lee, was born in 1807. The imposing brick-built mansion, one of the finest examples of Jacobean architecture in the US, is open to visitors year round.

A few miles west, on Route 204, is George Washington Birthplace National Monument. Despite the name, you cannot tour the original house in which George was born in 1732, because it was destroyed by fire in 1779. However, you can visit the pretty Memorial House built near the site and tour the gardens, the colonial farm and the family burial ground.

---

**RECOMMENDED WALKS**

You will do a lot of walking around plantation estates, battlefields and other historic places on this tour, but to get away from the crowds spend some time in Westmoreland State Park, near Stratford Hall, where you will find hiking trails and picnic spots overlooking the Potomac River.

---

Above: Jacobean-style Stratford Hall, built by Thomas Lee, is a fascinating restoration of a working colonial plantation

# **Birthplace of** Colonial Virginia

## BACK TO NATURE

If you have never seen a bald eagle in a natural setting, make for Caledon Natural Area on Route 218 by the Potomac River, just 4 miles (6km) west of Owens from US 301. Large numbers of these majestic birds congregate here in summer and can be seen from the walking trails.

Byrd Park in Richmond is good for sighting wintering wildfowl, which are usually quite tame.

▶ *Continue west on SR 3 to Oak Grove, then a further 10 miles (16km) to pick up US 301 southbound at Office Hall. Continue for 29 miles (47km) to Carmel Church and pick up I–95 southbound for 7 miles (11km) to Exit 98 for Paramount's Kings Dominion theme park.*

The Victory Monument, Yorktown, where British rule ended

## **8** **Paramount's Kings Dominion,** Virginia

One way to end a tour of Virginia's historic sites is at Paramount's Kings Dominion theme park at Doswell, north of Richmond. Open daily in the summer and weekends in the spring and fall, this 400-acre (160-hectare) park has rides and live shows in various theme areas including Wayne's World and Old Virginia.

### FOR HISTORY BUFFS

West of I–95, near Paramount's Kings Dominion, is Scotchtown, the white clapboard mansion bought in 1771 by patriot Patrick Henry, who gained fame for his 'Give me liberty or give me death' speech shortly before the Revolution. In 1776 he became the first governor of the newly-formed state of Virginia.

▶ *Continue south on I–95 for 22 miles (35km) to Richmond.*

## SCENIC ROUTES

Although this is not an itinerary with spectacular hill scenery, there are sections of highway that pass through lovely countryside and offer fine views over water. Most notable are SR 5, with its views of the James River; US 17, across the farmlands and marshes of the Tidewater region; and SR 3, up the Northern Neck.

## SPECIAL TO...

Tidewater Virginia has as much to please the palate as the eye. Don't finish your tour without sampling the succulent seafood from Chesapeake Bay or Virginia's famed Smithfield ham, accompanied, of course, by excellent native-grown wines. You can taste some of these on a tour of the Ingleside Winery, near Oak Grove on the Northern Neck.

# THE ATLANTIC SOUTHEAST

Historically and culturally this region is part of the Old South. Here a genteel white plantation society developed during the Colonial era, in which black slaves provided labor for fields and mansions. But, as Margaret Mitchell described in her epic story *Gone with the Wind*, this way of life was to be brusquely swept away by bitter defeat in the War Between the States of 1861–65.

The Confederate flag is still often seen, a nostalgic symbol of Southern pride. Other reminders of the past survive. There are Revolutionary War battle sites, old forts and plantation homes; the site of Sir Walter Raleigh's two ill-fated attempts to found England's first New World colony on Roanoke Island in the 1580s; and the North Carolina Colonial Governor's residence at Tryon Palace. Dotted throughout the region are historic small towns, like Old Salem, York, Camden and Madison. And the beautiful port cities of Charleston, Savannah and Wilmington preserve their atmospheric old streets and gracious town mansions.

Atlanta's State Capitol

The land is similar to the Mid-Atlantic states further north: flat coastal plain and marshes, fall line, rolling Piedmont Plateau, and Appalachian Mountains. Of these, it is the shoreline that shows greatest diversity. In North Carolina there is a maze of tidal inlets and marshes, broad river estuaries, sandy beaches, and offshore islands, known as the Outer Banks; in South Carolina, beaches, including the 55-mile (88km) Grand Strand, and resort sea islands such as Hilton Head; and in Georgia, the moss-draped, pine-clad Golden Isles of the Colonial Coast and, inland, the Okefenokee Swamp.

Woodlands and farm country, extending across the broad coastal plain and the more populated Piedmont, contrast with important manufacturing cities – Raleigh and Charlotte in North Carolina, Columbia in South Carolina, and Atlanta in Georgia.

The region's most beautiful scenery is packed into the forested ridges and valleys of the Appalachian Mountains, land of the hillbilly, log cabin and moonshine. Here, too, on a small reservation beside the Great Smokies, live the descendants of the proud Cherokee nation whose land this once was.

Sunset over Atlanta

## Charlotte

Named after Charlotte, George III's German-born consort, North Carolina's largest city is a financial, transportation and textile-manufacturing center at the hub of the 'Carolinas Crescent' industrial region. A pleasant, livable city of over 430,000 people, it sprawls across the wooded Piedmont, surrounded by tree-shaded residential districts like the attractive Fourth Ward; shopping malls, outlets and trade marts; sports and entertainment arenas; country clubs, golf courses and recreational lakes; and many other places of interest to visitors. Modern glass towers rise from the Uptown business district, location of the exciting hands-on science museum of Discovery Place, the Spirit Square Center for the Arts and the superb NC Blumenthal Performing Arts Center. South of town are the Mint Museum of Art, with art collections housed in a re-sited 1835 building from Charlotte's gold-producing era; the log cabins at the 1795 birthsite of President James K Polk; and the exciting Paramount's Carowinds theme park. On the east side of town you will find the area's oldest dwelling, the 1774 Rock House at the Hezekiah Alexander Homesite, and, further north, the Reed Gold Mine, where gold was discovered in 1799 by a 12-year-old boy, and the thrilling Charlotte Motor Speedway with its stock car races.

## Atlanta

Atlanta is probably best known as the Southern city burned to the ground by Yankees in the Civil War movie *Gone with the Wind*. Since then Georgia's capital has risen from the ashes like a phoenix to become the main business, financial and industrial hub of the Southeast. A vibrant, modern city, Atlanta boasts a flourishing cultural scene, with fine museums, galleries and performing arts events.

Amid the glittering glass towers that dominate the downtown skyline is the elegant Peachtree Center, a complex of hotels, offices, restaurants and shops. Its sleek modern architecture contrasts with the classic 1889 gold-domed State Capitol and government buildings nearby.

Among the many other places of interest to visit around the city are the shops and night spots of Underground Atlanta; the Martin Luther King Jr Historic Site along revitalized Auburn Avenue, which includes Dr King's birthplace and grave; Zoo Atlanta and the famous Cyclorama in Grant Park that tells the story of the Civil War battle of Atlanta; and the Wren's Nest, the home of writer Joel Chandler Harris, the creator of the beloved *Uncle Remus* tales. North along Peachtree Street are the art deco-style Fox Theatre; the Atlanta Botanical Garden in Piedmont Park; and the impressive Swan House in the smart residential neighborhood of Buckhead. For a final touch of nostalgia, drive out to Newnan, southwest of the city, to see many fine antebellum homes.

# Journey to the
## Land of the Sky

This journey starts with a drive across the green rolling country of central North Carolina to the pleasant town of Asheville, site of the Vanderbilts' famed Biltmore mansion, then enters the wild landscapes of the 'Land of the Sky', the Great Smoky Mountains, home of the proud Cherokee Indians. The Blue Ridge Parkway then leads you along the forested crests of the lovely Blue Ridge Mountains, past a succession of natural wonders, man-made attractions and unforgettable views.

**4/5 DAYS • 489 MILES • 782KM**

ITINERARY

| | | |
|---|---|---|
| **CHARLOTTE** | ▶ | **Gastonia (20m-32km)** |
| GASTONIA | ▶ | **Lake Lure (65m-104km)** |
| LAKE LURE | ▶ | **Asheville (30m-48km)** |
| ASHEVILLE | ▶ | **Cherokee (50m-80km)** |
| CHEROKEE | ▶ | **Great Smoky Mountains** |
| | | **(19m-30km)** |
| GREAT SMOKY | ▶ | **Blue Ridge Parkway** |
| MOUNTAINS | | **(16m-26km)** |
| BLUE RIDGE PARKWAY | ▶ | **Charlotte (289m-462km)** |

*i* 122 East Stonewall Street, Charlotte

▶ *Leave uptown Charlotte by Freedom Drive or Wilkinson Boulevard and enter I–85 westbound for the 20-mile (32km) drive to Gastonia.*

**❶ Gastonia,** North Carolina
One good reason to stop at Gastonia is to visit the Schiele Museum of Natural History, a 30-acre (12-hectare) showcase of the natural world at 1500 East Garrison Boulevard. Featuring a large collection of North American animals in habitat settings, it includes exhibits on minerals, fossils, archeology and local history. The museum also has a fine planetarium, a pioneer settlement, a nature trail and special events throughout the year.

---

**FOR HISTORY BUFFS**

In South Carolina, just 15 miles (24km) southwest of Gastonia via I–85, you can tour Kings Mountain National Military Park, site of a battle in 1780 that was a turning point in the Revolutionary War. Another reminder of Colonial times open for tours is Fort Dobbs, a State Historic Site near Statesville, built in 1756 to protect settlers during the French and Indian wars.

---

▶ *From Gastonia continue west on I–85 for 8 miles (13km), then US 74 for 57 miles (91km) through Shelby and Forest City to Lake Lure and Chimney Rock Park.*

**❷ Lake Lure and Chimney Rock Park,** North Carolina
Lake Lure lies in majestic forest country on the edge of the Blue Ridge Mountains, its shores a popular recreational area with facilities for swimming, boating, fishing and golf. Near by you can see the waterfalls of Bottomless Pools. For breathtaking views of the surrounding countryside

follow the picturesque 3-mile (5km) road from quaint Chimney Rock village, nestled between the cliffs of Hickory Nut Gorge, as far as the base of Chimney Rock itself. From here, either take the elevator inside the rock or follow the exciting, but more strenuous, trail up to the viewing platform at the top.

If you wish to explore further, you can follow one of the trails along the cliffs to 400-foot (122m) Hickory Nut Falls, one of the highest waterfalls in this part of the eastern United States.

▶ *Continue west along* US 74 *for 30 miles (48km) to Asheville.*

---

**SCENIC ROUTES**

Most of the itinerary between Chimney Rock and Blowing Rock is extremely scenic. The highlights include the Newfound Gap Road (US 441) north of Cherokee and the entire length of the Blue Ridge Parkway.

---

Chimney Rock Park

# TOUR
# 8

**Journey to the** Land of the Sky

**3 Asheville,** North Carolina
Asheville is the gateway to
North Carolina's scenic
Appalachian high country
region. It is also the location of
one of the state's greatest visitor
attractions, Biltmore Estate.
Designed by Richard Morris
Hunt for George Washington
Vanderbilt in the 1890s, the
colossal, luxuriously furnished
250-room mansion was built in
the grand style of a French
Renaissance château and set in
exquisite landscaped gardens
laid out by Frederick Law
Olmsted. Around it is a working
'gentleman's country estate'. In
keeping with the French-styled
château, the estate has a winery
(open to visitors), a large gift
shop and a picturesque English-
style village. Self-guided tours
take three to four hours.

Other places of interest you
can visit while you are here
include the Botanical Gardens;
the art and gem museums of
downtown Pack Place; the
boyhood home of novelist
Thomas Wolfe; and the Antique
Car Museum, next door to the
Biltmore Homespun Shop,
where you can see wool being
carded, spun and dyed.

*i 151 Haywood Street*

▶ *From Asheville follow I–40
heading west for 23 miles
(37km). Just before
Waynesville, take US 19 west
for 27 miles (43km) through
Maggie Valley to the Cherokee
Indian Reservation at
Cherokee.*

### FOR CHILDREN

At Maggie Valley, a town
devoted to family
entertainment, west of
Waynesville, take the kids up
the chair lift to Ghost Town in
the Sky on the mountain-top,
where they will enjoy the fun,
the mock gun-fights, the entertaining shows and the
stagecoach rides at the Wild
West frontier village.

**4 Cherokee,** North Carolina
Enclosed in lush forest at the
foot of the Great Smoky
Mountains is the home of the
eastern band of Cherokee
Indians. These are the descendants of the Cherokee who
remained in this region after the
majority were forced into exile
in what is now Oklahoma in
1838. The center of the reservation is the lively town of
Cherokee, which is packed with
visitor attractions, fun places for
children, shops, restaurants and
motels, so drop by the Visitor
Center on Main Street for useful
advice.

But don't miss the
Oconaluftee Indian Village,
where you can see the traditional Cherokee way of life as it
was in the 1700s; the Museum of
the Cherokee Indian, which
depicts Cherokee culture and
history; and the enticing Qualla
Arts and Crafts Shop. One of the
highlights of a visit here,
however, is a summer's evening
performance of the drama *Unto
These Hills*, which tells the exciting and moving story of the
Cherokee people.

*i Main Street*

### FOR CHILDREN

There is more entertainment
and a big zoo at Santa's
Land Theme Park at
Cherokee, where they say
Santa spends his summer
vacations.

▶ *From Cherokee it is just a few
miles north on US 441 to the
southern entrance of Great
Smoky Mountains National
Park.*

**5 Great Smoky Mountains
National Park,** North
Carolina and Tennessee
Shrouded in the permanent blue
haze that inspired its name, this
800-square-mile (2,072sq km)
jumble of worn-down, ancient
mountains, dense forests,
sparkling creeks and silvery

waterfalls is one of America's
most popular national parks.
More than 9 million visitors
come here each year to enjoy its
unspoiled beauty, rich wildlife
and recreational opportunities.
As you enter the park, stop for
information at the Visitor Center
and see the log buildings and
exhibits at the Pioneer
Farmstead. You can then follow
self-guiding trails, which include
the famed Appalachian Trail, for
a walk in the park.

But if you prefer a less strenuous visit, follow the 16-mile
(26km) scenic drive up
Newfound Gap Road (US 441),
then a 7-mile (11km) spur road
and a ½-mile (1km) trail to
Clingmans Dome, the Smokies'
highest point. From the observation tower at the 6,643-foot

### SPECIAL TO...

Boone, 9 miles (14km)
north of Blowing Rock on
US 321, offers nightly
outdoor performances in
midsummer of the historical
drama *Horn in the West*,
which tells how mountain folk
led by Daniel Boone rebelled
against the British and
moved over the Appalachians
to start a new life in the
West. The outdoor amphi-
theater is in a lovely mountain
setting.

Cataloochee Creek, in the Great Smoky Mountains National Park

(2,025m) summit, you will get marvelous views of the surrounding mountains, if there are no clouds.

*i* Oconaluftee Visitor Center, US 441

▶ *As you return from the Great Smoky Mountains on US 441, pick up the Blue Ridge Parkway on the left just before Cherokee for the 100-mile (160km) drive east as far as Blowing Rock.*

**6** **Blue Ridge Parkway,** North Carolina

A continuation of the Skyline Drive in neighboring Virginia, this marvelous road is one of America's finest scenic highways. Off-limits to commercial vehicles, it is used only for vacation travel. As it meanders at an average elevation of around 3,000 feet (914m) along the Blue Ridge Mountains, unfolding panoramas of forested mountain scenery can be viewed from many points. The Parkway also provides access to a wide range of visitor attractions.

On the first stretch of the parkway as far as Asheville, you can enjoy especially fine views of the wild Pisgah National Forest, an area of dramatic waterfalls and hiking trails. Just

beyond Asheville you can watch demonstrations of handicrafts at the Folk Art Center; visit the pioneer farmstead where Zebulon B Vance, governor of the state during the Civil War, was born (north at Weaverville); and tour lovely Craggy Gardens, famous for displays of blooming rhododendrons and flame azaleas in mid-June.

A few miles east you can drive almost to the top of 6,684-foot (2,037m) Mount Mitchell, eastern America's highest peak, for panoramic views from the lookout tower at the summit, before driving on to visit the fascinating Museum of North Carolina Minerals, near Spruce Pine. On this stretch of the parkway be sure to see the double-level Linville Falls, where the Linville River plunges into a deep, rugged gorge (a challenge for rock climbers), and the Linville Caverns nearby on US 221.

Continue along to Grandfather Mountain, at 5,964 feet (1,818m) the highest point in the Blue Ridge Mountains. Here you can enjoy the breathtaking scenery, walk the mile-high swinging suspension bridge and watch daring displays by hang-gliding experts. Leave the Parkway at Blowing Rock and visit the famed cliff-top viewpoint 3,000 feet (914m) above the John's River Gorge, where strong up-draughts make light

objects seem to fall upwards!

▶ *From Blowing Rock take US 321 south for 40 miles (64km) through Lenoir to Hickory, then go east on I-40 for 28 miles (45km) to Statesville. Pick up I-77 southbound for 42 miles (67km) to Charlotte.*

# Old Georgia's
## Antebellum Trail

This journey through Georgia's historic heartland east of Atlanta takes you back more than a century to those romantic pre-Civil War days when rich white folk of the Old South lived in grand plantation homes and elegant townhouses.

**3 DAYS • 262 MILES • 419KM**

**ITINERARY**

| | |
|---|---|
| **ATLANTA** | ▶ **Georgia's Stone Mountain Park (24m-39km)** |
| GEORGIA'S STONE MOUNTAIN PARK | ▶ **Athens (49m-78km)** |
| ATHENS | ▶ **Madison (30m-48km)** |
| MADISON | ▶ **Eatonton (21m-34km)** |
| EATONTON | ▶ **Milledgeville (20m-32km)** |
| MILLEDGEVILLE | ▶ **Clinton (24m-38km)** |
| CLINTON | ▶ **Macon (12m-19km)** |
| MACON | ▶ **Atlanta (82m-131km)** |

▶ From downtown Atlanta follow **I–20** eastbound for about 10 miles (16km), then **I–285** north to **Interchange 30**. Take **US 78** east for 6 miles (10km) to Georgia's Stone Mountain Park.

## ❶ Georgia's Stone Mountain Park, Georgia

The unmistakable rounded outline of Stone Mountain, an 825-foot (251m) bare granite monolith, looms over the vast family entertainment and recreational park at its foot. Along its side is carved a colossal relief sculpture of Confederate heroes: Jefferson Davis, Robert E Lee and 'Stonewall' Jackson. Kids will enjoy the many attractions, which include an exciting skylift up the mountain, a steam train, a paddlewheel riverboat, an antebellum (pre-Civil War) plantation and a summer laser show. There are also facilities for camping, fishing, swimming, ice skating, golf and tennis. Just west of the park, Stone Mountain Village has a range of enticements for shoppers.

▶ Continue east on **US 78** through Monroe to Athens.

## ❷ Athens, Georgia

The 'Classic City' of Athens, set in the green hills of northern Georgia, grew as a cultural center around the University of Georgia, chartered in 1785. Fine mansions built in the antebellum years still stand in magnolia-shaded gardens around its streets, among them Athens' oldest residence, the Church-Waddel-Brumby House of 1820. Here you can get information on self-guided tours of the university, neighborhoods with antebellum homes, and the downtown area, with its quaint shops and outdoor cafés. As you wander around, don't miss the city's two special curiosities: the Double-Barreled Cannon, a failed invention of 1862 that wreaked havoc when test-fired, and the Tree That Owns Itself, which stands in a small patch deeded to it by a professor who loved to sit in its shade. Garden lovers won't want to miss the 2½-acre (1-hectare) Founders Memorial Garden, on the university campus, or the beautiful 300-acre (120-hectare) State

Stone Mountain's natural face bears the mark of man's art

Botanical Garden, down by the Oconee River south of town. It is on the way to Watkinsville, where you can see the famous Eagle Tavern, built as Fort Edwards in 1789 and later used as a stagecoach stop and store.

E Dougherty Street

▶ Take **US 129/441** south through Watkinsville to Madison.

## ❸ Madison, Georgia

As early as 1864, this small community of tree-lined streets and beautiful old homes fronted with columns or lacy Victorian fretwork was praised as 'the most picturesque town in Georgia'. Fortunately, pleas by local citizens saved it from destruction during the Civil War, and it became known as 'the town that Sherman refused to burn'. Today most of Madison is designated as a National Historic District. You can get walking-tour maps and cassettes from the Chamber of Commerce and watch a short slide show on the town's historic homes at Heritage Hall on South Main Street. Among Madison's treasures are such beautiful mansions as Bonar Hall and the Kelly House, charming cottages, historic churches, Morgan County Courthouse, the Old Stagecoach Inn and the Madison-Morgan Cultural Center, a focus of performing and visual arts events.

> ℹ️ *115 East Jefferson Street*

> ▶ *From Madison continue south on US 129/441 to Eatonton.*

### RECOMMENDED WALKS

For gentler strolls in more countrified surroundings stop at the recreational areas along the tour. They include Lake Oconee, east of Madison, and Lake Sinclair and Oconee National Forest, between Eatonton and Milledgeville.

**4 Eatonton,** Georgia
Before entering Eatonton, make a stop at the Rock Eagle Center about 5 miles (8km) north of town to see one of the area's best-known attractions, the 5,000-year-old Indian Rock Eagle Mound. At Eatonton you will see fine examples of antebellum architecture, including the much-altered Bronson House, now occupied by the local historical society. The town is best known, however, as the home of Br'er Rabbit and the beloved 'critters' of the *Uncle Remus* tales written by Joel Chandler Harris, who lived in Eatonton until 1864. Kids enjoy discovering the statue of Br'er Rabbit on the courthouse lawn and visiting the slave cabin in nearby Turner Park, a replica of the one in which Uncle Remus lived. It serves as the Uncle Remus Museum and has many mementos of Harris's work.

> ℹ️ *Chamber of Commerce, 105 Sumter Street*

> ▶ *Follow US 441 south from Eatonton to Milledgeville.*

**5 Milledgeville,** Georgia
Milledgeville has a proud history as Georgia's capital during the prosperous years from 1803 to 1868 and boasts many imposing buildings in its Historic District. On Tuesday and Friday mornings there is a two-hour trolley bus tour starting from the tourist office on W Hancock Street. Among the highlights are the impressive Old State Capitol of 1807, which now forms part of the Georgia Military College; the Old Governor's Mansion of 1838, now a National Historic Landmark; St Stephen's Episcopal Church; and the beautiful 1812 Stetson-Sanford House. If you are here in May you will also enjoy a wide range of entertaining events and activities in the city's famed Old Capitol Celebration.

> ℹ️ *200 W Hancock Street*

### BACK TO NATURE

If you are interested in wild plants, don't miss a tour (free, by appointment weekdays) of the 50-acre (20-hectare) Lockerly Arboretum, just south of Milledgeville on US 441. A tour guide will tell you about the plants as you walk the pleasant wooded trails.

> ▶ *Take SR 22 southwest to Gray, then US 129 to Clinton.*

**6 Clinton,** Georgia
If you arrive here on a particular weekend in mid-April, you might think you have stumbled into a time warp and gone back to the Civil War. In their War Days festival each year at this time, Georgians re-enact, with terrifying realism, the fierce battles fought here in 1864. In those clashes the thriving little town was badly damaged and later began to decline. But about a dozen houses and the Methodist Church, all dating

Baldwin County Court House, Milledgeville

from 1810 to 1830, survived and have been preserved. Today Old Clinton is a place where you can feel history all around you. As Georgians say, it's 'the town that time forgot'.

> ℹ️ *McCarthy-Pope House*

### BACK TO NATURE

For a glimpse of Georgia's wildlife, visit Piedmont National Wildlife Refuge, some 12 miles (19km) north of Clinton via SR 11. The mosaic of abandoned farmland and forest – hardwoods, loblolly and shortleaf pines – harbors bobwhite quails, wild turkeys, red-cocked woodpeckers, tufted titmouse and numerous species of warblers.

> ▶ *Continue south on US 129/SR 22 for 12 miles (19km) to Macon.*

**7 Macon,** Georgia
Macon lies beside the Ocmulgee River at the southern end of Georgia's Antebellum Trail. Its downtown Historic District was originally laid out in the 1820s in a neat grid of broad streets and garden squares, and is now a showcase of carefully preserved and restored buildings, many of them on the National Register

of Historic Places. You can see them by following the Heritage Tour Markers.

The best way to see the city is to take Sidney's Old South Historic Tour from the Convention and Visitors Bureau. Be sure to visit elegant Hay House (1850s); Old Cannonball House (1853) and Confederate Museum; Woodruff House

Macon, a town of delightfully preserved and restored houses

(1836); the pretty cottage where the Georgia poet Sidney Lanier was born in 1842; and the elegant Grand Opera House (1906). For an evening's entertainment you might catch a concert or play here, or a show or sporting event at the Macon Coliseum across the river.

*i* *Terminal Station, 200 Cherry Street*

▶ *From Macon take I-75 northbound for 82 miles (131km) back to Atlanta.*

# THE SUNSHINE STATE

Florida has for many years been the place to escape the snowbound northern states in the winter. More recently, it has also become a popular year-round destination for overseas visitors, who come to enjoy the climate, the superb beaches, the vast family entertainment complexes, outdoor recreational opportunities and the exotic wildlife.

Long after the arrival in 1513 of Spanish explorer Ponce de León, the peninsula remained largely unexploited. Except for its idyllic coastline, it seemed an unlikely place for colonization – a huge, flat, waterlogged slab of limestone pockmarked with lakes, sinkholes and springs, and blanketed in moss-draped forests, mangroves and swamps. It was also inhabited by fearsome alligators and even more hostile Seminole Indians. But in the 1880s and '90s railroads were brought down its coasts to Tampa Bay and Miami, and Florida's destiny was sealed.

Aerial view of Panama City Beach

Florida's attractions are many and varied. The Atlantic coast is fringed with beaches, lagoons, islands and resort towns. Here you will find the charming old city of St Augustine; Daytona Beach and its International Speedway; the NASA Kennedy Space Center; Fort Lauderdale, the 'Venice of America'; the glitzy oceanfront hotels of Miami Beach; and the skyscrapers and cruise ships of Miami. At the southern tip lie the Everglades, whose waters are now threatened by Miami's relentless growth. The Florida Keys arch into the ocean to the bustling vacation center of Key West. Known for tarpon fishing, seashells, sponges and pirates, Florida's Gulf Coast boasts delightful seaside communities and more superb beaches. The most popular stretch is the Pinellas Suncoast, near St Petersburg and Tampa and linked by fast highway to Orlando's entertainment parks.

Florida's 220-mile-long (350km) panhandle has the state capital, Tallahassee, and historic Pensacola. It is a region of pine forests, salt marshes, springs and sun-splashed beaches, where the atmosphere of the Old South survives.

## Miami

With an average year-round temperature of 76°F (24°C) and 15 miles (24km) of silvery beaches shelving into a warm, blue-green sea, Miami, not surprisingly, is a major international vacation center drawing about 7 million visitors each year. Clustered around the glittering skyscrapers of the downtown business district, the 26 municipalities known as Greater Miami are linked by causeways across Biscayne Bay to a necklace of offshore resort islands, from the Sunny Isles in the north to fabled Miami Beach and Key Biscayne in the south. And sheltered in the bay, sleek cruise ships line the wharves of the busy Port of Miami.

A rich potpourri of ethnic groups – South American, Cuban, Black, and white Anglos – has produced an exciting cultural mix, creating a lively performing and visual arts scene, colorful festivals, and a mouthwatering range of international cuisine. Following large influxes of Cubans in the early 1960s and '80s, Miami has acquired an especially strong Latin flavor, so you are just as likely to hear Spanish spoken as English.

Although the press and the TV series *Miami Vice* have spotlighted its high crime rate in recent years, Miami remains a fascinating and alluring place for the visitor, with a range of attractions too numerous to list. Apart from fine museums like the downtown Historical Museum of Southern Florida, sightseeing musts in Miami include the Latin enclave of Little Havana, centered on colorful Calle Ocho, or SW 8th Street; Bayside Marketplace, with its eye-catching boutiques and street performers down by the waterfront; the nostalgic 1920s and '30s architecture in the Art Deco district of South Miami Beach; and the performing dolphins and other marine animals at the Miami

A fine example of Miami Beach's Art Deco architecture

Seaquarium on Rickenbacker Causeway. There are also enjoyable one-day cruises with on-board entertainment from the Port of Miami, and yacht and sportfishing charters from the area's many marinas. But for sheer relaxation, you still can't beat soaking up the sun on one of the fabulous palm-dotted beaches.

## Tampa

The manufacturing port city of Tampa lies at the head of the immense natural harbor of Tampa Bay, midway along Florida's Gulf Coast. A notable landmark is the old Moorish-style Tampa Bay Hotel built in 1891. At this time Cuban cigar-makers set up business in the nearby neighborhood of Ybor City, now Tampa's Latin Quarter. You can recall those days as you tour the cobbled streets, now lined with colorful restaurants and shops. Other shopping highlights are Old Hyde Park Village and The Shops on Harbour Island. Tampa's other visitor attractions include fine museums such as the Museum of Science and Industry; the new Florida Aquarium; and the Tampa Bay Performing Arts Center, which offers everything from ballet to jazz. There are also boat cruises, sailing, water skiing and sailboarding, and lots of fun at the water theme park of Adventure Island. But not to be missed is a visit to fabulous Busch Gardens, an amusement park on an African theme, with live entertainment, animal shows and exhibits, shops, exciting rides and a huge zoo.

# The Everglades
## & Coral Keys

Head off south through the sprawling suburban communities of Miami – with a pause to explore the refreshing oases of Coconut Grove and Coral Gables and tourist attractions along the way. Then it's on to the sawgrass-and-alligator swampland of Everglades National Park and the Florida Keys, a necklace of sparkling coral islands.

**4/5 DAYS • 341 MILES • 545KM**

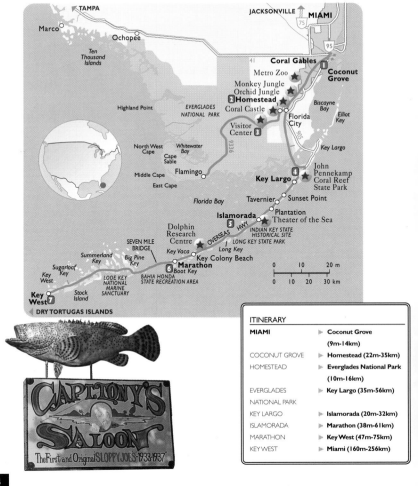

**ITINERARY**

| | |
|---|---|
| **MIAMI** | ► **Coconut Grove** (9m-14km) |
| COCONUT GROVE | ► **Homestead** (22m-35km) |
| HOMESTEAD | ► **Everglades National Park** (10m-16km) |
| EVERGLADES NATIONAL PARK | |
| KEY LARGO | ► **Key Largo** (35m-56km) |
| ISLAMORADA | ► **Islamorada** (20m-32km) |
| MARATHON | ► **Marathon** (38m-61km) |
| KEY WEST | ► **Key West** (47m-75km) |
| | ► **Miami** (160m-256km) |

*i* Bayside Marketplace, 401,
G Miami

▶ From downtown Miami take
either I–95 or Brickell Avenue
and South Bayshore Drive for
the short drive to Coconut
Grove and Coral Gables.

**❶ Coconut Grove and
Coral Gables,** Florida
Just minutes from downtown
Miami, these two communities
have a special appeal. Coconut
Grove draws visitors with its
smart boutiques, outdoor cafés,
art galleries and night spots,
centered on CocoWalk and its
frequent festivals. Among its
sightseeing attractions are
magnificent Villa Vizcaya and its
fine gardens. Planned by the
poet George Merrick as the ulti-
mate 'city beautiful', Coral
Gables is an architectural showcase, with Spanish-style buildings, tree-lined boulevards,
shady plazas and fountains, and
imposing entrance gates. Take a

drive around to see the shops on
the Miracle Mile (Coral Way),
the Venetian Pool, the
marvelous Lowe Art Museum,
and the Fairchild Tropical
Garden's rare plant house and
rainforest.

*i* 2820 McFarlane Road, Coconut
Grove; 50 Aragon Avenue, Coral
Gables

---

### FOR CHILDREN

Children will enjoy the hands-
on exhibits at the excellent
Miami Museum of Science and
Space Transit Planetarium at
Coconut Grove. The museum's
attractions include computer
exhibits, minitheater shows on
flora and fauna in Florida and
the Everglades, and an aviary
and wildlife center, while the
Planetarium houses changing
displays and offers multimedia
laser and star shows daily.

---

▶ From Coral Gables pick up the
South Dixie Highway (US 1)
southbound for the 22-mile
(35km) drive to Homestead.

**❷ Homestead,** Florida
The urban sprawl of Greater
Miami South has little interest
for passing visitors except for a
few special attractions with
names that are self-explanatory.
Even if you are not into performing animals, you will probably
enjoy Parrot Jungle, on SW 57th
Avenue; the immense, state-of-
the-art, cageless MetroZoo, on
SW 152nd Street; and Monkey
Jungle, on SW 216th Street,
where, in an ironic reversal, you
will be put in a cage to be
watched by free-roaming
animals.
    For plant lovers there is a
colorful show of blooms at
Orchid Jungle, just north of
Homestead; and for the romantic at heart, Homestead itself

*Enjoying a drink in Coconut Grove*

*Exploring the mysterious peace of the Everglades by airboat*

boasts the amazing Coral Castle, built single-handedly by a jilted lover over a period of 20 years. The center of Florida's nursery and fruit production, Homestead is also the gateway to Everglades National Park. Don't miss a visit to the Fruit and Spice Park, on SW 187th Avenue, which has over 500 species of spice trees, nuts and fruit from 50 tropical countries.

ℹ️ *160 US Highway 1, Florida City*

▶ *From the Homestead-Florida City area follow **SR 9336** southwest for 10 miles (16km) to Everglades National Park.*

### ❸ Everglades National Park, Florida

This immense natural wilderness and wildlife haven at the southern tip of Florida was created by spillage flowing south to the sea from Lake Okeechobee. Stretching into the distance are great expanses of sawgrass – Florida's 'River of Grass' – which grows in the shallow water. Here and there, islands of semitropical vegetation, called hammocks, provide a home for black bears, white-tailed deer, alligators, herons, egrets and many other wild creatures (especially mosquitoes!). And among the mangrove forests and mudflats along the coast, you can see white ibis, brown pelicans, roseate spoonbills and even flamingos.

Stop at the main Visitor Center near the park entrance and follow the paved road which meanders for 36 miles (58km) to the seaside community of Flamingo. Along the way take a closer look at this unique natural habitat by exploring some of the side roads leading to walking trails and points of interest. You can also take boat tours into the park from Flamingo.

ℹ️ *Parachute Key Visitor Center, park entrance, SR 9336*

---

### BACK TO NATURE

The Everglades National Park is accessible via Homestead and visitors should not miss the ½-mile (800m) Anhinga Trail at Royal Palm Hammock and Eco Pond at Flamingo, where hundreds of roosting wading birds can be seen flying at dusk.
Look for alligators, terrapins, anhingas, egrets, herons, turkey vultures and black vultures.

---

▶ *From Flamingo return by the same road (**SR 9336**) to Florida City. Then take **US 1** south for about 20 miles (32km) to Key Largo, the first of the islands on the 110-mile (177km) drive on the Overseas Highway along the Florida Keys to Key West.*

### ❹ Key Largo, Florida

Key Largo is your first sight of the string of coral islands known as the Keys, which arch westward into the sea from Florida's southern tip. A popular year-round vacation spot, the Keys are a mecca for boating, fishing, swimming, scuba diving, camping, biking, walking, or just lying in the sun. With their exotic cuisine, they are also a gourmet's paradise.

Key Largo is known around the world for the Bogart-Bacall movie of the same name, and it still preserves Bogart's old boat from *The African Queen*. But its star visitor attraction is undoubtedly the underwater wonderland encompassed by the John Pennekamp Coral Reef State Park. By snorkeling, scuba diving or just sitting in a glass-bottom boat, you can see a dazzling array of colorful

fish darting around the beautiful coral and the incongruous spectacle of a submerged statue, 'Christ of the Deep'. Even more unusual is Jules Undersea Lodge, an ocean-floor hotel five fathoms down.

*i* *106 Plaza, Key Largo*

▶ *Drive southwest for 20 miles (32km) to Islamorada.*

**5 Islamorada,** Florida

West of Key Largo, the group of islands known collectively as Islamorada, or 'Purple Isles', is a major center for charter fishing but also has other visitor attractions.

Not to be missed are the dolphin and sealion shows and other sea creatures at the Theater of the Sea on Windley Key; the tropical hardwood forest on Lignumvitae Key; the reefs and historic wrecks off the southern shores; and the beach and nature trails in Long Key State Park.

▶ *Continue on **US 1**.*

Key Largo captivates with its silver sand and azure sea and sky

---

### FOR HISTORY BUFFS

Scattered along the Florida Keys are historic sites that tell the colorful story of these lovely islands. You can visit the wreck of the Spanish galleon *Herrera* off Islamorada; Indian mounds and village sites on the Lower Keys; and romantic Fort Jefferson, a National Monument on the Dry Tortugas Islands, 70 miles (113km) off Key West, accessible by charter boat or seaplane.

---

**6 Marathon and the Lower Keys,** Florida

Midway along the Keys, the Marathon group of islands is best known for golf, sportfishing, and angling from 'the world's longest fishing pier' – still-standing segments of the former highway bridge. The spectacular new Seven-Mile Bridge that replaced it links Marathon to the Lower

Keys. The main attraction for visitors to the Lower Keys is the unspoiled forest wilderness and abundant wildlife in the specially protected areas. When you have sampled the pleasures of Bahia Honda's fine beach, be sure to see the beautiful undersea reefs at Looe Key National Marine Sanctuary and the rare miniature Key deer and great white herons at the special refuges on Big Pine Key.

*i* *3330 Overseas Highway, Marathon*

---

### BACK TO NATURE

The Keys are generally rather built up and have lost much of their wildlife interest. However, shorebirds, herons and gulls are found almost anywhere, and magnificent frigatebirds are ever present in the skies as you approach Key West. A few sanctuary areas are set aside for the diminutive and endangered Key deer.

---

Audubon House, named after the renowned naturalist

▶ *Continue on **US 1** to Key West.*

**7 Key West**, Florida

With its sophisticated, free-and-easy lifestyle, this lively island community has long been a favorite retreat for the rich and famous and a popular play-ground for vacationers. For a taste of Key West's unique atmosphere, walk the Pelican Path or ride an Old Town Trolley or the Conch Tour Train; explore the colorful shops, bars and outdoor cafés; sample the exotic local cuisine; and mingle with the evening crowds who gather in Mallory Square to watch free entertainment and the breath-taking sunsets.

Rent a charter boat for some deep-sea fishing and tour the many sightseeing attractions. Not to be missed among these are the town's 'gingerbread' mansions (ornate Victorian style); Hemingway House and Audubon House, commemorating two of Key West's best-known celebrities; historic Fort Zachary Taylor; and the Mel Fisher Maritime Heritage Society Museum, with its booty from wrecked Spanish galleons. For underwater wildlife visit the Key West Aquarium or take a cruise on a glass-bottom boat. And if you have time, take a walk to the town's picturesque cemetery. You will find it hard not to chuckle when you read some of the epitaphs, like the one from a grieving widow which wryly observes: 'At least I know where he's sleeping tonight!'

ℹ *402 Wall Street (Old Mallory Square)*

▶ *From Key West follow the Overseas Highway and **US 1** back to Miami.*

---

**SCENIC ROUTES**

The highlight of the itinerary is the island-hopping drive along the Florida Keys on the Overseas Highway, with its bridges and constantly changing views of the ocean, beaches, craggy bays and forest wilderness.
The Seven-Mile Bridge between Marathon and the Lower Keys is an especially exciting section, with expansive views of the ocean and of the old unused bridge which runs alongside, now frequented by anglers.

---

**SPECIAL TO...**

Key West's festive atmosphere is punctuated each year by three major celebrations. During Old Island Days (February 2 through April) houses are opened to visitors, and a series of special events highlighting the history, culture and architecture of the island take place.
The Hemingway Days Festival (mid-July) features a Hemingway look-alike contest and a short-story contest. In the lively Fantasy Fest (late October), the town is seized with a carnival atmosphere with colorful events climaxing in the Grand Parade.

---

**RECOMMENDED WALKS**

In addition to the trails off the highway through Everglades National Park, there are enjoyable walks on the Keys in John Pennekamp State Park, Long Key State Park, Indian Key State Historic Site, Bahia Honda State Recreation Area and around Key West.

# Florida's Family
## Funland

This drive out of Tampa spans the whole width of Central Florida from
the Gulf Coast to the Atlantic, from the superb beaches of the Pinellas
Suncoast to the launchpads at Cape Canaveral. It is a tour of man-made
entertainments rather than scenic attractions but with enough variety to
satisfy most tastes and interests.

**4/5 DAYS • 406 MILES • 650KM**

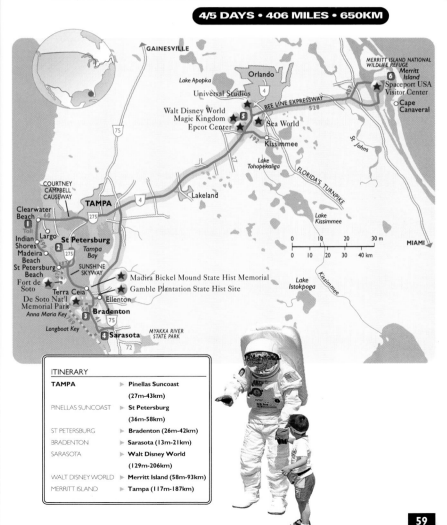

## ITINERARY

| | | |
|---|---|---|
| **TAMPA** | ▶ | **Pinellas Suncoast** (27m–43km) |
| PINELLAS SUNCOAST | ▶ | **St Petersburg** (36m–58km) |
| ST PETERSBURG | ▶ | **Bradenton** (26m–42km) |
| BRADENTON | ▶ | **Sarasota** (13m–21km) |
| SARASOTA | ▶ | **Walt Disney World** (129m–206km) |
| WALT DISNEY WORLD | ▶ | **Merritt Island** (58m–93km) |
| MERRITT ISLAND | ▶ | **Tampa** (117m–187km) |

*i* *Corner of Ashley and Madison streets, Tampa*

▶ *From downtown Tampa follow I–275 west for 5 miles (8km), turn on to **SR 60** and continue via the Courtney Campbell Causeway, Gulf-to-Bay Boulevard and Clearwater Causeway to Clearwater Beach. Cross the Clearwater Pass toll bridge and follow Gulf Boulevard (**SR 699**) south for about 18 miles (29km) along the Pinellas Suncoast.*

## **0 The Pinellas Suncoast,**
Florida

With its unbroken sunshine and 28 miles (45km) of sparkling white beaches shelving gently into the Gulf of Mexico's warm blue waters, the coast of Pinellas County and its string of offshore sandbar islands are among America's top vacation destinations. Here you will find accommodations and dining

establishments from the inexpensive to the luxurious. High on the list of popular outdoor activities – in addition to swimming and soaking up the sun – are windsurfing, waterskiing, parasailing, golf and tennis. Boat cruises are available, and there are opportunities for fishing.

On the drive south from Clearwater Beach visit the Suncoast Seabird Sanctuary at Indian Shores, where nearly 5,000 injured birds get hospital treatment every year; take a walk around the shops at John's Pass Village, a re-created turn-of-the-century fishing community at Madeira Beach; and take a sightseeing cruise on the bay to glimpse dolphins and feed seabirds at St Petersburg Beach, location of the old Don CeSar hotel resort, a noted landmark along the seafront.

The impressive Salvador Dalí Museum in St Petersburg

### FOR HISTORY BUFFS

On exhibit at Heritage Park and Museum, in Largo, adjacent to Clearwater, is a replica of a Benoist airboat, the plane that began the age of scheduled commercial air services with a flight from St Petersburg across the bay to Tampa in 1915. The park also displays a collection of historic buildings in the wooded grounds. The museum portrays aspects of pioneer life, with frequent displays of weaving, spinning and other crafts.

*i* *Welcome Center, 3550 Gulf-to-Bay Boulevard, Clearwater*

▶ *Follow the Pinellas Bayway (**SR 682**; toll) from the southern end of St Petersburg Beach and after about 4 miles (6km) take **I–275** north to downtown St Petersburg.*

### SPECIAL TO...

Among the myriad events and festivals that draw thousands of visitors to Florida's central west coast every year are the Fun 'n' Sun Festival, a 10-day extravaganza in late April at Clearwater, with music, sports events and a regatta.

### 2 St Petersburg, Florida

Once known as a retirement area for senior citizens, St Petersburg, on Tampa Bay, is now blossoming at the hub of Florida's west coast tourism boom. New hotel resorts and sightseeing attractions have sprouted to cater for visitors' needs. On your way into town you will pass one of the newest facilities, the Florida Suncoast Dome, an impressive arena for baseball, concerts, shows and other events. Jutting into the bay on the waterfront is St Pete's most famous landmark, the Pier, with its unusual, inverted pyramid-shaped marketplace.

North of the Pier you will find lovely Straub Park; the Museum of Fine Arts, with its fine collections, including ancient and oriental art and pre-Columbian goldware and pottery; and the famed Sunken Gardens, home to exotic birds and animals in a beautiful jungle setting. Drive south from the Pier and take in a show or concert at the Bayfront Center or explore St Petersburg's past at the Historical and Flight One Museum. Children on the tour will surely enjoy the fascinating hands-on science, nature and art exhibits at the Great Explorations Museum. Not to be missed is the unique and comprehensive collection of surrealist art at the excellent Salvador Dalí Museum.

*i* 100 Second Avenue North

▶ *From St Petersburg take I-275 and the Sunshine Skyway south across Tampa Bay, then US 41 (the Tamiami Trail) south to the town of Bradenton.*

*Exquisite orchids at the Marie Selby Botanical Gardens, Sarasota*

### SPECIAL TO...

The big Festival of States, held at St Petersburg over two weeks in March and April, features band competitions, concerts, three parades, various sports events and fireworks displays. The St Petersburg Grand Prix, held every fall, has racing cars roaring around the waterfront circuit.

### 3 Bradenton, Florida

Several places of cultural and historic interest are scattered around the Bradenton area. You can view the historic buildings at the Manatee Village Historical Park; see displays of ancient Indian relics at the Madira Bickel Mound State Historic Site, on Terra Ceia Island, and also at Bradenton's South Florida Museum; and tour a 19th-century sugar planter's home at the Gamble Plantation State Historic Site at Ellenton, off US 301. Drive west out of Bradenton on SR 64 and you will find the De Soto National Memorial Park, which commemorates the Spanish explorer's landing in 1539, an event re-enacted every year in April.

*i* 5030, US 301 North, Ellenton

### FOR CHILDREN

The sun, sea and sand of the Pinellas beaches, the excitement of Walt Disney World and the marvels of Spaceport USA are probably enough for most kids on this tour. But for something different, take them to see Snooty, one of Florida's endangered manatees and a playful performer at the South Florida Museum in Bradenton.

▶ *Continue south from Bradenton for 13 miles (21km) on **US 41** to the resort of Sarasota.*

**4 Sarasota,** Florida
Sarasota is another popular west coast vacation center offering a wide range of seaside activities. But it is especially known for its important cultural attractions, which owe much to the contributions made to the town by the circus impresario John Ringling. North of town he built his lavish dream home, Ca'd'Zan (John's House, in Venetian dialect). It is now part of the complex that also includes the John and Mabel Ringling Museum of Art, containing his priceless Rubens collection and other treasures; the nostalgic Circus Galleries; and the reconstructed 18th-century Asolo Theater from Italy.

Near by is another popular attraction, Bellm's Cars and Music of Yesterday, featuring antique automobiles, mechanical musical boxes, and early arcade games and pinball machines. For a complete change of mood, go to see the tropical plants, Gardens of Christ, alligators and flamingos on show at the Sarasota Jungle Gardens on Bayshore Road.

Also of interest to nature lovers are the Pelican Man's Bird Sanctuary; the undersea life at the Mote Marine Aquarium; and the performing horses at Hermann's Lippizan Ranch, out at Myakka.

[i] *655 North Tamiami Trail (US 41)*

▶ *Pick up **I–75** northbound from Sarasota, then take **I–4** east for the 129-mile (206km) drive to Walt Disney World.*

**5 Walt Disney World,** Florida
Don't expect scenic beauty or natural wonders in this part of Florida. This is 'Vacationland USA' – a brash and breezy fantasy world created specifically, and successfully, to entertain you. The variety of theme parks, water parks, entertainment complexes and other attractions here are enough to make any adventurous soul, from seven to 70, wide-eyed with wonder. At the top of the list, without question, is Walt Disney World, off I–4 at Exit 25. This huge resort complex includes the Magic Kingdom, the Epcot Center, Disney/MGM Studios, Typhoon Lagoon, River Country and Shopping Village and much more. But be warned: a brief visit simply cannot do it justice, so plan your day carefully and get there early.

A few miles further along I–4 you can watch the antics of performing killer whales and dolphins at Sea World of Florida (Exit 28) and enjoy the fun in

The space shuttle 'Discovery', at Kennedy Space Center

The Valiant Air Command Museum has an outstanding collection of military aircraft

favorite movie settings at Universal Studios Florida (Exit 30B), two of the area's other outstanding attractions.

---

### SCENIC ROUTES

The most scenic routes on this tour are those sections of SR 60 and the Sunshine Skyway, a suspension bridge, that span Tampa Bay.
For an additional treat, instead of taking US 41 from Bradenton to Sarasota, follow the more pleasant shoreline route on Routes 64 and 789 along Anna Maria Island and Longboat Key, with its broad views of rolling dunes, dazzling beaches and the ocean.

---

▶ Leave I–4 at **Exit 28** and continue east for about 55 miles (89km) on the Beeline

*Expressway and* **SR 407** *to Merritt Island and Spaceport USA.*

**❻ Merritt Island and Spaceport USA,** Florida Merritt Island and the other offshore barrier islands and lagoons of Florida's eastern shoreline – the 'Florida Space Coast' – are home not only to seabirds but also to the rockets and spacecraft launched from famous Cape Canaveral. If you can't watch a launch, do the next best thing and tour the awesome complex and the technological marvels on display at Spaceport USA at the Kennedy Space Center, where every aspect of space flight – past, present and future – is explored. You can watch the birds in the peace and quiet of Merritt Island National Wildlife Refuge, which surrounds the space complex.

▶ *Follow the Beeline Expressway* (**SR 528**) *and* **I–4** *westbound for the 117-mile (187km) return drive to Tampa.*

---

### RECOMMENDED WALKS

Pleasant places for a stroll are the boardwalk at John's Pass Village and the waterfront and Pier at St Petersburg. There is also the nature trail by the Manatee River at De Soto National Memorial Park, at Bradenton, and quiet walks along the dunes and beaches of Anna Maria Island, Longboat Key and little Egmont Key, off the coast between Bradenton and Sarasota.

---

### BACK TO NATURE

Unexpected encounters with Florida's wildlife can happen anywhere on the tour. However, it is more than likely you will see pelicans fishing and egrets stalking fish on a walk along the boardwalk at John's Pass Village, Madeira Beach.

# THE MIDWEST

America's Midwest region stretches across the center of the country from the Appalachians to the Rockies and from the northern forests and lakes of Minnesota and Wisconsin to the Ozark Mountains of Arkansas. Drained by the Mississippi, Missouri, Ohio and other great rivers, this huge territory is the nation's agricultural heartland. From Ohio to Nebraska an immense checkerboard of fields known as the Corn Belt yields abundant harvests of farm produce, while in the west, treeless expanses of wheat and vast cattle ranches extend across the Great Plains that border the Rockies from Montana to Kansas.

This region conjures up eternal images of sultry, hot summers and bleak, snowy winters; isolated farmsteads with tall shiny silos, red-painted barns and water tanks on towers; and quiet little towns with no more than a few clapboard houses, a church, wooden schoolhouse, diner and general store. Yet there are also big manufacturing cities, often hugging the great river arteries, like Cincinnati, Minneapolis and St Paul, or the shores of the Great Lakes, like Chicago, Milwaukee, Detroit and Cleveland.

The tranquility of today's Midwest belies its often violent past. Stories tell of the early Indian inhabitants and great buffalo herds; the region's exploration by the French; westward expansion by settlers and the railroads and the lawless Wild West.

Statue of the Founding Fathers, Chicago

## Cincinnati

Cincinnati lies on the north bank of the Ohio River in an amphitheater of hills in southwest Ohio. Established in 1788, it developed as an important river port linked to the Mississippi and the newly opened-up lands in the west. The city's German heritage is reflected in its vibrant cultural life, fine restaurants, and its famous Oktoberfest.

A steamboat cruise on the river today takes you beneath photogenic old bridges and past the landmark Riverfront Stadium and the Riverfront Coliseum entertainment complex. Other fine views of the city are available from the top of the 49-story Carew Tower. Not to be missed is a tour of the charming old hilltop neighborhood of Mt Adams, with its fashionable boutiques and restaurants, and prestigious Cincinnati Art Museum; Playhouse in the Park professional theater, and the Krohn Conservatory botanical showcase. For family fun there are also the superb Cincinnati Zoo and several amusement and water parks, including the Kings Island theme park.

## Chicago

Three of the world's five tallest buildings puncture the magnificent skyline of America's third largest city, at the southern tip of Lake Michigan. Since its birth in 1830, immigrants, many of them Poles, have helped turn the Windy City into a major business, financial and manufacturing center, transportation hub and lake port.

Chicago is a sophisticated, cosmopolitan place with fine hotels, restaurants and shops, exciting entertainment, nightlife and spectator sports, and numerous cultural and sightseeing attractions. Outstanding among these are museums such as the Art Institute of Chicago and the Museum of Science and Industry. On the lakefront are the Navy Pier, with its boat cruises; Grant Park and the Buckingham Fountain; and the Adler Planetarium, John G Shedd Aquarium and Field Museum of Natural History. Among the skyscrapers of the downtown business and shopping district, known as the Loop, are small plazas embellished with modern sculptures, and old architectural landmarks like the Carson Pirie Scott and Marshall Field department stores. North of here are the shops of Oak Street and North Michigan Avenue, Chicago's 'Magnificent Mile', and the throbbing nightlife of Rush Street. Breathtaking bird's-eye views are available from the observation decks in the 110-story Sears Tower and the 100-story John Hancock Center.

*Chicago's impressive city skyline*

## Minneapolis and St Paul

The Twin Cities of Minneapolis and St Paul lie together on the Mississippi River amid the rolling farmlands of southeast Minnesota. Minneapolis is the dynamic business and financial center of the Upper Midwest, while more conservative St Paul serves as state capital. Minneapolis presents a bold skyline of sleek modern architecture, while St Paul still preserves many renovated old landmarks among its newer structures. Together they enjoy a thriving cultural life, which adds to their appeal.

Minneapolis is known for the IDS building's Crystal Court; the shops of Nicollet Mall, quaint St Anthony Main and the Riverplace mall; Guthrie Theater; and fine museums like the Walker Art Center and the American Swedish Institute. St Paul highlights include the impressive State Capitol complex, and new Minnesota History Center; the Cathedral of St Paul; the renovated Landmark Center; the magnificent Ordway Music Theater; the shops of Grand Avenue, St Paul Center and Bandana Square; the fine 19th-century homes along Summit Avenue; and the marvelous hands-on Science Museum with its superb Omnitheater.

# Kentucky &
# Mammoth Cave

Mention Kentucky and many things spring to mind: Kentucky Fried Chicken and bluegrass music, the Kentucky Derby and thoroughbred horses, bourbon whiskey, tobacco and mint juleps – and, of course, Daniel Boone and young Abraham Lincoln. All of these appear on this tour, which includes the big-city attractions of Louisville and Lexington and the natural delights of Bluegrass Country and Mammoth Cave.

**3/4 DAYS • 437 MILES • 699KM**

| ITINERARY | | |
|---|---|---|
| **CINCINNATI** | ▶ | Louisville (103m-165km) |
| LOUISVILLE | ▶ | **Mammoth Cave** |
| | | **(95m-153km)** |
| MAMMOTH CAVE | ▶ | **Hodgenville (48m-77km)** |
| HODGENVILLE | ▶ | **Bardstown (27m-43km)** |
| BARDSTOWN | ▶ | **Lincoln Homestead** |
| | | **(23m-37km)** |
| LINCOLN HOMESTEAD | ▶ | **Frankfort (36m-58km)** |
| FRANKFORT | ▶ | **Lexington (23m-37km)** |
| LEXINGTON | ▶ | **Cincinnati (82m-131km)** |

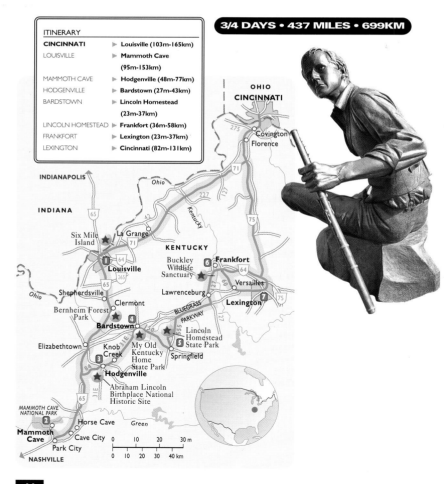

**i** *300 West 6th Street, Cincinnati*

▶ *From downtown Cincinnati take I–71/75 south across the Ohio River via the Brent Spence Bridge to Covington and northern Kentucky and continue south on I–71 for about 103 miles (165km) to Louisville.*

**❶ Louisville,** Kentucky
One of the world's great meccas of horse racing, Louisville is the home of the prestigious Kentucky Derby, the climax to 10 days of varied events in the city's annual Kentucky Derby Festival in early May. Even if you are not there on the day, you can experience the thrills of the race by watching the multi-image show in the Kentucky Derby Museum at the Churchill Downs track south of downtown.

But first explore this historic city's other attractions. At the entrance to the city, just off I–71, don't miss Locust Grove, the plantation home built around 1790 by Louisville's founder, General George Rogers Clark. Then drive to the Ohio riverfront to see the famous Louisville Falls Fountain and the sternwheeler *Belle of*

*Louisville.* Wander through the downtown streets and you will see the Museum of History and Science, Kentucky Center for the Arts, the Actors Theater and the Galleria shopping center. Then make your way south along Third Street to charming Old Louisville, location of the marvelous J B Speed Art Museum and the Rauch Memorial Planetarium, minutes from Churchill Downs track.

**i** *400 S First Street*

---

### SPECIAL TO....

No tour of Kentucky would be complete without touring enterprises that produce two of its major products: tobacco and bourbon.
You can watch the cigarette-making process at Philip Morris USA in downtown Louisville, where the famous Kentucky barley tobacco is blended in the region's only cigarette-production facility, and learn some of the secrets of bourbon production at any of the distilleries open for tours along the route.

---

Riverboat on the Ohio at Cincinnati

▶ *Follow the Henry Watterson Expressway (I–264) east to pick up I–65 southbound. Continue for 95 miles (153km) through Elizabethtown to Mammoth Cave National Park.*

**❷ Mammoth Cave National Park,** Kentucky
About 45 miles (72km) out of Louisville take a break at Elizabethtown to visit the unique Schmidt's Museum of Coca-Cola Memorabilia, with displays, memorabilia and collectibles connected with this popular drink over the last 100 years, before driving on to Kentucky's Cave Country. Here the three small towns of Horse Cave, Cave City and Park City lure visitors to the area with their varied attractions both above and below ground. The center of interest here, however, is Mammoth Cave, with more than 346 miles (557km) of known passageways and caverns below ground and 52,830 acres (21,380 hectares) of forested hill country teeming with wildlife on the surface. In the cave, guided walking tours of varying lengths

start at the Visitor Center and take you past amazing, colorfully named rock formations and caverns shaped by the underground Echo River. And if you get hungry, don't worry: there is even a restaurant down there. On the surface the park's beautiful scenery and wildlife can be enjoyed either by walking the many self-guiding nature trails or by taking the delightful one-hour boat trip along the Green River.

*i* Mammoth Cave National Park

## RECOMMENDED WALKS

At Mammoth Cave there is a choice of guided underground tours lasting from 1¼ to 4½ hours. Here you will see fantastic rock formations and huge caverns with names like Frozen Niagara, Onyx Colonnade and Bottomless Pit and historic relics recording mankind's long use of the cave. There are also special tours available for the disabled. Above ground, you can take a short walk on the Cave Island Nature Trail which starts and finishes near the Historic Entrance.

▶ *From Mammoth Cave drive north on* **I–65** *for about 38 miles (61km) to* **Exit 81** *and turn east (right) on to* **SR 84** *for another 10 miles (16km) to Hodgenville.*

**❸ Hodgenville,** Kentucky
Within a few miles of this old town, Abraham Lincoln was born and lived until he was seven. In historic Lincoln Square you will see a statue of Honest Abe as a man, and a museum that traces his life.

Drive south out of town for 3 miles (5km) on US 31E and SR 61 and you will find the Abraham Lincoln Birthplace National Historic Site, with a shrine and log cabin in the 116-acre (47-hectare) park. In the opposite direction, on US 31E at

Knob Creek, is the Lincoln Boyhood Home, a reconstructed cabin on or near the site where he lived from 1811 to 1816.

▶ *Continue north on* **US 31E** *to Bardstown.*

**❹ Bardstown,** Kentucky
You can see many of this historic town's attractions if you take a walking tour or the free one-and-a-half-hour tourmobile ride from Stephen Foster Avenue. Among them are several fine historic houses; the Old Nelson County Jail; the Talbott Tavern of 1779; the Civil War Museum and old frontier community re-created at Old Bardstown Village; and paintings donated by King Louis-Philippe of France in St Joseph's Proto-Cathedral. Not to be missed, either, is the Bardstown house that really did inspire Stephen Foster, the great 19th-century song-writer, to write his immortal ballad *My Old Kentucky Home.* It is Federal Hill, his cousin's

1818 plantation house, which is now the focal point of My Old Kentucky Home State Park just outside town on US 150. Here

### FOR HISTORY BUFFS

Spalding Hall, in Bardstown, is perhaps an odd choice for the location of the Oscar Getz Museum of Whiskey History, when you consider it was once a Catholic seminary and college, a hospital, an orphanage and a school. It chronicles the role of whiskey over 200 years, and collections exhibited include advertising posters, rare documents and memorabilia from pre-Colonial days to Prohibition years. Among the containers and bottles is an 1854 E C Booz bottle, the brand which gave its name to 'booze'.

Hodgenville, birthplace of Abraham Lincoln in 1809

you can see an outdoor evening performance of the popular show *The Stephen Foster Story*, featuring the composer's music.

▶ *Follow* **US 150** *southeast to Springfield, then go north on* **SR 528** *and* **SR 438** *to Lincoln Homestead State Park.*

### 5 Lincoln Homestead State Park, Kentucky

This park occupies land originally settled by the Lincoln family in the 1780s. Among several historic buildings preserved here is the original house in which Abraham's mother, Nancy Hanks, lived when being courted by his father, Thomas Lincoln, and a replica of the cabin in which Thomas and his brothers were raised. In Springfield you can see Nancy and Thomas's marriage certificate among other documents preserved at the County Courthouse.

▶ *Continue north on* **SR 438** *and* **SR 555** *for about 8 miles (13km) and join the Bluegrass Parkway at eastbound* **Entry 42***. After 11 miles (18km) take* **Exit 59** *north on to* **US 127** *and continue for about 17 miles (27km) through Lawrenceburg to Frankfort.*

### 6 Frankfort, Kentucky

The Bluegrass State's capital city since 1792, Frankfort lies in the pleasant Kentucky River valley, overlooked by the grave of Daniel Boone, the intrepid pioneer who first opened up this territory. Get a brochure and map at the Visitor Center on Capital Avenue before starting a marked walking tour of the city's historic sights. Highlights include the majestic State Capitol and the Governor's Mansion; the Old State Capitol and the Old Governor's Mansion; and the smart 'Corner in Celebrities' district, where

The Old Kentucky Home, Stephen Foster's inspiration in Bardstown

top people lived in such elegant homes as the Vest-Lindsey House, Liberty Hall and the Orlando Brown House. History buffs will also find much to see at the Kentucky Historical Museum, next to the Old Capitol, and at the Kentucky Military History Museum, with its fine collection of uniforms, flags, medals and weapons. But for something quite different, go and see bourbon whiskey candies being made at Rebecca-Ruth Candies or take a guided tour of the Ancient Age Distillery, where its well-known bourbon is produced.

ⓘ *100 Capital Avenue*

▶ *For the 23-mile (37km) drive from Frankfort to Lexington, take* **I-64***,* **US 60** *or scenic* **SR 421***.*

# Kentucky & Mammoth Cave

Lexington is the country's chief producer of bluegrass seed and white barley

**7 Lexington,** Kentucky

Lexington lies in the heart of the state's rolling Bluegrass Country, surrounded by horse farms with manicured paddocks, smart fences and splendid barns. Internationally recognized as the horse capital of the world, the city plays host to large numbers of visitors at The Red Miles and Keeneland race tracks, the Kentucky Horse Center, and the horse industry's major showcase, the Kentucky Horse Park, with its International Museum of the Horse, north of town.

Take a walking or driving tour from downtown Triangle Park, or a horse-drawn carriage ride, to see the city's other attractions. These include Henry Clay's Ashland Estate, Federal-style Hunt-Morgan House, Mary Todd Lincoln's girlhood home, the Greek Revival mansions of Waveland Estate, Lexington's historic cemetery, and the Headley-Whitney Museum, with its fine art collections.

*i* *430 West Vine Street*

### RECOMMENDED WALKS

Raven Rum Nature Sanctuary has beautiful hiking trails along the Kentucky River Palisades, 6 miles (10km) from Lexington on Jacks Creek Pike.

▶ *Pick up I–75 north of downtown Lexington for the 82-mile (131km) drive back to Cincinnati.*

### FOR CHILDREN

Additional attractions for children on the itinerary include Louisville Zoo and Kentucky Kingdom Amusement Park; Guntown Mountain Wild West amusement park, Cave City; America's Miniature Soldier Museum, Bardstown; and the hands-on Children's Museum, Lexington.

### SCENIC ROUTES

Away from the interstate highways, the smaller country roads between Hodgenville and Frankfort, the US 31E, and SR 528, SR 438, and SR 555, offer scenic views of the Kentucky Bluegrass Country.

### BACK TO NATURE

The famed bluegrass of northern Kentucky is just one of the state's natural wonders. The lush countryside and forests abound with wild animals, birds and plants, including the state symbols – the gray squirrel, the cardinal and goldenrod. Among the best places to observe wildlife are the three state Nature Preserves around Louisville (Beargrass Creek, Blackacre and Six Mile Island); Bernheim Forest Park, off I–65 south of Louisville; Mammoth Cave National Park; and Buckley Wildlife Sanctuary, off US 60 south of Frankfort.

# The Black
## Hawk Hills

A 90-minute drive from downtown Chicago, the nine-county region of northern Illinois, the Black Hawk Hills, lures many visitors with scenery of timeless beauty. It is a world of rolling hills and rich farmlands, woodlands and orchards, sparkling rivers and lakes, and historic towns where the past lives on in traditional festivals, gracious old homes and atmospheric museums – all bound on the west by the mighty Mississippi.

**3 DAYS • 355 MILES • 567KM**

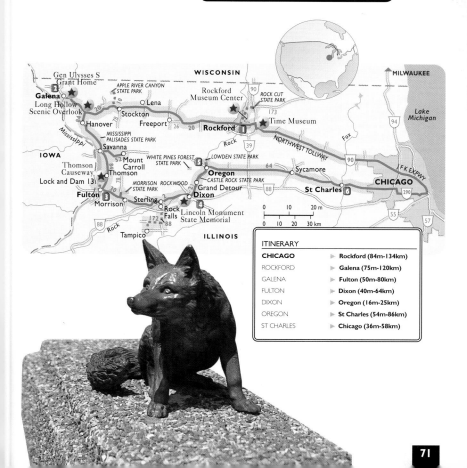

| ITINERARY | | |
|---|---|---|
| **CHICAGO** | ▶ | **Rockford (84m-134km)** |
| ROCKFORD | ▶ | **Galena (75m-120km)** |
| GALENA | ▶ | **Fulton (50m-80km)** |
| FULTON | ▶ | **Dixon (40m-64km)** |
| DIXON | ▶ | **Oregon (16m-25km)** |
| OREGON | ▶ | **St Charles (54m-86km)** |
| ST CHARLES | ▶ | **Chicago (36m-58km)** |

[i] 78 E Washington Street, Chicago

► From downtown Chicago follow the John F Kennedy Expressway and Northwest Tollway (I–90) to Rockford.

**❶ Rockford,** Illinois

Illinois' second largest city was founded in 1834 at a crossing point on the Rock River used by travelers on the way to the booming town of Galena further west. It still has four well-preserved historic districts around the downtown area and many fine old buildings that you can visit, such as the Tinker Swiss Cottage (1865) and the Erlander Home (1871).

But your first stopping point should be at the tollway exit on your way into town to see the fabulous collection of antique timepieces at the Time Museum in the Clock Tower Resort. For a change of pace in your tour of the city, board the *Forest City Queen* for a pleasant cruise on the Rock River, and ride an old trolley bus to the lovely Sunken Gardens in Sinnissippi Park. Leave enough time, though, to see the reconstructed turn-of-the-century village at Midway Village and Rockford Museum Center and to browse the shops at Victorian Village.

Before driving on to Galena, head north out of town on SR 173 for an enjoyable walk in beautiful Rock Cut State Park.

[i] 211 N Main Street

► From Rockford follow **US 20** west for 75 miles (120km) past Freeport and Stockton to Galena.

---

#### SPECIAL TO...

The dairy country around Freeport in Stephenson County is said to produce some of the best cheeses and cream in America. The Torkelson Cheese Company on Louisa Road, off Highway 73 north of Lena, is noted for its semisoft Muenster and brick cheeses.

---

**❷ Galena,** Illinois

Along the highway to Galena, amid the beautiful Black Hawk Hills just beyond Stockton, there is an enjoyable 7-mile (11km) side trip to the scenic splendors of Apple River Canyon State Park. There is also fine scenery along US 20 further on as you drive into Galena, a charming old town clinging to the steep, wooded slopes above the river of the same name.

Galena's name derives from the soft, heavy mineral galena, consisting of lead sulphide. The town came into existence as a lead-mining community and prospered until the mid-1800s. Since then, it has remained much as it was, with its quaint streets studded with historic buildings. Many lovely old homes, like the Belvedere Mansion, Dowling House and Turney House, are open to visitors, as is the home of General Ulysses S Grant.

As Galena is a compact town and its streets are narrow and difficult for driving, leave your car here and cross the footbridge into the center. Here you will find Main Street, an enticing gold mine of antique shops, art galleries, craft shops and restaurants. While in this area, be sure to see the Old Stockade, with its pioneer exhibits, the Old Market House and the Old General Store. Enjoy a tasting at Galena Cellars Winery, then drive out to the Vinegar Hill Historic Lead Mine for a nostalgic look back at Galena's early mining days.

---

#### FOR CHILDREN

Places with kids especially in mind are scattered along the tour. Rockford has the Zitelman Scout Museum, with uniforms, badges and other items going back to 1910; the Burpee Museum of Natural History, with dinosaurs and Illinois wildlife among the exhibits; the hands-on Discovery Center Museum, all about science; and water fun at the Magic Waters theme park.

---

*i* *101 Bouthillier Street*

Galena was once the largest Mississippi port north of St Louis

### FOR CHILDREN

Children will enjoy Lolly's Doll and Toy Museum in Galena and toy trains at the Thomson Depot Train Museum.

▶ *From Galena follow the Great River Road by retracing **US 20** for 12 miles (19km) to the **SR 84** intersection, then continue south through Hanover, Savanna and Thomson to Fulton.*

### ❸ Fulton, Illinois

Before turning on to SR 84 from US 20, stop at the Long Hollow Scenic Overlook rest stop to enjoy the views of the countryside from the observation tower. As you drive south beyond Hanover, with its huge mallard duck hatchery, the road approaches the Mississippi River, and you will get some spectacular views of it from the wooded bluffs and trails in Mississippi Palisades State Park.

A few minutes away are the boat marinas of Savanna, a riverfront town lying amid prime fishing and duck-hunting country where you can visit the little Hiawatha Train Museum. Plagues of shadflies (mayflies) in this area each August have been turned to an advantage by local folk as an excuse to have a little fun in a celebration called Shadfly Days!

South of Savanna there is another train museum at Thomson and, further on, more engineering marvels to watch as Mississippi riverboats negotiate Lock and Dam 13. Before leaving the river at Fulton, take a walk through the woods to see the quaint old village created at Heritage Canyon.

▶ *From Fulton drive east on **SR 136** for 2 miles (3km) and join **US 30** for about 24 miles (39km) to the twin cities of Sterling and Rock Falls. Follow the Rock River Valley on **SR 2** to Dixon.*

### ❹ Dixon and the Rock River, Illinois

If you need a break on the drive from Fulton, turn on to SR 78 just north of Morrison for a stroll by the lake in Morrison Rockwood State Park. If it is August you might then catch the fun at the Whiteside County Fair in Morrison. When you reach Sterling call at the historic Dillon Home where, in addition to opulent furnishings, you will find yet another mini-railroad museum. In Dixon itself, there is a statue of Abraham Lincoln, who served in the Black Hawk

Ronald Reagan's Boyhood Home in the town of Dixon

War that raged up this valley in 1832. He later confessed that he fought no Indians but had 'a good many bloody struggles with the mosquitoes'. On South Hennepin, in Dixon, is Ronald Reagan's Boyhood Home, which is open for tours. If you want to see his birthplace, you will have to drive out to Tampico, 16 miles (26km) south of Rock Falls on SR 88 and 172.

▶ Continue on **SR 2** through Grand Detour to Oregon.

**5 Oregon,** Illinois
At the quaint little town of Grand Detour, on a great bend in the Rock River, you can tour the John Deere Homestead, complete with its own reconstructed blacksmith's shop, where, in 1837, he made the first steel plow that revolutionized prairie farming. A scenic drive along wooded bluffs then brings you to the riverfront town of Oregon, nestled amid the beauty of three forested state parks: Castle Rock, White Pines Forest and Lowden. A landmark in Lowden State Park is a huge statue of an Indian popularly referred to as Chief Black Hawk.

▶ From Oregon follow **SR 64** east through Sycamore to the town of St Charles.

**6 St Charles,** Illinois
If you are a browser, a collector of knick-knacks or a lover of good food, you will be happy in St Charles, one of the picturesque towns clustered along the Fox River west of Chicago. Three markets in Old St Charles, on the west bank of the river, are just bursting with antiques, while out at the fairgrounds on Randall Road they claim to have the 'largest antique flea market in the world'. In Old St Charles, at Fox Island Square and Piano Factory, and, on the other side of the river, in the Century Corners district, there are more than 50 restaurants and enough tempting shops to wear out your credit card. But don't miss a tour of the St Charles History Museum to see how the town was in the past or a pleasant riverboat cruise along the lovely Fox River valley aboard the *St Charles Belle* or *Fox River Queen*.

Above: view over Rock River, from Castle Rock
Opposite: Lincoln Statue, New Salem State Historic Site

ℹ *311 North Second Street*

▶ *Continue east on SR 64 and I-290 for the return to Chicago.*

### SCENIC ROUTES

Although the entire Black Hawk Hills region of northern Illinois is an area of remarkable natural beauty, there are especially attractive sections of highway along US 20 (the Great River Road) between Freeport and Galena; along SR 84 south from Galena to Fulton; and up the Rock River Valley on SR 2, especially between Dixon and Grand Detour and north to Oregon.

### BACK TO NATURE

Along the itinerary you are quite likely to come across Illinois' varied wildlife, such as white-tailed deer, squirrel, raccoon, opossum, fox, skunk and perhaps even coyote. Among the birds you might see various species of duck, Canada geese, wild turkey, quail and pheasant. Good places for sightings are the trails in state parks and special places along the Mississippi River, such as the Thomson Causeway, a favorite spot for great blue heron, and Lock and Dam 13, where you can watch for eagles from the observation deck.

### RECOMMENDED WALKS

Beautiful walks abound on this tour. In addition to the walking tours around the historic streets of Rockford and Galena, there are pleasant trails in Mississippi Palisades State Park, near Savanna, in the state parks along the Rock River near Oregon, and along the Fox River at the delightful old town of St Charles.

# In Lincoln's
## Footsteps

This trip across the prairie farmlands of Illinois follows much of the route of the historic Illinois-Michigan Canal and the Illinois River Valley. The focal point of the tour is the cluster of towns and log cabins in the center of the state, where the memory of Abraham Lincoln remains strong.

**3/4 DAYS • 492 MILES • 787KM**

### ITINERARY

| | | |
|---|---|---|
| **CHICAGO** | ▶ | **Starved Rock** (94m–150km) |
| STARVED ROCK | ▶ | Peoria (67m–108km) |
| PEORIA | ▶ | Lincoln (49m–78km) |
| LINCOLN | ▶ | Petersburg (34m–54km) |
| PETERSBURG | ▶ | Springfield (21m–34km) |
| SPRINGFIELD | ▶ | Decatur (41m–66km) |
| DECATUR | ▶ | Champaign (46m–75km) |
| CHAMPAIGN | ▶ | Kankakee (77m–123km) |
| KANKAKEE | ▶ | Chicago (62m–99km) |

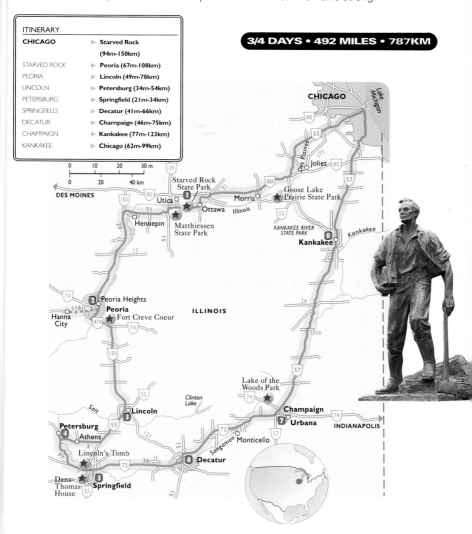

Starved Rock State Park has 18 canyons formed by glacial meltwater some 15,000 years ago

## BACK TO NATURE

In addition to its scenic attractions, Starved Rock State Park is also an excellent spot for observing wildlife and wild flowers. Springtime is best for birdwatching when resident woodland species mingle with migrant warblers and thrushes passing through the region. Within the Chicago area there are also several good locations: Lincoln Park, McGinnis Slough Wildlife Refuge and Palos Park Forest Preserve are among them. They harbour a mixture of woodland birds and mammals as well as freshwater species.

## FOR HISTORY BUFFS

An important factor in the development of Illinois' central region was the construction of the Illinois-Michigan Canal, which linked the Great Lakes and Mississippi River through the valleys of the Chicago, Des Plaines and Illinois rivers. You can trace the history of this waterway at the Illinois-Michigan Canal Museum at Lockport, which recalls 19th-century life along the canal, and at the Illinois Waterway Visitor Center at Utica.

*i* *78 E Washington Street, Chicago*

▶ *From downtown Chicago take the Adlai E Stevenson Expressway (**I–55**) southwest for 47 miles (75km) and at **Exit 250** turn west on to **I–80**. Continue for 36 miles (58km) past Morris to Ottawa, then go another 11 miles (18km) on **SR 71** to Starved Rock State Park.*

### ❶ Starved Rock State Park, Illinois
This spectacular state park beside the Illinois River is one of the most popular visitor attrac-

tions in Illinois. Together with Matthiessen State Park, which adjoins it on the west, Starved Rock is a jumble of sandstone bluffs, ravines, streams and waterfalls that vie for your attention as you walk along the network of trails. Once the site of a French trading post, the park got its name from an Indian legend of the 1760s, which relates how a band of braves, cornered on a high rock in a war with another tribe, refused to surrender and so starved to death.

*i* *Park Visitor Center*

▶ *Continue west on **SR 71** past Hennepin for about 24 miles (39km) and join **SR 29** southbound along the Illinois River to Peoria.*

### ❷ Peoria, Illinois
The Peoria area was settled by the French more than 300 years ago and today contains many historic gems. As you enter the city from the north, drive up to Tower Park in Peoria Heights for fine views of the Illinois River from the top of the observation

Above: reconstructed buildings at New Salem State Historic Park
Right: *Abraham Lincoln: on the Prairie*, New Salem

tower. Touring the city you will see the elegant mansions on Grand View Drive, the Pettengill-Morron House in the historic Moss District, the John C Flanagan House of about 1837, and the grand old Hotel Père Marquette, set amid the office towers and public buildings in the heart of downtown. For a different experience board the *Par-A-Dice* Riverboat casino for a dining and gaming cruise on the Illinois River. Other attractions are the Lakeview Museum of Arts and Science and, west of town via SR 116, the Wildlife Prairie Park, where you can see buffalo, bears, elk, bald eagles and other native Illinois animals.

Not to be missed as you leave Peoria is Fort Creve Coeur, a reconstruction of the defensive fortress built by the French on the east bank of the Illinois River back in 1680, now the location for the Fort Creve Coeur Rendezvous festivities every September.

ℹ️ *403 NE Jefferson*

▶ *From Creve Coeur drive east on I–474 and I–74 for about 13 miles (20km) and take* **Exit 101** *on to* **SR 121** *southbound for the 36-mile (58km) drive to Lincoln.*

**8 Lincoln,** Illinois
At the marked Christening Site, Abraham Lincoln christened this town himself with the juice of a watermelon in 1853, and henceforth Postville was known as Lincoln. It was here, during his sessions at the Postville Courthouse as a traveling attorney and judge, that the future president earned his nickname, 'Honest Abe'.

When you visit the reconstruction of this historic building today, you might meet huge Charlie Ott, a convincingly tall presidential look-alike, before going on to see the memorabilia about Lincoln and other presidents displayed at the Lincoln College Museum.

And if you are here during September, you can enter the

The Lincoln Law Office where Lincoln practised law in Springfield

annual National Railsplitter Contest, an art at which young Abe excelled. Other places to see are the Logan County Courthouse and the Aiprort Heritage in Flight Museum.

ℹ️ *303 South Kickapoo Street*

▶ *From Lincoln follow I–55 for about 17 miles (27km) to Exit 109. Continue west through Athens on the marked Lincoln Heritage Trail for about 17 miles (27km) to Petersburg.*

### ❹ Petersburg and New Salem, Illinois

At Petersburg is an authentic reconstruction of the log cabin village of New Salem, where Abraham Lincoln worked as postmaster and store clerk and studied to be a lawyer in the 1830s. Today costumed interpreters re-enact village life of the time, and on summer evenings there is a thrilling outdoor performance by the Great American People Show company that retraces Lincoln's life. There are also pleasant short cruises along the Sangamon River on the stern-wheeler *Talisman*.

▶ *Follow the Lincoln Heritage Trail (SR 97) to Springfield.*

### ❺ Springfield, Illinois

The spirit of Abraham Lincoln pervades this city, the place where he lived for much of his life and now lies buried. As you approach across the prairie, the tall dome of the New State Capitol looms up in the distance, announcing that this is the seat of Illinois' government. Many places here are associated with Lincoln, and on a tour of the city you will visit the Old State Capitol, where he made his famous speech referring to slavery with the words 'a house divided against itself cannot stand'; Lincoln's Home, a National Historic Site in the pleasant restored district along 8th Street; the Lincoln-Herndon Building, where Lincoln practised law with William Herndon; and Lincoln's Tomb, a moving monument dominated by a tall obelisk in Oak Ridge Cemetery, where visitors traditionally rub the nose on a bust of the president at the entrance for good luck. In a different vein, don't miss the Dana-Thomas House on East Lawrence, one of architect Frank Lloyd Wright's famed 'prairie houses'.

*i* 109 North 7th Street

### FOR CHILDREN

If the children get bored they can, for example, see life on the farm at the McGlothlin Farm Park in East Peoria; pet barnyard animals at the Henson C Robinson Children's Zoo in Springfield; or climb aboard a steam locomotive or caboose at the Sangamon Valley Railway Museum at Monticello on I-72 between Decatur and Champaign.

▶ Follow I-72/US 36 east for 41 miles (66km) to Decatur.

### ⑥ Decatur, Illinois

Set beside Lake Decatur, this pleasant old city, with its numerous parks and golf courses, also has many associations with Abraham Lincoln. At Lincoln Square he delivered his first political speech, and at the Lincoln Log Cabin Courthouse, he won his first court case. Other interesting places to visit are the

downtown Historic District, with its famous octagonal ticket office and shelter, the Transfer House; the Oglesby Mansion on West Wiliam Street; imposing James Millikin Homestead on North Pine Street; and the Macon County Museum with its outdoor Prairie Village. But for something quite different, visit the Mari-Mann Herb Farm and Gingerbread House, where the products on sale are hard to resist.

*i* 202 E North Street

▶ Continue northeast on I-72 past Monticello to Champaign/Urbana.

### ⑦ Champaign/Urbana, Illinois

One good reason for stopping at these twin cities in the heart of the Illinois cornbelt is to visit the cultural and architectural attractions on the University of Illinois campus. The highlights are the Krannert Art Museum, which has major collections of paintings, sculpture, textiles, pottery and glassware; the Krannert Center for the Performing Arts, a showcase for music, drama and dance, which is open for tours in addition to performances; and the World Heritage Museum, with exhibits tracing the story of mankind.

*i* 40 East University Avenue, Champaign

### SPECIAL TO...

The rural communities of Illinois' prairie country are in full swing throughout the year with all sorts of festivals and celebrations. Among the big-city events are the bubbling river festivities during Steamboat Days at Peoria in June; the July 4 weekend Lincolnfest and the huge Illinois State Fair over two weeks in August at Springfield; and National Outboard Motorboat Race at Decatur.

### SCENIC ROUTES

Driving across flat prairielands on interstate highways is rarely ever scenic, but you will enjoy the ride along SR 71 beside the Illinois River west of Ottawa and the marked routes on the Lincoln Heritage Trail around Petersburg.

### RECOMMENDED WALKS

As well as 12 miles (19km) of walking trails in Starved Rock State Park, suitable and interesting places for a stroll include Decatur's community parks and Rock Springs Center for Environmental Discovery, with its nature trails and wagon rides for the weary; the gardens at Allerton Park in Monticello; and charming Lake of the Woods Park, with its forest trails and delightful bridges, on I-74 west of Champaign.

▶ Pick up I-57 west or north of Champaign and continue north for 77 miles (123km) to Kankakee.

### ⑧ Kankakee, Illinois

Just an hour's drive from Chicago, this industrial city and county seat has an Indian name meaning 'beautiful river', a reference to the relatively unspoiled river which runs through the area.

If you feel like a break before driving on to Chicago, make for the Kankakee River State Park, a recreation area along the river northwest of town, where you will find opportunities for walking, picnicking and doing other outdoor activities in pleasant surroundings.

▶ Continue north for about 62 miles (99km) on I-57 and the Dan Ryan Expressway to downtown Chicago.

# The Great River
## Road Ramble

This tour from the Twin Cities of Minneapolis and St Paul begins with a drive through the rolling farmlands and woods of southeast Minnesota. Here you will see a bank that was raided by Jesse James, an opera house where they still stage old melodramas, and one of the finest medical institutions in the world. A wide variety of other sights and experiences then accompanies you as you drive up the Mississippi and St Croix river valleys.

**3 DAYS • 345 MILES • 554KM**

### ITINERARY

| | |
|---|---|
| **MINNEAPOLIS** | ▶ **Northfield (42m-67km)** |
| NORTHFIELD | ▶ **Rochester (64m-103km)** |
| ROCHESTER | ▶ **Winona (45m-72km)** |
| WINONA | ▶ **Wabasha (28m-45km)** |
| WABASHA | ▶ **Pepin (9m-14km)** |
| PEPIN | ▶ **Red Wing (30m-48km)** |
| RED WING | ▶ **Hastings (24m-39km)** |
| HASTINGS | ▶ **Stillwater (24m-39km)** |
| STILLWATER | ▶ **Taylors Falls (30m-48km)** |
| TAYLORS FALLS | ▶ **Minneapolis (49m-79km)** |

*i* *375 Jackson Street, Minneapolis*

▶ *Take I–35W from Minneapolis or I–35E from St Paul south for about 35 miles (56km) to Exit 69. Take SR 19 east for 7 miles (11km) to Northfield.*

**1 Northfield,** Minnesota
If you are enjoying your ride through the pleasant farmlands of southeast Minnesota and suddenly see a busload of visitors being hijacked by bandits, don't be alarmed. It is just a dramatic promotion stunt to highlight the little town of Northfield's main claim to fame: the attempted robbery of the local bank by Jesse James and his gang in 1876. If you are here in early September, you will also witness a shoot-out on the town's streets as the event is re-enacted in the annual Defeat of Jesse James Days celebration. For an account of the raid call in at the museum housed in the still-surviving bank building during your walking tour of Northfield's historic preservation district.

*i* *105 East Fourth Street*

▶ *Continue east on SR 19 to Cannon Falls, then head south on US 52 and SR 57 through Hader to Mantorville. Three miles (5km) south of here take US 14 east to Rochester.*

**2 Rochester,** Minnesota
On the drive to Rochester pause for a walk around old Mantorville, a former stagecoach stop with a boardwalk and restored historic buildings, including an opera house where you can enjoy a lively melodrama during the summer months.
Rochester, the largest city in this part of Minnesota, is a manufacturing center with a vibrant music and theater scene. But it is best known as the home of the world-famous Mayo Clinic, a medical research and treatment complex in the heart of the town. Take the guided tour of its facilities and visit the Mayo Medical Museum. Then

drive out to see the local history exhibits at the Olmsted County History Center southwest of town and take the special tour bus from here to visit impressive Mayowood, the 1911 home and estate of one of the Mayo Clinic's founders. Other sightseeing musts in Rochester include the restored 1875 Heritage House in downtown Central Park and the lovely Old English-style Plummer House completed in 1917.

*i* *150 South Broadway, Suite A*

▶ *From Rochester continue east on US 14 for 45 miles (72km) through St Charles to Winona.*

> ## SPECIAL TO...
>
> Among the many memorable experiences you can savor on this tour are a concert recital played on the 56-bell Mayo Carillon at Rochester's Plummer Buildings; a taste of delicious Wisconsin cheeses as you tour the Nelson Cheese Factory north of Wabasha or the cider and apples at Hay Creek Apple Farm just outside Red Wing; and a look at the piano that was twice dumped in the Mississippi River while on its way to the Octagon House at Hudson on the St Croix River.

**3 Winona,** Minnesota
From the 554-foot (169m) bluffs in Garvin Heights Park there is a spectacular view of the old river port of Winona lying along the sand plain beside the Mississippi River. Now the largest city on this stretch of the river, Winona has a fine County Courthouse and many 19th-century buildings. Its river town heritage is brought vividly to life at the Julius C Wilkie Steamboat Center, a replica old steamboat housing a museum. If you would like to sail on one of these old-timers down the Mississippi, you can take a short cruise aboard the *Jollie Ollie*.

*i* *67 Main Street*

▶ *Follow the Great River Road (US 61) north along the Mississippi River to Wabasha.*

**4 Wabasha,** Minnesota
North of Winona as far as Hastings, the Great River Road, on both the Minnesota and the Wisconsin sides of the Mississippi, passes through a scenic patchwork of farmlands, wooded hillsides and historic river towns nestled beneath towering rock bluffs. For an authentic old river town atmosphere, explore historic Wabasha. Here you will find the renowned Anderson House, a gracious old

Lamberton House, Winona

inn dating from 1856, where you can get, if you wish, tasty Pennsylvania Dutch food, a house cat for overnight company and hot bricks to warm your bed. The Arrowhead Bluffs Exhibits has a large collection of pioneer and native American artifacts, with mounted displays of wildlife and a fine collection of firearms, including every Winchester model made from 1866 up to 1982.

▶ *From Wabasha take SR 25 across the Mississippi River to Nelson, Wisconsin. Then follow the Great River Road (SR 35) north for 20 miles (32km) through Pepin to Maiden Rock.*

## 5 Pepin and Maiden Rock, Wisconsin

North of Nelson, where the Mississippi broadens to form Lake Pepin, stop at the town of Pepin to visit the Laura Ingalls Wilder Wayside Park, which commemorates the author of the *Little House* books. Seven miles (11km) out of town on SR 183 is a replica of the log cabin in which she was born. North along the lake, Maiden Rock is named for the 400-foot (122m) bluff from which, according to legend, a young Indian woman jumped to her death rather than marry a man she did not love.

Stillwater, on the St Croix River

▶ *Continue north from Maiden Rock on SR 35 before taking US 63 south across the Mississippi River to Red Wing.*

## 6 Red Wing, Minnesota

The old community of Red Wing lies below Barn Bluff on a lovely stretch of the Mississippi known as the Hiawatha Valley. There is a fine view of its setting from the top of nearby Sorin's Bluff. The town's many architectural treasures include the St James Hotel, T B Sheldon Auditorium Theatre and historic Mall District. If you don't want to walk, you can take a delightful 45-minute narrated tour of the streets on a San Francisco-style cable car.

Leave enough time, though, to visit the fine Goodhue County Historical Museum and to browse through the shops at Pottery Place, a restored former pottery factory at the west end of town. And to round off your visit, board the riverboat *Red Wing Princess* for a relaxing two-and-a-half-hour cruise on the Mississippi.

ℹ️ *416 Bush Street*

▶ *Take US 61 northwest for 24 miles (39km) to Hastings.*

### RECOMMENDED WALKS

Stop the car at any rivertown or state park along the Mississippi or St Croix and you will have an opportunity for a pleasant stroll. A rewarding walk follows the trail to the top of Barn Bluff from East 5th Street in Red Wing, where you will enjoy a fine view of the Mississippi River.

## 7 Hastings, Minnesota

You can savor the 19th-century atmosphere of Hastings, a quiet rivertown with streets lined with historic buildings. The impressive Dakota County Courthouse, the Gardner House and the LeDuc-Simmons Mansion are just some of its notable landmarks.

ℹ️ *1304 Vermilion Street*

▶ *From Hastings follow SR 95 north up the St Croix River valley to Stillwater.*

## 8 Stillwater, Minnesota

The old logging community of Stillwater, on the lower St Croix River, is a bustling town with fine shops and restaurants housed in beautifully restored

19th-century buildings. Historic landmarks include the gracious Lowell Inn, County Courthouse, Staples Mill, and the old prison warden's house presently used by the Washington County Historical Museum. Every July townsfolk recall their heritage and celebrate Lumberjack Days.

Head north out of town on SR 95 and you will find opportunities to walk by the lovely St Croix River at the picturesque Marine on St Croix and nearby William O'Brien State Park.

*i* 423 South Main Street

### FOR HISTORY BUFFS

The story of human settlement in this part of America is well documented in the museums along the itinerary. At the Ice Age Center in Interstate Park at St Croix Falls, you can see how the land itself was dramatically shaped by glaciation much further back in time.

▶ *Continue on SR 95, then take US 8 east to Taylors Falls.*

**❾ Taylors Falls,** Minnesota
As you near Taylors Falls you will see the mood of the river change from the placid meanderings of the broad lower reaches to the turbulent surge through the rugged gorge of the Dalles, at Interstate Park, a favorite spot for both canoeists and rock climbers.

At Taylors Falls don't miss the view of the river from the bridge, the old jail now used as a guest house (complete with barred windows) and, up the hill, the W H C Folsom House of 1855, which is open to visitors at Angel Hill.

▶ *Go west on US 8 for 13 miles (21km) before turning southeast on to SR 98 for 6 miles (10km) to Wyoming. Pick up I–35 southbound and continue for about 30 miles (48km) to downtown Minneapolis (I–35W) or St Paul (I–35E).*

### SCENIC ROUTES

The most scenically spectacular sections of the itinerary are along the Great River Road between Winona and Red Wing and along SR 95 up the St Croix valley between Stillwater and Taylors Falls.

### FOR CHILDREN

Seven miles (11km) north of Taylors Falls, children can ride the chair lift and water slide at Wild Mountain Ski Area.

### BACK TO NATURE

With their abundant wildlife, the Mississippi and St Croix valleys are a paradise for nature lovers, hunters and anglers alike.

In remote spots you may glimpse a black bear, coyote, beaver, otter, mink or raccoon, and down by the water, great blue herons, woodcocks and all sorts of ducks.

Among the special places are Reads Landing, near Wabasha, for bald eagles, and Whitewater State Park on SR 74 north of St Charles, for a wide variety of bird life and trout.

Taylors Falls, Interstate Park

# THE MISSISSIPPI HEARTLAND

On the last lap of its long journey south to the Gulf of Mexico, the Mississippi River flows through a region of low plains that stretch for miles across the states of Arkansas, Tennessee, Alabama, Mississippi and Louisiana. Much of the land is rich farmland, forests and man-made reservoirs, while the coast is edged with white sandy beaches, lagoons, barrier islands, the swamps and bayous of the Mississippi's waterlogged delta, and the offshore oil rigs of Louisiana. After brief, relatively mild winters these southern states swelter through long, sultry summers, which culminate dramatically in spectacular thunderstorms and the occasional hurricane that lashes the coast.

This is the heart of the traditional Deep South. Nothing evokes its spirit so powerfully as a cruise on an old-time sternwheeler down the Mississippi from St Louis to New Orleans. In your mind you can recapture the world of Huckleberry Finn, with its imposing old plantation houses, fields white with cotton, and soul-baring spirituals and gospel songs.

Many memories of the past linger on in this region. Old communities like Sainte Genevieve, Cape Girardeau, even New Orleans itself, recall the time when it was part of the enormous French territory of Louisiana, before it was finally bought by the United States in 1803. Battle sites, like the one at Vicksburg, Mississippi, commemorate the War Between the States, while beautiful antebellum homes and gardens survive as melancholy reminders of the now-vanished way of life over which it was fought.

New Orleans' French Quarter

The cultural identity of America's Mississippi heartland is especially colored by its music – blues, jazz, bluegrass, country, gospel and rock 'n' roll, not forgetting the music of Louisiana's Cajun folk. Cajun is some of the region's finest cuisine, with dishes like andouille, boudin, jambalaya and gumbo offering more exotic flavors than the traditional fried chicken and grits. Everywhere there are year-round festivals and gatherings to celebrate, though few can match the exuberance of New Orleans' renowned Mardi Gras.

## St Louis

St Louis, Missouri, an important Mississippi river port and manufacturing city, lures visitors with sightseeing attractions, live entertainment, riverboat rides and gaming, fine shopping malls, and museums ranging from art and history to transport, magic and dogs.

Founded by the French in 1764, St Louis became the gateway for settlers moving into the newly opened-up western territories after the Louisiana Purchase of 1803. Many buildings and homes of the 1800s still stand in the city, and colorful riverboats, now packed with sightseers, still throng the busy waterfront. Here the city's most famous landmark, the spectacular 630-foot (192m) Gateway Arch, offers marvelous views for miles around from the observation room at the top. At its foot is the Museum of Western Expansion and, nearby, the Old Cathedral, Old Courthouse, impressive Busch Stadium, and the shops, restaurants and night spots of the revitalized old riverfront district of Laclede's Landing. Other major visitor attractions include the redeveloped old Union Station; the imposing New Cathedral; the Missouri Botanical Garden and its Climatron greenhouse; and the varied attractions of immense Forest Park, which include the St Louis Art Museum, the Science Center, the Zoo, and the popular outdoor entertainment amphitheater known as The Muny.

St Louis' Gateway Arch on the Mississippi River

## New Orleans

New Orleans is one of America's most fascinating cities. Founded by the French in 1718 on a bend in the Mississippi River, Louisiana's 'Crescent City' exhibits a unique cultural blend derived from its French, Spanish and Creole heritage.

The historic heart of the city is the Vieux Carré, or French Quarter, a potpourri of little shops, houses, museums, restaurants, cafés, bars and night spots, where music and spicy aromas constantly waft on the air. A walking tour or carriage ride along the narrow streets takes you past colorful old buildings, many with lacy ironwork balconies, and small hidden courtyards filled with exotic greenery. At night, Bourbon Street bubbles with jazz clubs, burlesque revues and lively bars, while Preservation Hall, the mecca of jazz, is around the corner on St Peter Street. Focal point of the French Quarter is lovely Jackson Square, flanked by the 1794 St Louis Cathedral and other historic buildings. Nearby is the bustling French Market, where the Café du Monde serves its famous *café au lait* and *beignets*.

From Canal Street, with its hotels and department stores, you can take a St Charles Avenue streetcar ride past the elegant 19th-century homes of the Garden District on the way to Audubon Park and Zoo. Another ride north takes you to immense City Park and the excellent Museum of Art, while back on the riverfront there are wonderful old-style steamboats offering nostalgic narrated cruises.

# Land Between
## the Rivers

This drive takes you through the historic towns of the Mississippi River region and into the forested hill country lying between the Mississippi and Ohio rivers at the southern tip of Illinois. This beautiful region, known as the Shawnee Hills or the Illinois Ozarks, is a land of great scenic beauty and abundant wildlife.

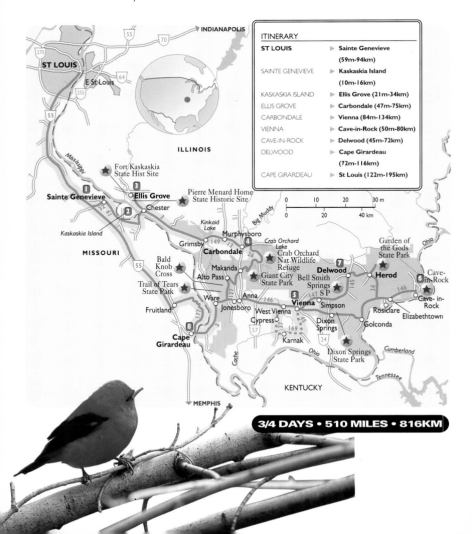

**ITINERARY**

| | | |
|---|---|---|
| ST LOUIS | ► | **Sainte Genevieve** |
| | | **(59m–94km)** |
| SAINTE GENEVIEVE | ► | **Kaskaskia Island** |
| | | **(10m–16km)** |
| KASKASKIA ISLAND | ► | **Ellis Grove (21m–34km)** |
| ELLIS GROVE | ► | **Carbondale (47m–75km)** |
| CARBONDALE | ► | **Vienna (84m–134km)** |
| VIENNA | ► | **Cave-in-Rock (50m–80km)** |
| CAVE-IN-ROCK | ► | **Delwood (45m–72km)** |
| DELWOOD | ► | **Cape Girardeau** |
| | | **(72m–116km)** |
| CAPE GIRARDEAU | ► | **St Louis (122m–195km)** |

**3/4 DAYS • 510 MILES • 816KM**

St Louis' historic old Courthouse, framed by the Gateway Arch

**2 Kaskaskia Island,** Illinois
Kaskaskia Island is an enclave of Illinois on the Missouri side of the Mississippi River. From 1818 to 1820 it was the site of Illinois' first state capital, washed away long ago by the river. All that remains is the Liberty Bell of the West, a gift from King Louis XV of France in 1741.

▶ *Continue for another 7 miles (11km) on* **Highway H** *and* **SR 51** *across the Missouri River to Chester and north on* **SR 3** *to Ellis Grove.*

---

### BACK TO NATURE

Botanists and wildlife lovers will find much of interest on this tour, which lies on the Mississippi Flyway used by migrating birds.
If you are in luck you will spot not only the more common wild creatures but perhaps also beavers, otters, bobcats and bald eagles – even timber rattlers and water moccasins in out-of-the-way places in the Shawnee Forest.

---

[i] *10 South Broadway, St Louis*

▶ *Follow* **I–55** *south from downtown St Louis for about 55 miles (88km), then turn east on* **SR 32** *for another 4 miles (6km) to Sainte Genevieve.*

**1 Sainte Genevieve,**
Missouri
This charming small town, Missouri's oldest permanent community, was established beside the Mississippi River by French settlers in about 1735. Despite a devastating flood in 1785, many fine buildings dating from those early years have survived, including the Amoureaux House of 1770 and the Green Tree Tavern of 1790. French tradition remains very much alive, as you will see if you

are here during the Jour de Fete celebrations in August. On your walk around the town don't miss the Felix Valle Historic Site, a store and home built in 1818 in the American Federal style of the time; the local history exhibits at the Sainte Genevieve Museum, which has Indian relics, Civil War items and birds mounted by John James Audubon when he lived here; and the charming Inn St Gemme Beauvais. Take a look, too, inside the Catholic Church and visit the town's winery on Merchant Street.

[i] *66 South Main Street*

▶ *Follow* **US 61** *south for about 10 miles (16km) to Kaskaskia Island.*

**3 Ellis Grove,** Illinois
Across the Mississippi at Ellis Grove, north of Chester, you can visit the elegant period-furnished home of Illinois' first lieutenant governor at the Pierre Menard Home State Historic Site, with its small museum of local history, herb garden and smokehouse, and enjoy panoramic views of the river from the remains of historic Fort Kaskaskia.

As you drive back through Chester, look out for the statue of Popeye and, just south of town, stop at the Turkey Bluffs Scenic Overlook for more fine views of the river.

▶ *Continue southeast on* **SR 3,** **SR 149** *and* **SR 13** *for 47*

*miles (75km) through Grimsby and Murphysboro to Carbondale. From **SR 13**, just east of Carbondale, meander south on **SR 26** back roads past Crab Orchard Lake and through Makanda to Alto Pass.*

## 4 Carbondale and the Western Shawnee Hills,
Illinois

Beyond Grimsby, in the recreational area centered on Kinkaid Lake and Big Muddy River, you pass through the orchard country around Murphysboro, where there is a lively Apple Festival every September. You then come to Carbondale, site of Southern Illinois University and gateway to the western end of the Shawnee Hills, a spectacularly beautiful region of rugged, forested hills and valleys and quaint little towns.

Drive on through Crab Orchard National Wildlife Refuge, with its three recreational lakes, where you might see beavers, coyotes, bald eagles or migrating Canada geese. But stop for a walk in Giant City

State Park, near Makanda, where spectacular sandstone bluffs soar above the thick forest, before driving on to Alto Pass, a little town known for its quilts. Near by, offering superb views of the surrounding hills from the top of Bald Knob Mountain, is a well-known Illinois landmark, the impressive Bald Knob Cross, a Christian monument 111 feet (34m) high, which is illuminated at night.

*i* 714 E Walnut Street, Carbondale

---

### SCENIC ROUTES

In addition to magnificent panoramas of the Mississippi and Ohio rivers from the viewpoints and riverfront towns mentioned along the itinerary, there are many wonderful mountain vistas to be enjoyed along the roads through the Shawnee Hills, especially the back roads around Makanda, Alto Pass, Herod and Delwood.

---

Cave-in-Rock State Park

▶ *From Alto Pass take **SR 127** and **SR 146** to Jonesboro, then follow **SR 146** east for 19 miles (30km) to West Vienna. Make a 28-mile (45km) detour south on **SR 37** through Cypress, east on **SR 169** through Karnak and north on **US 45** to Vienna.*

## 5 Vienna, Illinois

It is hard to believe you are in Illinois when you explore the remote unspoiled swamp country among the lower Cache River south of Vienna. Here you can see stands of majestic white oaks, cypresses standing in the water, and all sorts of wildlife, perhaps even beavers, otters and bobcats, and colonies of great blue herons nesting amid the peace of Heron Pond Nature Preserve.

▶ *Continue east on **SR 146** through Dixon Springs, Golconda and Elizabethtown for 50 miles (80km) to Cave-in-Rock.*

**6 Cave-in-Rock,** Illinois
After stretching your legs in Dixon Springs State Park, drive on to the historic little town of Golconda, tucked away amid deer-hunting country beside the mighty Ohio River. There is a lively little Deer Festival here every November. Further east, don't miss the historic Illinois Iron Furnace on Hog Thief Creek, before turning south on a side road to visit the Fluorspar Museum at the small riverfront town of Rosiclare. At Cave-in-Rock you must see the colossal cavern that gave the town its name. Two centuries ago it was a famous landmark for pioneers sailing down the Ohio River on their way west. It was also a notorious hideout for the river pirates who preyed on them.

▶ Retrace **SR 146** for about 17 miles (27km) through Elizabethtown and turn north on **SR 34** for about 15 miles (24km) to the Garden of the Gods, near Herod, and west on the local road for about 13 miles (21km) to Delwood.

### RECOMMENDED WALKS

Although many of the best-known state park trails in this region are quite long and strenuous, there are stretches which you can follow for a gentle stroll. Among them are the Pirates Bluff and Hickory Ridge trails at Cave-in-Rock State Park and the famed Red Cedar Trail and shorter trails in Giant City State Park near Makanda. You will also find pleasant walking trails in Trail of Tears State Park, near Cape Girardeau.

**7 Delwood,** Illinois
Weave your way along the trails in Garden of the Gods State Park and you will understand how this scenic wonderland got its name. Set against the dark forest are spectacular rock formations, with such colorful names

as Camel Rock, Buzzard's Roost, Tower of Babel and Fat Man's Squeeze. To the west, hidden in the breathtaking scenery around Delwood, there are more beautiful trails in Bell Smith Springs State Park, along which you will see a winding canyon, Indian caves, a lovely waterfall and, nearby, a natural stone bridge.

▶ From Delwood take **SR 145** and **SR 147** south to Vienna, then continue west on **SR 146** for 30 miles (48km) through Anna and Jonesboro to Ware. Turn south on **SR 3** for 16 miles (26km) across the Mississippi River to Cape Girardeau.

**8 Cape Girardeau,** Missouri
Despite the French name it acquired during French Colonial times, Cape Girardeau was not laid out as a planned riverfront town until 1806, just after it became part of the United States. So the historic buildings you see on a downtown walking tour are not French but 19th-century American. Among them are the imposing Common Pleas Courthouse of 1854; the Gothic-style Old St Vincent's Church dedicated in 1853; the lovely Hoche House of 1838; and the elegant Glenn House of 1883. As you walk around, see if you can also spot the old Opera House and General Grant's headquarters, now disguised behind other uses. Don't miss a stroll along Riverfront Park and a tour of the Cape River Heritage Museum before driving out to see the famed Rose Display Garden at Capaha Park and Arena Park, the site of the Southeast Missouri District Fair in September. Then make your way northeast of town to enjoy Mississippi River views from Cape Rock Park and Trail of Tears State Park.

ⓘ 1707 Mount Auburn Road

▶ From Trail of Tears State Park continue on **SR 177** to Fruitland and pick up **I–55** northbound for St Louis.

### FOR HISTORY BUFFS

According to legend, the monument in Trail of Tears State Park, near Cape Girardeau, marks the grave of Princess Otahki, just one of the 4,000 who died during the forced removal of 15,000 Cherokee Indians from their homeland in the southern Appalachians to Oklahoma in the winter of 1838. Their march into exile, the cruel 'Trail of Tears', took them through southern Illinois and across the Mississippi at Cape Girardeau.

### FOR CHILDREN

If there is too much to see and not enough to do for the children on the tour, give them a ride, complete with clanging bells and hissing steam, on the St Louis Iron Mountain and Southern Railway. It starts at weekends from Jackson, just north of Cape Girardeau. (It is just possible there will be a 'murder' on the train to solve, or a 'hold-up' by Bonnie and Clyde or other outlaw gangs played by local people.)

### SPECIAL TO...

Cape Girardeau's unusual method of recording local history will probably catch your eye on this tour. Look out for the big colored murals. The Water Street Riverfront Mural is a brightly colored celebration of life on the Mississippi River at Cape Girardeau, and the Missouri Murals on Lorimer Street are made of tiles and depict the local role in the story of printing, while the Jake Wells Mural at Kent Library on the campus of the University of Southeast Missouri portrays the history and natural resource of southeast Missouri.

# The Bayous of
## Acadiana

This tour takes you through the steamy swamps and along the sleepy bayous of the Mississippi delta to experience the unique atmosphere of Louisiana's Cajun Country. You will visit the historic communities of the French-speaking Cajun people, gather memories of live oaks and cypresses festooned with Spanish moss, alligators, swamp tours, a cruise on the bayou, and gracious old sugar plantations.

**4 DAYS • 332 MILES • 531KM**

| ITINERARY | |
|---|---|
| **NEW ORLEANS** | ▶ **Houma** (61m–98km) |
| HOUMA | ▶ **Thibodaux** (14m–22km) |
| THIBODAUX | ▶ **New Iberia** |
| | (78m–125km) |
| NEW IBERIA | ▶ **St Martinville** (10m–16km) |
| ST MARTINVILLE | ▶ **Lafayette** (17m–27km) |
| LAFAYETTE | ▶ **Baton Rouge** (53m–85km) |
| BATON ROUGE | ▶ **Burnside** (45m–72km) |
| BURNSIDE | ▶ **New Orleans** (54m–86km) |

*i* 529 St Ann Street, New Orleans

▶ *Cross the Mississippi River from New Orleans on either Greater New Orleans Bridge or Huey P Long Bridge and follow* **US 90** *west for the 55-mile (89km) drive to Houma.*

**❶ Houma,** Louisiana
Nicknamed the 'Venice of America' on account of its many waterways and bridges, Houma is a shrimp-fishing and seafood-processing center. From here you can take boat excursions into the surrounding cypress swamps to see alligators and other wild creatures. Walk around the Historic District and see the porcelain birds and other exhibits at Southdown Plantation's Terrebonne Museum, on SR 311 on the way to Thibodaux. Further north see the Ardoyne and Magnolia plantations.

*i* S St Charles Street at US 90

▶ *Follow* **SR 311** *north to Thibodaux.*

### FOR CHILDREN

Waterland USA, on SR 311 north of Houma, offers children all the usual fun activities of a water park.

**❷ Thibodaux,** Louisiana
The university city of Thibodaux is another community with fine 19th-century architecture. Here you should visit the Laurel Valley Village and Rural Life Museum, southeast of town on SR 308, where you will learn about life on a sugar plantation. Still in operation, the complex includes a schoolhouse, general store, boarding house and the remains of an old sugar mill.

*i* On SR 1 at Raceland

▶ *Go south on* **SR 24** *and pick up* **SR 20** *going southwest for 16 miles (26km) to Gibson, then* **US 90** *west through Morgan City, Patterson and Franklin to New Iberia.*

### FOR HISTORY BUFFS

Historic houses, plantations and museums are plentiful along this itinerary, but for a break from the long Thibodaux to New Iberia drive, stop to explore the historic districts and houses at Morgan City and Franklin and to see exhibits depicting life along Bayou Teche at the small Jeanerette Museum further west.

Shadows-on-the-Teche, restored by the builder's great-grandson

### FOR CHILDREN

If the kids prefer familiar animals to wild alligators and swamp creatures, they can see and feed farm animals at the Barnyard Zoo in Morgan City.

**❸ New Iberia,** Louisiana
The old city of New Iberia, on Bayou Teche, is the center of Louisiana's sugarcane industry. A tour of its downtown Historic District reveals many architectural treasures and, surprisingly, a genuine 2nd-century Roman statue of the Emperor Hadrian. Not to be missed is the beautiful and romantic Shadows-on-the-Teche mansion, standing by the bayou amid moss-draped live oaks. Be sure to drop by Trappey's famous Cajun shop for a tour of the adjoining hot pepper sauce factory, or to visit the Konriko Company Store to see the rice mill and watch the slide show on Cajun culture. If you then feel like relaxing, take a pleasant cruise on the bayou. For trips out of town visit beautiful Live Oak Gardens, Jefferson Island, or Jungle Gardens and the Tabasco Sauce factory, Avery Island.

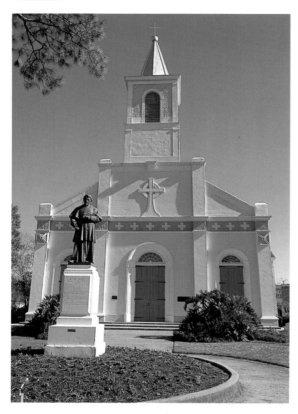

see the historic exhibits in the adjacent Petit Paris Museum. And, for a leisurely one-hour cruise on the bayou, board a boat at Evangeline Oak.

▶ *Leave St Martinville on **SR 96** and after 7 miles (11km) pick up **US 90** northbound to Lafayette.*

**5 Lafayette,** Louisiana
This city of more than 94,000 people is the cultural capital of Acadiana, with busy restaurants that serve traditional Cajun and Creole cuisine and foot-stomping music. The best times to be here are spring, when there is a big Mardi Gras celebration and the city is ablaze with azalea blossom, and September, for the Festivals Acadiens. Downtown landmarks include the Old City Hall, the Cathedral of St John the Evangelist, the Lafayette Museum and the Lafayette Natural History Museum and Planetarium. But the highlight for visitors is a tour of the reconstructed Acadian Village southwest of town, which captures the atmosphere of a small 19th-century Cajun community. There is also the living history museum of Vermilionville, on Surrey Street, which presents the traditional culture of Cajun and Creole people.

*i* | *Near US 90/SR 14 junction*

St Martin de Tours Church has a replica of the Grotto of Lourdes

▶ *Follow West Main Street and SR 31 from New Iberia for about 10 miles (16km) to St Martinville.*

**4 St Martinville,** Louisiana
It helps if you have already read Henry Wadsworth Longfellow's poem *Evangeline* when you visit this quiet little town with its strong French atmosphere beside Bayou Teche. It was here that Longfellow's heroine (in real life, Emmeline Labiche), like many other Acadian settlers, ended her journey into exile from Nova Scotia in the 1760s. On a tour of the town you will see Evangeline's statue and grave, the Evangeline Oak, beneath which she disembarked, and the Longfellow-Evangeline State Commemorative Area, a 157-acre (63-hectare) park dedicated to the early settlers north of town. Be sure, too, to visit St Martin de Tours Church and to

---

### SCENIC ROUTES

Get off the main highways in this part of Louisiana and you will be driving through swamplands with tall cypresses trailing Spanish moss, vast expanses of sugarcane and little communities with old Cajun-style cabins shaded by ancient live oaks. Not spectacular mountain scenery, it is true, but scenic nonetheless, and you can enjoy it anywhere between Houma and Lafayette, not to mention along the Great River Road.

---

### SPECIAL TO...

Everything about Cajun Country is different and therefore special: the geography, the climate, the vegetation, the wildlife and the people and their language, food and music. There are also those unique experiences you will always remember, like the crawfish farm at Houma; the carillon tower that plays in Brownell Memorial Park at Morgan City; the old airplanes on show at the Wedell-Williams Aviation Museum of Louisiana at Patterson; and the horse races at New Evangeline Downs in Lafayette.

*i* *1400 NW Evangeline Thruway*

▶ *Take I–10 eastbound from just north of downtown Lafayette for 53 miles (85km) across the Atchafalaya Swamp and Mississippi River to the state capital, Baton Rouge.*

**6 Baton Rouge,** Louisiana
This vibrant Mississippi river port, with its lovely old homes and tree-lined streets, has been the capital of Louisiana since 1850, and today it is home to a quarter of a million people.

For a panoramic view of it, go to the top of the 34-story State Capitol, which was constructed from 26 varieties of marble from every marble-producing country in the world. The Old Governor's Mansion, which Mark Twain once dismissed as a 'sham little castle', is another of the government buildings you can tour (by appointment) in this city.

Along the riverfront you can explore the Catfish Town old warehouse area, tour the World War II destroyer USS *Kidd*, and take a one-hour narrated cruise aboard the steamboat *Samuel Clemens*. But not to be missed is the representation of a working 19th-century plantation at the Rural Life Museum, one of Louisiana State University's four excellent museums in the south part of town. For the real thing, you can visit Magnolia Mound Plantation not far away.

*i* *State Capitol*

**FOR CHILDREN**

Another favorite with kids is the Greater Baton Rouge Zoo at Baker, north of Baton Rouge, with animals from around the world in naturalistic outdoor habitats. There is a small zoo for children, with goats and rabbits and a variety of rides.

▶ *Cross the Mississippi River bridge from downtown Baton Rouge and follow the Great River Road (SR 1) south for 35 miles (56km) through Plaquemine to Donaldsonville. Cross the Mississippi on SR 70, then turn north on to SR 44 to Burnside.*

**7 Burnside and the Mississippi River Plantations,** Louisiana
As you drive through the sugar-cane fields along this stretch of the Mississippi, you will be reminded of the vanished way of life of the old plantations. A few miles beyond historic Plaquemine, with its old locks and fine views of the river, be sure to visit the imposing Nottoway Plantation, the biggest of them all.

Then, if you have time, drive on down SR 18 to see the impressive avenue of live oaks at Oak Alley Plantation, near Vacherie. Across the river, at Burnside, you will see other fine mansions, none more beautiful than the Greek Revival Houmas House Plantation. Rebuilt in 1840, it is furnished with early 19th-century antiques, and especially interesting are a graceful, three-story spiral staircase and a collection of armories.

▶ *Leave Burnside on SR 44, then take SR 22 to join I–10 eastbound back to New Orleans (54 miles/86km).*

**BACK TO NATURE**

Alligators, nutria (coypu), crawfish, herons, egrets and a long list of other wild creatures inhabit the moss-draped cypress swamps, marshes, bayous and creeks of southern Louisiana. An easy way to see this rich variety of flora and fauna is to visit such special places as the Wildlife Gardens at Gibson, the Original Swamp Gardens at Morgan City, and Cypress Lake/Swamp on the University of Southwestern Louisiana campus at Lafayette.

**RECOMMENDED WALKS**

Walks in Louisiana's hot and humid summer climate are best kept to a short stroll at the many places of interest along the itinerary. You will find easily walkable trails at Lafayette's Acadiana Park and a pleasant walk along the Great Wall on Front Street overlooking the Atchafalaya River at Morgan City.

Lafayette was founded by French exiles from Nova Scotia

# THE LONE STAR STATE

Decades of Hollywood movies and TV series have helped to perpetuate the image of Texas as one vast dusty plain swarming with cattle and slow-talking John Wayne-style cowboys, and dotted with cities of glittering mirror-glass skyscrapers where tough business entrepreneurs play for high stakes. This is the larger-than-life version of Texas, but one which Texans enjoy acting out. They walk around downtown Dallas or Houston, for example, wearing cowboy boots, jeans and wide-brimmed Stetsons; they play the cowboy at the state's many dude ranches and rodeos; and they will dance the Cotton-Eyed Joe or Two Step at country music honkytonk one night and be seated at the opera or a symphony concert the next.

Dallas's glass skyscraper's are transformed by night

Until Alaska joined the Union in 1959, Texas was America's largest state, with 267,339 square miles (692,408sq km) of territory between the Oklahoma state line on the Red River and the Mexican border on the Rio Grande. Larger than France, Italy or Britain, it was a country in its own right for nine years after Texans won their independence from Mexico in 1836. Texas then became the 28th state of the US, and from the 1840s to the '80s, the Golden Age of the cowboy, vast herds of cattle were driven from its ranches along the legendary Chisholm Trail and others to markets elsewhere in the country. Oil transformed the economy after 1901, building the fortunes of Houston and Dallas.

Geographically, Texas encompasses terrain of considerable diversity. Behind the long, sandy beaches and islands of the Gulf shoreline, the flat coastal plain extends in an arc from the fertile farmlands, lakes and forests of the Piney Woods region of East Texas to the semitropical croplands near the Mexican border south of San Antonio. Inland, the wheat prairies and ranches of the Great Plains stretch north from the Hill Country near Austin to the Oklahoma line. West Texas has the rugged canyon country of the Panhandle around Amarillo and, west of the Pecos River, the desert and mountain scenery that includes the Guadalupe Mountains and Big Bend National Parks.

## Dallas

Dallas has grown along the Trinity River on the plains of northeast Texas. As a business center it has an atmosphere of wealth and sophistication and boasts well-manicured parks, beautiful residential districts, fine shops and restaurants and a flourishing cultural life. Glistening skyscrapers rise above the clean downtown streets, where many of the buildings are linked by underground and elevated walkways. Of special interest here is the permanent exhibit called 'The Sixth Floor' in the former Texas School Book Depository, which commemorates the assassination of President Kennedy in Dallas in 1963. Near by are the revitalized West End Historic District, with its shops, restaurants and night spots, and the Arts District, which contains the Dallas Museum of Art, and the stunning Morton H Meyerson Symphony Center.

Other premier attractions near Dallas include Southfork Ranch, the setting of the famous *Dallas* TV series; the cluster of family amusement parks west of the city; and the Stockyards and outstanding art museums of Fort Worth.

## Houston

A cluster of historic pioneer buildings stands today in Houston's downtown Sam Houston Park, dwarfed by the surrounding futuristic skyscrapers – an eloquent symbol of this vibrant port city's remarkable development since its modest beginnings by a hot swampy bayou back in 1836. Now America's fourth largest city, Houston has many attractions for visitors, and shopping opportunities such as the popular Galleria west of downtown. The city has an especially lively performing arts scene, offering ballet, opera, symphony concerts and theater. There are also fine museums, such as the Museum of Fine Arts, Menil Collection and Museum of Natural Science. South of downtown are the AstroWorld amusement park and the huge Astrodome arena, which hosts year-round spectator sports, and many other events, such as the exciting Houston Rodeo and Livestock Show every February.

## San Antonio

The downtown Tower of the Americas offers marvelous bird's-eye views of this captivating southwest Texas city, founded by the Spaniards on the San Antonio River in 1718. But the city's best-known landmark is the Alamo, the old mission where Davy Crockett and a band of Texas volunteers were massacred by Mexican forces in the struggle for Texas independence in 1836. Near by, you can enjoy the festive atmosphere of the Paseo del Rio, or River Walk, with its mariachi bands, outdoor cafés, restaurants and shops, and explore the quaint adobe craft shops and galleries of La Villita, where the city began. Other city attractions include the old San Fernando Cathedral, the Spanish Governor's Palace and El Mercado the Mexican Market.

South of town are the 19th-century homes of the King William Historic District and a chain of old Spanish missions; north, several impressive art museums and Brackenridge Park, with koalas in the fine San Antonio Zoo; west, Sea World of Texas, the showcase of marine animal entertainment; and northwest, Fiesta Texas theme park.

San Jose Mission, San Antonio, was founded in 1720

# Piney Woods of
## East Texas

With its wide range of attractions, this relatively unknown corner of Texas east of Dallas may come as a pleasant surprise. Much of its appeal derives from the natural beauty of its dense forests, lakes and streams and its rich wildlife. There are also charming towns with lovely old homes and historic sites that tell of the Indians and early Spanish colonists. At each point on the tour something new awaits you – a rose garden, a doll museum, a replica oil-boom town and a delightful steam train – all tucked away amid the timeless scenery.

**3 DAYS • 470 MILES • 751KM**

**ITINERARY**

| | |
|---|---|
| **DALLAS** | ▶ **Tyler** (98m-157km) |
| TYLER | ▶ **Rusk** (42m-67km) |
| RUSK | ▶ **Alto** (12m-19km) |
| ALTO | ▶ **Nacogdoches** (27m-43km) |
| NACOGDOCHES | ▶ **Kilgore** (59m-94km) |
| KILGORE | ▶ **Marshall** (37m-59km) |
| MARSHALL | ▶ **Karnack** (15m-24km) |
| KARNACK | ▶ **Jefferson** (11m-18km) |
| JEFFERSON | ▶ **Dallas** (169m-270km) |

ℹ️ *Union Station, 400 S Houston Street, Dallas*

## SPECIAL TO...

If you are on I–20 east of Dallas on the first Monday of the month (or the weekend before), don't miss the Canton flea market, one of the nation's biggest.

▶ *For the 98-mile (157km) drive to Tyler, take **US 80** east from downtown Dallas and pick up I–20 eastbound. At **Exit 556** turn south on to **US 69** to Tyler.*

### 🄮 **Tyler,** Texas

Every September large crowds descend on this manufacturing center and college town to attend the six-day East Texas State Fair, a major livestock event linked to the local agricultural business. Roses, however, are Tyler's best-known product, and they feature in magnificent displays at the 22-acre (9-hectare) Municipal Rose Garden on West Front Street. Another popular visitor attraction is Caldwell Zoo, designed with children especially in mind. Animals from Texas, South America and Africa live in simulated natural habitats. A well-known city landmark is the Goodman-LeGrand Home, a stately mansion of 1859 that now houses a museum displaying historic artifacts.

## SCENIC ROUTES

Lovely forest scenery awaits you along this tour of the Piney Woods region. The drive along US 69 through Cherokee County between Tyler and Alto is exceptionally enjoyable, with vistas of hills, woodlands and lakes bordering the highway. For especially fine views of the countryside, stop at Love's Lookout Park just north of Jacksonville.

▶ *Drive south on Broadway and **US 69** for 42 miles (67km) through Jacksonville to Rusk.*

### 🄯 **Rusk,** Texas

Highway 69 passes through beautiful rolling forest country. Between the towering pines of Jim Hogg State Historic Park and Rusk State Park is the historic community of Rusk, birthplace of two Texas governors; James S Hogg and Thomas M Campbell. Here you can walk across the nation's longest foot-

Tyler is well known for its field-grown rose bushes

bridge at 546 feet (166m), and enjoy a ride on the antique steam train operated by the Texas State Railroad between Rusk State Park and Palestine, 25 miles (40km) away.

▶ *Continue on **US 69** for 12 miles (19km) to Alto.*

## FOR HISTORY BUFFS

For an interesting 30-mile (48km) side trip, follow the old Camino Real (SR 21) southwest from Alto to Weches. Just outside town, at Mission Tejas State Park, you will see a replica of the first Spanish mission in East Texas, built in 1690. Also in the park is the historic Rice Stagecoach Inn, of 1828.

### 🄳 **Alto,** Texas

Where US 69 crosses the old Spanish *Camino Real*, or Royal Highway (SR 21), is the little town of Alto, famous for tomatoes. It is also the gateway to the Caddoan Mounds State Historic Site, an ancient Indian site 6 miles (10km) southwest of town on SR 21. Here you can see a reconstructed Caddoan Indian dwelling which resembles a beehive, two ceremonial mounds and various exhibits at the Visitor Center, which also has an audio-visual presentation about the excavation of the site. The whole site is thought to date back some 15 centuries.

▶ *From Alto take **SR 21** east for 27 miles (43km) to Nacogdoches.*

### 🄴 **Nacogdoches,** Texas

This charming old city, a paradise for history buffs, was the site of an Indian settlement long before the arrival of the Spaniards. Hernando de Soto's lieutenant probably stayed in the area in 1541 en route to Mexico after de Soto's death. The main gateway to Texas from the east, the city grew at the crossroads of an old Indian highway (named the *Calle del Norte* by the Spanish, now North Street) and the Camino Real, which was blazed through the area by the Spaniards in 1691. You can see ancient Indian arti-

facts excavated from local archeological sites, and other historic exhibits at the Old Stone Fort, a reconstruction of the Spanish trading post built here in 1779.

Other historic city landmarks worth seeing date from the 1800s; they include the fine group of buildings at Millard's Crossing; the Sterne-Hoya Home (1828), which houses a library; Oak Grove Cemetery, with several historic monuments, including the graves of four of the signatories of the Texas Declaration of Independence; Old Nacogdoches University (1845), now used as a museum of antique furniture and silver; and Old North Church (1852), just outside town off US 59.

### FOR CHILDREN

Attractions along the itinerary include the Hudnall Planetarium and the space vehicle exhibits at Tyler Junior College; the hands-on learning displays and buildings at the Depot Museum and Children's Discovery Center, at Henderson; and the fine doll collection at Jefferson's Carnegie Library.

▶ *Follow **US 259** north from Nacogdoches through Henderson to Kilgore, 59 miles (94km).*

### 🖪 **Kilgore,** Texas

One good reason to visit this oil-producing town is to tour the excellent East Texas Oil Museum on Kilgore College campus. You can relive the exciting boom days that followed the discovery of the East Texas oilfield in 1930 as you wander around the realistic dioramas, the boomtown street scene and other fascinating exhibits explaining the oil industry. Downtown, in the block at Main and Commerce streets nicknamed 'The World's Richest Acre', you can still see one of the 24 derricks that once stood on this site, one of them actually piercing the terrazzo floor of the Kilgore National Bank.

ⓘ 107 South Martin Street

▶ *Continue north on **US 259** for 5 miles (8km) and pick up I–20 eastbound for 32 miles (51 km) to Marshall.*

### 🖪 **Marshall,** Texas

As a wealthy manufacturing center back in the 19th century, Marshall played an important

The Dallas skyline

part in keeping the Confederacy supplied with ammunition and other equipment during the Civil War – hence the Confederate Monument on the lawn of the courthouse. You will learn more about such aspects of the city's past if you stop by the Harrison County Historical Society Museum. Also worth visiting are the 1896 Ginocchio Hotel and 1877 Allen House Museum in the three-block Ginocchio National Historic District downtown.

Another prominent city landmark open for tours is the impressive 1870 Italianate mansion, built by J Franklin Starr, in the Starr Family State Historic Site. But don't leave town without seeing the T C Lindsey and Company General Store, opened in 1807 and still operating; the fine collection of 1,200 dolls and other toys at the Franks Doll Museum on Grand Avenue; and the famous Marshall Pottery southeast of town. Here you can watch the potters at work and see their creations in the showrooms.

▶ *From Marshall take **SR 43** northeast for 15 miles (24km) to Karnack and Caddo Lake.*

### 7 Karnack and Caddo Lake, Texas

Along the highway just south of Karnack you will pass the birthplace of Mrs Lyndon B Johnson, a fine, two-story brick house dating from before the Civil War (it is not, however, open for tours).

North of Karnack you will come to Caddo Lake, shrouded in parts by lush, moss-draped forest and an atmosphere of mystery. Mississippi steamboats once plied its waters on their way up Big Cypress Bayou. Access to the lake is by Caddo Lake State Park, where you will find facilities for camping, boating and fishing, and hiking and nature trails.

▶ *From Caddo Lake follow* **SR 143** *west for about 11 miles (18km) to Jefferson.*

### 8 Jefferson, Texas

In the historic little community of Jefferson, time almost seems to have stood still since its citizens refused to let businessman Jay Gould bring a railroad through the town more than a century ago. Before then it was a flourishing river port on Big Cypress Bayou, with an ironworks, a lumber industry, an ice plant and gas street lighting. With no railroad, however, Jefferson failed to develop, so

today you can see it more or less as it was.

The town is packed with historic homes and bed-and-breakfast inns, most of them listed on the National Register of Historic Places. Many are

> #### SPECIAL TO...
>
> Jefferson hasn't totally spurned the railroad, for on display is the luxurious private railroad car used by tycoon Jay Gould. It is across the street from the Excelsior House hotel, in whose register Gould left his prediction of 'the end of Jefferson' when townsfolk rejected his railroad proposals. It is a nice touch of irony.

regularly open for tours, others only during the annual Historical Pilgrimage in early May. One of the most famous is Excelsior House, a beautifully furnished old hotel, where many prominent people have stayed, including Ulysses S Grant and Irish writer Oscar Wilde.

The red-eyed vireo, a Texan resident

> #### RECOMMENDED WALKS
>
> Numerous hiking and nature trails crisscross the Piney Woods region of East Texas: for example in Tyler State Park, in Jim Hogg State Park, near Rusk, and beside Caddo Lake. You can also stroll through the pleasant gardens and the Goodman-LeGrand House and the Rose Garden and Park at Tyler.

When you have seen the exhibits depicting Jefferson's colorful past at the Historical Society Museum, take a 45-minute narrated tour around the streets in a horse-drawn surrey. Then cast your mind back to the days of the steamboats with a cruise along Big Cypress Bayou departing from Polk Street Bridge landing.

ℹ️ *223 West Austin Street*

▶ *Follow* **US 59** *south from Jefferson for 19 miles (30km) through Marshall and pick up* **I–20** *westbound for another 150 miles (240km) to Dallas.*

> #### BACK TO NATURE
>
> If you thought Texas was just one great expanse of grass, the Piney Woods of East Texas will be a pleasant surprise with its jungle-like forests of loblolly pines and all sorts of hardwood trees, often festooned with Spanish moss, vines and creepers and shading a dense undergrowth of dogwood, sumac, sassafras, ferns and countless wildflowers. This 'Garden of Eden' is home to white-tailed deer, squirrels, wild turkeys, barred owls, Acadian flycatchers and pine warblers.

# The Gulf Coast
# & Big Thicket

This tour of the East Texas Gulf Coast and the Big Thicket forest region takes you along the shoreline where you will see fine sandy beaches, fishing piers, the historic seaside city of Galveston and modern oil refineries. Inland you will drive through old logging towns nestled in dense forests where you can look for wild animals or rare plants.

**3/4 DAYS • 410 MILES • 656KM**

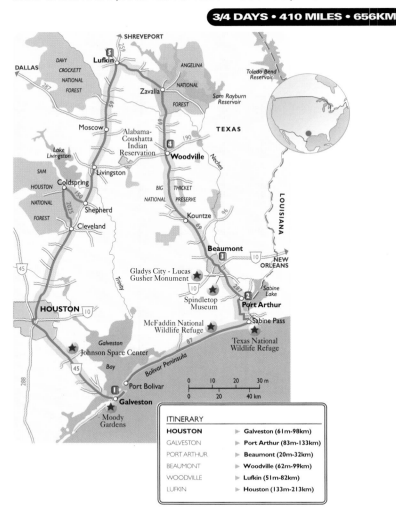

| ITINERARY | |
|---|---|
| **HOUSTON** | ▶ **Galveston (61m-98km)** |
| GALVESTON | ▶ Port Arthur (83m-133km) |
| PORT ARTHUR | ▶ Beaumont (20m-32km) |
| BEAUMONT | ▶ Woodville (62m-99km) |
| WOODVILLE | ▶ Lufkin (51m-82km) |
| LUFKIN | ▶ Houston (133m-213km) |

*i* *3300 Main Street, Houston*

▶ *Follow the Gulf Freeway (I–45) south from downtown Houston to Galveston, with a stop at the Johnson Space Center.*

---

### SPECIAL TO...

The NASA space complex, southeast of Houston off I-45, has the excellent hands-on Space Center Houston. Here you can experience flying in space, watch real flights on giant screens and see spacecraft and other exciting exhibits.

---

**❶ Galveston,** Texas
This historic port city, at the eastern end of Galveston Island, boasts excellent beaches and a growing number of visitor attractions. The most enjoyable way to see them is to ride the Galveston Flyer trolley or the Treasure Island Tour Train. A major city attraction is the revitalized Strand National Historic District, the 19th-century commercial area once known as the 'Wall Street of the West', which now bustles with shops, restaurants, pubs, galleries and even a candy factory. Other historic landmarks are the Bishop's Palace of 1886, the opulent Ashton Villa, built in 1859, and the fascinating Railroad Museum, in the old Santa Fe Depot. On the waterfront you can enjoy the varied attractions of Pier 21; tour the restored 1877 sailing ship *Elissa*, now a museum of seafaring technology; and board the paddlewheeler *Colonel* for a two-hour cruise around Galveston Bay. You can catch it at Moody Gardens, the huge botanical and entertainment complex west of downtown.

*i* *2106 Seawall Boulevard*

▶ *Take the free ferry across the ship channel between Galveston and Port Bolivar and follow SR 87 along the Bolivar Peninsula for 77 miles (123km) to Port Arthur.*

Galveston's Railroad Museum

Gladys City–Spindletop Boomtown, a re-created oil field boomtown just outside Beaumont

**❷ Port Arthur,** Texas
This important oil-refining center lies inland on Sabine Lake and is linked to the Gulf by a broad ship channel. You will

see the tankers pass by from Sabine Pass Battleground State Historical Park, south of Port Arthur, which commemorates a Confederate Civil War victory. You can discover more about the battle and local history at the Port Arthur Historical Museum downtown. Also of interest is the Pompeian Villa, a mansion built in grand style in 1900 by a local industrialist.

### BACK TO NATURE

Some of Texas' rich wildlife can be viewed at the McFaddin National Wildlife Refuge near Port Arthur, which has a large population of American alligators. The refuge at nearby Texas Point contains great numbers of shorebirds and waterfowl. In the lush forests inland look out for the pileated woodpecker and such exotic plants as wild orchids and insectivorous pitcher plants.

▶ *Follow **US 69/287** from downtown Port Arthur for 20 miles (32km) to Beaumont.*

## ❸ Beaumont, Texas
Now a major industrial city and port on the Neches River, Beaumont was suddenly transformed from a small logging community when an oil rig at Spindletop struck black gold in 1901. Exhibits recording those times are displayed at the Spindletop Museum on the Lamar University campus, while nearby, at the Gladys City-Lucas Gusher Monument, there is an excellent re-creation of the old town in the early days of the oil boom. Also worth visiting are the John Jay French Trading Post of 1845; the richly furnished McFaddin-Ward House of 1906, with its silver, china, porcelain and oriental rug collections; and the Babe Didrikson Zaharias Memorial Museum, containing golfing trophies and other memorabilia of the famous American sportswoman who was one of the world's greatest athletes.

### FOR CHILDREN

In addition to the Space Center Houston and Galveston's fine beaches, places of interest to kids include the Edison Plaza Museum at Beaumont, with its exhibits of scientific inventions from Edison's time to the present and into the future, and Lufkin's Ellen Trout Zoo Park, which has a miniature railroad.

▶ *Continue north on **US 69/287** through Kountze for 62 miles (99km) to Woodville in the Big Thicket.*

## ❹ Woodville, Texas
The Big Thicket National Preserve is a vast area of dense woodlands, marshes, bayous and streams containing a rich variety of wildlife and exotic plants. It extends north from Beaumont in 13 units penetrated by nature and canoe trails. Walking is the best way to see the preserve and there are a variety of guided walks on weekends throughout the year. For details stop at the Information Station on Route 420 just north of Kountze.

In the midst of the area is the small logging town of Woodville, where you can visit the Shivers Library and Museum, the restored Victorian home of Allan Shivers, former Texas governor.

West of town on US 190 is the Heritage Village Museum, with

Below and right: exhibits at Houston Space Center. Tram tours guide visitors behind the scenes at this fascinating, hands-on experience of space exploration

its outdoor historic exhibits depicting Texas life. The Alabama-Coushatta Indian Reservation, further on, is the oldest in the state; its excellent visitor program includes craft-making displays, swamp tours, miniature railroad rides, and Indian dances on weekends in fall and spring.

▶ *Continue north for 51 miles (82km) through Zavalla to Lufkin.*

**8 Lufkin,** Texas
Settled in 1882, this important manufacturing and logging center city lies in the heart of the East Texas Piney Woods region, where the Davy Crockett and Angelina National Forests and Sam Rayburn Reservoir provide facilities for camping, hiking, swimming, hunting and fishing. Worth a visit in Lufkin are the Texas Forestry Museum, which has botanical exhibits, an old railroad and depot and sawmill steam engines, and the Museum of East Texas, with changing art exhibits featuring the works of regionally, nationally and inter-nationally known artists, a general store and the Angelina Room containing porcelain, china and other artifacts belonging to early Lufkin residents.

▶ *Follow US 59 south to Shepherd. Make a 28-mile (45km) detour west on SR 150 through Coldspring, then south on Route 2025, and rejoin US 59 near Cleveland. Continue south for 43 miles (69km) to Houston.*

## RECOMMENDED WALKS

Opportunities for walking include the short Moscow Trail, just south of Moscow on US 59; nature trails beside Lake Livingston, just west of Livingston; and hiking trails in Sam Houston National Forest, south of Coldspring and northwest of Cleveland.

## FOR HISTORY BUFFS

In the quaint Old Town area of Coldspring is the San Jacinto County Museum, housed in a restored jail of about 1887 and complete with hangman's drop, jailer's quarters and cell block. Exhibits such as household objects, old photographs and farming implements depict the early settlers' life.

# The Texas
## Hill Country

Close to San Antonio and Austin, the state capital, is the scenic Hill
Country. It is a land of limestone hills dotted with gnarled trees and wildflowers, of canyons and caverns, sparkling streams and green valleys,
and historic communities where folk still speak German, enjoy western
music and dance the Cotton-eyed Joe. Here, too, you can sample the
outdoor life at the ranches of Kerrville and Bandera.

**4 DAYS • 318 MILES • 509KM**

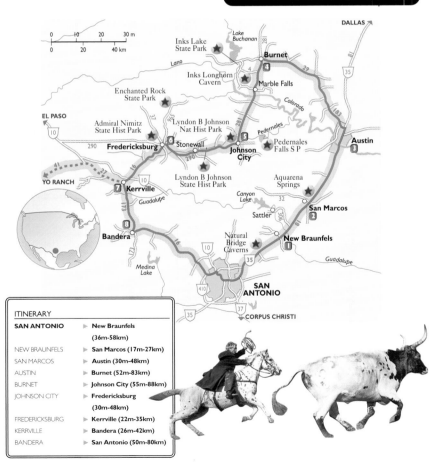

| ITINERARY | | |
|---|---|---|
| **SAN ANTONIO** | ▶ | **New Braunfels** |
| | | **(36m-58km)** |
| NEW BRAUNFELS | ▶ | San Marcos (17m-27km) |
| SAN MARCOS | ▶ | Austin (30m-48km) |
| AUSTIN | ▶ | Burnet (52m-83km) |
| BURNET | ▶ | Johnson City (55m-88km) |
| JOHNSON CITY | ▶ | Fredericksburg |
| | | (30m-48km) |
| FREDERICKSBURG | ▶ | Kerrville (22m-35km) |
| KERRVILLE | ▶ | Bandera (26m-42km) |
| BANDERA | ▶ | San Antonio (50m-80km) |

ⓘ *317 Alamo Plaza, San Antonio*

▶ *Pick up the Pan Am Expressway (I–35/US 81) northbound from downtown San Antonio and continue to New Braunfels.*

**❶ New Braunfels, Texas**
There is a strong German flavor to New Braunfels, established by German settlers in 1845. It is especially evident during the colorful 10-day Wurstfest celebration held in November to honor the German sausage. You will notice it, too, in the architecture of historic buildings like the Baetge House and the Lindheimer Home, built in the 1850s. Take a drive around the historic Gruene district, with its old homes, shops, galleries and 1880 dance hall; visit the Museum of Texas Handmade Furniture; and take a look at pioneer life at the Sophienburg Museum. For outdoor recreation, there are good facilities for golf, boating and swimming in Landa Park, while on the river you can enjoy canoeing, rafting and tubing. Don't miss Natural Bridge Caverns, west of town.

The Alamo, San Antonio, where Davy Crockett and Colonel Jim Bowie volunteered to die for freedom fighting the Mexican army

with glass-bottom boats, submarine theater shows, sky rides, alligator pits, historic buildings, Old West village and more. The cavern and varied attractions at Wonder World are another highlight. As a contrast, visit the Belvin Street Historic District, with its beautiful 19th-century homes and shady live oaks.

ⓘ *390 S Seguin Street*

---

**FOR CHILDREN**

Of special interest to children are the Schlitterbahn Water Park at New Braunfels and the animals at the Wildlife Wilderness and the Natural Bridge Wildlife Ranch out of town. There are also exciting rides and petting animals at Wonder World, San Marcos.

---

▶ *Continue north on I–35/US 81 to San Marcos.*

**❷ San Marcos, Texas**
This city was laid out for Anglo-American settlers in 1851 in an idyllic setting beside a crystal-clear river fed by natural springs. The site is now occupied by the Aquarena Springs family entertainment complex, complete

---

**RECOMMENDED WALKS**

Special places for a stroll include the San Marcos River Walkway, San Marcos; lovely Zilker Park, location of the popular Barton Springs swimming hole, Austin; the trails in Inks Lake State Park, near Burnet; and Pedernales Falls State Park, near Johnson City.

---

▶ *Continue north on I–35/US 81 for 30 miles (48km) to Austin (Exit 233) for the free parking lot on West Riverside Drive.*

**❸ Austin, Texas**
The Lone Star State's capital, a city of fine shops and a thriving cultural and entertainment center, stands on the Guadalupe River, its skyline pierced by the unmistakable shapes of the pink-granite Capitol and the

Tower of the University of Texas. Leave your car on West Riverside Drive and take a green 'Dillo (Armadillo) trolley to see the main downtown sights. In addition to the Capitol, you should see the Governor's Mansion; the Old Bakery and Emporium and Old Paramount Theater on Congress Avenue; and the revitalized center of city life, historic Sixth Street (Old Pecan Street), with its shops, restaurants, bars, night spots and street entertainers. Best reached by car are the historic French Legation, established in 1841 when Texas was an independent republic; and on the University of Texas campus, the Lyndon B Johnson Library and Museum and the Harry Ransom Center, whose treasures include a priceless Gutenberg Bible. For outdoor recreation, Zilker Park is the place.

ⓘ *State Capitol*

---

**FOR HISTORY BUFFS**

Austin has many special places of interest, including the 50-year-old Treaty Oak on Baylor Street, beneath which agreements with local Indians were made; the home of the writer O Henry on E 5th Street; and the Elisabet Ney Museum, with sculptures by the famous artist at her studio on E 44th Street.

---

▶ Follow **US 183** *north, then take* **SR 29** *west to Burnet and the Lake Buchanan area, a distance of 52 miles (83km).*

### ❹ Burnet and Lake Buchanan, Texas

Make a stop at Burnet to see the historic exhibits at the site of Fort Croghan. The museum here preserves a variety of artifacts, including antique saddles, horse-drawn farm machinery and pianos, while in the grounds are several restored 19th-century buildings.

Then drive on to explore the area around Lake Buchanan. The lake lies amid the rugged scenery of the Texas Hill Country, the highest of the seven man-made Highland Lakes along the Colorado River northwest of Austin. Visitor attractions in the area include facilities for swimming, boating and fishing at Black Rock Park and Inks Longhorn Cavern on Park Road 4; and the 2½-hour Vanishing Texas River Cruise on Lake Buchanan, during which you will see towering cliffs, waterfalls and Texas wildlife.

▶ *From Burnet, take* **US 281** *south for 37 miles (59km) to Johnson City and on to Lyndon B Johnson National Historical Park.*

### ❺ Johnson City and Lyndon B Johnson National Historical Park, Texas

Dedicated to the memory of the 36th president, this popular visitor attraction has two separate units: one in Johnson City, the other at Stonewall, 14 miles (23km) west along the Pedernales River valley on US 290. Stop first at the Visitor Center in Johnson City for a guided tour of the president's boyhood home and his grandparents' homestead (the Johnson Settlement). Near Stonewall make another stop at the LBJ State Historical Park, where you can see native Texas animals, historic frontier buildings, and costumed interpreters re-enacting German pioneer life at the Sauer Beckmann Farmstead. From the Visitor Center a free National Parks Service bus takes you on a tour of President Johnson's birthplace, boyhood school, Texas White House and ranch and his grave.

▶ *Continue west on* **US 290** *for 30 miles (48km) to Fredericksburg.*

### ❻ Fredericksburg, Texas

Established by German settlers in 1846, this picturesque old town has a distinct German atmosphere and many German-style buildings in its National Historic District. Be sure to see the old Vereins Kirche, a rebuilt eight-sided church, the Pioneer Museum, and the tiny stone 'Sunday Houses' used as weekend town homes by pioneer farmers. The town's best-known visitor attraction, however, is the Admiral Nimitz State Historical Park, dedicated to those who served with the admiral in World War II. In the complex are the Museum of the Pacific War, Garden of Peace, and History Walk, with displays of guns, tanks and aircraft. The area also boasts fine wineries.

*Historic Fredericksburg – many of the town's stone houses have been restored by the present owners*

> ⓘ *106 N Adams Street*

▶ *Follow* **SR 16** *south for 22 miles (35km) to Kerrville.*

### ❼ Kerrville, Texas

Nestled beside the Guadalupe River in the heart of the Hill Country, Kerrville attracts large numbers of visitors, both young and old, to its annual summer camps and to guest ranches offering a taste of traditional cowboy life, with horseback riding, hayrides and cookouts. A popular destination is the Y O Ranch – 30 miles (48km) west via Routes 27 and 41 – with its Longhorn cattle and its collection of native Texas animals, zebras, ostriches and giraffes. Among Kerrville's other attractions are its music festivals and its museums, including the Classic Car Showcase and Wax Museum and the fine Cowboy Artists of America Museum, just south of town. This showcase for contemporary cowboy artists displays paintings and sculpture on Western subjects.

### SCENIC ROUTES

There are many fine stretches of highway in this area. Highlights include the winding River Road to Canyon Lake north of New Braunfels and the 'Devil's Backbone', Route 32 west of San Marcos; Route 2341 to the Vanishing Texas River Cruise, east of Lake Buchanan; roads off US 281 in the Marble Falls area; the roads to the Y O Ranch and to Enchanted Rock north of Fredericksburg; and SR 173 between Kerrville and Bandera.

*i* *1200 Sidney Baker Street*

▶ *Follow SR 173 south for 26 miles (42km) to Bandera.*

### 8 Bandera, Texas

Bandera was established in 1853 when settlers, attracted by the fine cypress trees in the area, set up a lumber mill here. This small Hill Country town claims to be the 'Cowboy Capital of the World'. Here you can sample the outdoor life of the Old West at the area's many working and guest ranches, watch thrilling rodeos and join in country-and-western dancing on sawdust floors at honky-tonks like Arkey Blue's Silver Dollar.

You can also look back at pioneer life as you tour the exhibits at the Frontier Times Museum with its Old West relics and the Old Jail Museum and Art Gallery's exhibits of local history.

▶ *From Bandera take SR 16 for 50 miles (80km) to San Antonio.*

Enchanted Rock State Park

### BACK TO NATURE

Among the wildflowers that color the Texas Hill Country are the bluebonnet (state flower), Indian blanket and Mexican hat. Wild animals that frequent this natural paradise include white-tailed deer, wild goats, coyotes, wild boars and armadillos. You may also see bald eagles, golden eagles, wild turkeys, great blue herons and perhaps even roadrunners or a rare golden-cheeked warbler.

### SPECIAL TO...

Things to do and see: footprints of prehistoric monsters at Dinosaur Flats, near Sattler, north of New Braunfels; nine days of parades, water fun, races and other events at Austin's Aqua Festival in July and August; and spectacular Enchanted Rock, off scenic Route 965 north of Fredericksburg.

# THE MOUNTAIN WEST

Whether you call it the Old West or even the Wild West, this is that ruggedly romantic part of America which decades of Western movies have taught us to associate with stagecoaches, wagon trains, leather-faced cowboys and dusty cattle drives, saloon brawls, shoot-outs, Indian ambushes and US Cavalry rescues.

Bryce Canyon, Utah

The Mountain West covers an immense tract of territory stretching from Canada to Arizona and New Mexico and from the Rocky Mountains to the Sierra Nevada of California. Along the eastern edge, the Rockies rise from the Great Plains just west of Denver in a series of spectacular forested ranges that run from Montana to New Mexico. Scenery of indescribable beauty is encompassed in Glacier, Grand Teton and Rocky Mountain National Parks, while in places like Yellowstone National Park hot-water springs, geysers and mud pools provide dramatic evidence of continuing volcanic activity.

West of the Rockies, in western Colorado, Utah and Nevada, a vast arid wilderness extends across rugged plateaux, parallel mountain ridges, blazing desert basins and shimmering salt flats, where nature has carved immense flat-topped mesas and buttes, towering pinnacles and precipitous canyons. Utah's magnificent national and state parks showcase the region's amazing natural wonders.

The only major centers of population in this sparsely inhabited part of the Mountain West are Salt Lake City, Utah, and Las Vegas, Nevada. Cliff dwellings in places like Mesa Verde National Park, Colorado, show that Indian peoples lived in the area long before the arrival of the white man. The first Americans to see the wonders of the Mountain West were the explorers, mountain men, fur trappers and traders who wandered through the area in the early 1800s. They paved the way for the exodus of pioneer wagon trains along the Oregon and California Trails to the west coast in the 1840s and '50s. Gold and silver strikes across the region brought floods of prospectors, miners and all sorts of adventurers.

## Denver

Denver, the 'Mile High City', lies at the foot of the Rocky Mountains on Colorado's Great Plains. Born in the gold rush of 1859, it prospered as the gateway to the mining communities in the west. Today it is the main business and cultural center of the entire Mountain West region.

Among Denver's many attractions are the shops of 16th Street Mall, Larimer Square and the big Cherry Creek Shopping Center; museums such as the Denver Art Museum, with its fine collection of American Indian art, the Museum of Western Art and the Museum of Natural History in City Park; busy nightlife and entertainment. Major sightseeing highlights include the gold-domed State Capitol, the US Mint, the Denver Botanic Gardens, and such historic buildings as the Molly Brown House, the Victorian home of the unsinkable survivor of the Titanic disaster.

## Salt Lake City

Salt Lake City was founded by Mormon pioneers led by Brigham Young at the end of their great trek west to Utah in 1847. It lies 4,300 feet (1,312m) above sea level between the Great Salt Lake and the Wasatch Mountains to the east. The heart of the city is Temple Square, a walled precinct containing the main buildings of the Mormon faith.

Near by are other Mormon buildings, including the historic Beehive House; the Utah State Capitol; the Pioneer Memorial Museum; and the Salt Palace Center. Other visitor attractions include the Trolley Square shopping center and, east of town, Pioneer Trail State Park, which contains a reconstructed Mormon settlement and the monument which commemorates the Mormons' arrival in Utah.

Assembly Hall, Salt Lake City

## Las Vegas

Surrounded by awesome desert scenery, the gaudy, neon-lit resort city of Las Vegas has been a mecca for gamblers since the 1930s. Fronted by glittering billboards, fantasy-style hotel-casinos like Caesar's Palace, Circus-Circus and the Aladdin line the famous 3½-mile (5.6km) boulevard known as 'The Strip' and the streets of the downtown Casino Center, labeled 'Glitter Gulch'. To tempt you inside, there is non-stop gambling at roulette, blackjack, craps, poker, baccarat and keno; gargantuan drinks bars and subsidized food buffets; and spectacular entertainment featuring top-name stars, unusual specialty acts, and dancing girls. Most spectacular are the new 'megaresorts': the MGM Grand, with its own theme park; the Egyptian-style Luxor; and Treasure Island, featuring an outdoor pirate battle. Grand Slam Canyon is a new fun park.

There are also excellent golf courses, theaters, concerts and museums, spectator sports at Cashman Field, the spectacular Helldorado festival every May – and lots of little wedding chapels offering instant marriage ceremonies for a fee.

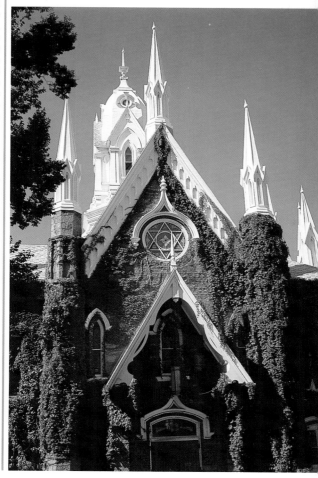

# The Rocky
## Mountains

One of America's great scenic experiences is the drive along the magnificent Trail Ridge Road around the the breathtaking mountain scenery of the 12,000-foot (3,600m) peaks of Colorado's Rocky Mountain National Park, northwest of Denver.

**2/3 DAYS • 229 MILES • 366KM**

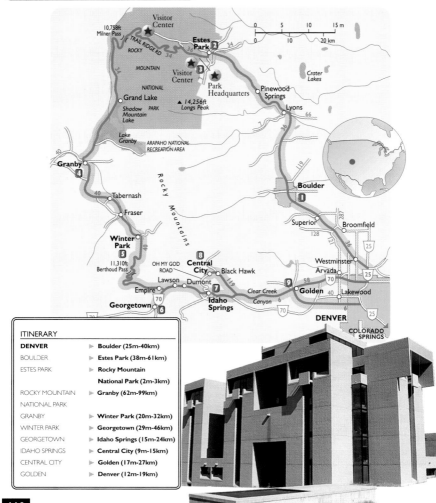

**ITINERARY**

*225 W Colfax Avenue, Denver*

▶ *From downtown Denver pick up I–25 northbound, and at* **Exit 217** *take* **US 36** *northwest to Boulder.*

**❶ Boulder,** Colorado
The town of Boulder lies at the edge of the Rockies overlooked by the red-rock cliffs of the Flatirons. Four blocks of its old Victorian downtown district now form Pearl Street Mall, a lively pedestrian area of boutiques, art galleries and outdoor cafés. Most of the year Boulder is home to the 20,000 students of the University of Colorado, who periodically enliven the town with events like the zany Kinetic Conveyance Parade and Challenge in May or the more dignified Shakespeare Festival, in July and August. If you are interested in the Old West, drop in at the Leanin' Tree Museum of Western Art on Longbow Drive. Sample, too, the exotic teas at the Celestial Seasonings Tea Company. But if you are more scientifically minded, you might prefer to learn about the weather and solar astronomy at the National Center for Atmospheric Research on Table Mesa Drive.

*2440 Pearl Street*

▶ *Continue north on* **US 36** *through Lyons to Estes Park.*

**❷ Estes Park,** Colorado
This popular resort village, the location of the old Stanley Hotel, a noted landmark, lies amid beautiful forest-clad mountain scenery at the eastern gateway to the Rocky Mountain National Park. Visitors flock here in the summer to enjoy the shops and restaurants along Elkhorn Avenue and the area's varied attractions. You can tour the Estes Park Area Historical Museum, go horseback riding at one of the local guest ranches and take the exciting Aerial Tramway for views from 8,700-foot (2,652m) Prospect Mountain.

*Junction of US 34/US 36*

▶ *Follow* **US 36** *west to Rocky Mountain National Park.*

**❸ Rocky Mountain National Park,** Colorado
This scenic mountain wonderland is one of America's most impressive spectacles. Clustered within its 415-square-mile (1,074sq km) area are more than

The foothills of the Rocky Mountains, Colorado
Opposite: National Center for Atmospheric Research, Boulder

18 rugged peaks towering way above 13,000 feet (3,963m). To appreciate its grandeur, see the orientation filmshow at Park Headquarters before starting the 50-mile (80km) drive along Trail Ridge Road. Closed during the winter, this famed – and sometimes busy – highway winds above the timberline across the Continental Divide at 12,183 feet (3,713m), offering breathtaking mountain vistas, with glaciers and snowfields, cold alpine lakes, streams and waterfalls, wildflower meadows, stands of aspen and pine and perhaps glimpses of the abundant wildlife.

After a break at the Trail Ridge Store, turn south down the Kawuneeche (Colorado River) Valley and leave the park at the yachting and boating center of Grand Lake. This pleasant lakeside town in its idyllic setting, offering facilities similar to Estes Park, has an Old West-style main street, complete with a boardwalk and historic log buildings, and a small sandy beach.

### BACK TO NATURE

Wild things almost seem to pale into insignificance in the awesome grandeur of Rocky Mountain National Park. But keep your binoculars and camera handy for a possible sight of mountain goats, elk, mule deer, chipmunks and Colorado's state animal, the bighorn sheep. Keep a lookout for eagles, hummingbirds and the curious American dipper – a bird which lives beside rivers and often submerges itself to feed. In season, colorful wildflowers like the wild rose, snow buttercup, pasque flower and the state flower, the beautiful blue columbine, can be seen, not forgetting the gorgeous yellow displays of aspen in the fall.

▶ *From Grand Lake follow US 34 south for 16 miles (26km) to Granby.*

**4 Granby,** Colorado
Guest ranches, rodeos, hunting and fishing are the main visitor attractions of the area around Granby. This former railroad center is now the western gateway to the Arapaho National Recreation Area. Lake Granby Pumping Station provides water for northeastern Colorado and is open for informative tours in summer.

▶ *Take US 40 south for 46 miles (74km) through Winter Park and over Berthoud Pass to Empire.*

**5 Winter Park and Empire,** Colorado
The winter ski resort of Winter Park draws visitors in summer with its fine restaurants, weekend rodeos and art and jazz festivals. Beyond Berthoud Pass, where the highway climbs over the Continental Divide at 11,310 feet (3,447m), is Empire, where you can see the restored 19th-century Peck House, Colorado's oldest hotel still in operation.

### FOR HISTORY BUFFS

Well worth a stop on the road between Fraser and Winter Park is the Cozens Ranch House, built between 1874 and 1881 to serve as a family home, small hotel, stage stop and post office, and now restored as a museum to recall those pioneer days.

▶ *From Empire pick up I–70 southbound for 4 miles (6km) to Georgetown.*

**6 Georgetown,** Colorado
In the 1860s Georgetown, on Clear Creek, blossomed as a silver-mining town and soon became Colorado's third largest city. Justifying its tag as 'Silver Queen of the Rockies', it quickly acquired the usual lavish Victorian houses, hotels, gambling saloons, restaurants and the obligatory opera house. It also had a first-rate fire brigade, so, unlike other wood-built mining towns of the time, it suffered no major conflagrations. What you will see today is a quaint little town with more than 200 restored Victorian buildings lining its atmospheric streets. Don't miss the Hamill House (with its delightful six-seater privy), and the famous Hotel de Paris, built by the eccentric French restaurateur Louis du Puy, in 1875. An irresistible attraction is the exciting ride on the narrow-gauge Georgetown Loop Railroad to the nearby old mining town of Silver Plume, an excursion which also includes a fascinating mine tour.

▶ *Backtrack on I–70 and continue east to Idaho Springs.*

**7 Idaho Springs,** Colorado
Named for its hot mineral springs, the Victorian resort town of Idaho Springs, on Clear Creek, was the site of Colorado's first big gold strike in 1859. A monument southwest of Chicago Creek Road marks the

spot. More than 200 mines in the area still produce gold, lead, silver, zinc, tungsten and molybdenum. In summer you can follow the old-timers and pan for gold yourself on a tour of the Argo Mine and Mill.

▶ *Follow US 6 northeast for about 3 miles (5km), then take SR 119 northwest through Black Hawk to Central City.*

**8 Central City,** Colorado
In the same year as the 1859 gold strike at Idaho Springs, the discovery of a rich gold-bearing lode in the mountains created the new boom town of Central City, 'the richest square mile on earth'. Despite a big fire in 1874, the town survived, was rebuilt in brick and is now a National Historic Landmark. Its colorful Victorian streets are lined with old saloons with swing doors, boisterous museums, fine restaurants and shops have now been turned into gambling casinos.

Remaining landmarks are the splendid old Opera House, built in 1878 and still offering a summer season of opera and, next door, the 1872 Teller House hotel, where you will see the famous 'Face on the Barroom Floor', painted in 1936. Other visitor attractions include an underground tour of the Lost Gold Mines. Colorful festivals and events draw the crowds throughout the year, such as the internationally known Jazz Festival in August.

### FOR HISTORY BUFFS

Among the fascinating buildings you can visit on a tour of Central City's historic streets is the Thomas-Billings Home at 209 Eureka Street. It stood fixed in a silent time warp for some 70 years after being closed up around 1916, and now you can see it just as it was, furnishings and all, when it was lived in all those years ago.

### FOR CHILDREN

By the time you reach Golden the children may be tired with all the sights and adventures on the tour. But for a final fling of fun you should visit Heritage Square, off US 40 south of town, a family enter-tainment and shopping park designed as a Victorian village. There are lots of rides, a Ferris wheel and the exciting Alpine Slide.

▶ *From Golden follow **US 6** (W 6th Avenue) or **US 40** (W Colfax Avenue) eastbound for about 12 miles (19km) to downtown Denver.*

### RECOMMENDED WALKS

Many hiking trails cross the spectacular landscapes of Rocky Mountain National Park. Two of the shorter trails are the Tundra World Nature Trail, where you will get magnificent panoramic views of the Continental Divide; and the half-mile (1km) walk along East Inlet, east of Grand Lake, to impressive Adams Falls. You can get details of routes at the park's visitor center.

### SPECIAL TO...

Central City's glorious past included a colorful establishment run by Madam Lou Bunch that was very well patronized in its heyday. In June every year grateful citizens honor her memory with a day-long celebration that features a costume parade and bed races down Main Street, culmi-nating in a grand Madams and Miners Ball.

▶ *Backtrack through Black Hawk on **SR 119** and continue on **US 6** for another 12 miles (19km) through Clear Creek Canyon to Golden.*

**9 Golden,** Colorado
At the edge of the Rocky Mountain foothills lies the city of Golden, Colorado's first terri-torial capital of the 1860s and gateway to the goldfields, and now perhaps best known as the home of Coors beers. You can

Central City is perhaps one of the best preserved mining towns in the Rocky Mountains

visit the famous brewery – one of the largest in the world – and sample the products while tour-ing the nearby Historic District along 12th Street. Other places of interest are the Pioneer Museum, the Foothills Art Center and the Geology Museum and National Earthquake Center at the presti-gious Colorado School of Mines. Two of the most popular attrac-tions, however, are just outside town.

To the west, atop Lookout Mountain via the Lariat Loop Trail, is the Buffalo Bill Memorial Museum, with a large observation deck, and the famous old scout and frontiers-man's grave.

To the north, on W 44th Avenue, there is the excellent Colorado Railroad Museum, with its impressive collection of historic locomotives and passenger cars.

### SCENIC ROUTES

Extra special sections of this outstanding scenic tour include the mountain-top Trail Ridge Road in Rocky Mountain National Park; US 40 over Berthoud Pass; and the rugged US 6 route through Clear Creek Canyon west of Golden. For a special adventure, however, take the unpaved, twisting, wild scenic route from Central City to Idaho Springs on the appropri-ately named 'Oh My God Road' (Virginia Canyon). It is not for the faint-hearted!

# Great Salt Lake
## Country

This route takes you from the shores of the Great Salt Lake to the edge of the desert, then up lush green valleys into the cool, forested wildernesses of Utah's highest mountains. Along the way you will see breathtaking natural scenery, historic mining towns, old stagecoach inns, dazzling rock caverns, quiet mountain villages and glossy ski resorts.

**4 DAYS • 341MILES • 545KM**

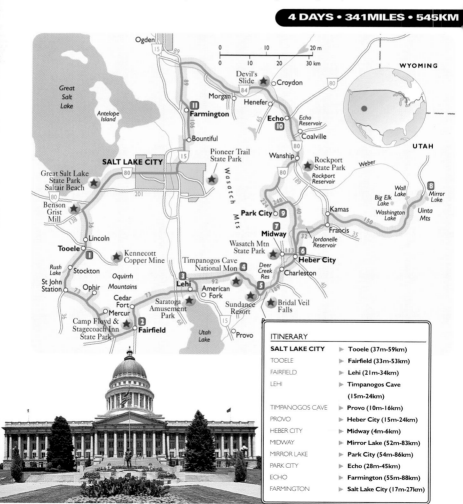

| ITINERARY | | |
|---|---|---|
| **SALT LAKE CITY** | ▶ | **Tooele (37m–59km)** |
| TOOELE | ▶ | **Fairfield (33m–53km)** |
| FAIRFIELD | ▶ | **Lehi (21m–34km)** |
| LEHI | ▶ | **Timpanogos Cave (15m–24km)** |
| TIMPANOGOS CAVE | ▶ | **Provo (10m–16km)** |
| PROVO | ▶ | **Heber City (15m–24km)** |
| HEBER CITY | ▶ | **Midway (4m–6km)** |
| MIDWAY | ▶ | **Mirror Lake (52m–83km)** |
| MIRROR LAKE | ▶ | **Park City (54m–86km)** |
| PARK CITY | ▶ | **Echo (28m–45km)** |
| ECHO | ▶ | **Farmington (55m–88km)** |
| FARMINGTON | ▶ | **Salt Lake City (17m–27km)** |

*i* *Council Hall, Capitol Hill, Salt Lake City*

▶ *The tour begins on **I–80**, west from Salt Lake City near the south shore of the Great Salt Lake. After about 20 miles (32km) turn south on to **SR 36** for 23 miles (37km) to Tooele.*

**1 Tooele,** Utah
About 15 miles (24km) west of Salt Lake City the highway reaches the Great Salt Lake, where you can experience the strange sensation of bobbing like a cork in water so salty it is almost impossible to sink. Inland, just off Route 138 at Mills Junction, the renovated Benson Grist Mill, built by the Mormons in 1854, makes an interesting stop before driving on to Tooele. Pronounced 'Too-will-a', this is the region's biggest town, and it lies between two rugged mountain ranges. Of interest are several historical museums. A 9-mile (14km) drive (unsuitable for some vehicles) east up Middle Canyon into the Oquirrh Mountains brings you to one of America's most awesome sights: the vast open pit nearly two-and-a-half miles (4km) wide and half a mile (0.8km) deep excavated at the famous

Kennecott (or Bingham) Copper Mine. From the mountaintop overlook there are magnificent views of the mine, the populated Salt Lake Valley in the east, and the forested mountains topped by 11,031-foot (3,362m) Deseret Peak in the west.

▶ *Continue south from Tooele on **SR 36** to St John Station. Then follow **SR 73** to Fairfield.*

**2 Fairfield,** Utah
Along the Rush Valley south of Tooele you will find once-booming gold- and silver-mining communities such as Stockton, now better known for sailboating and windsurfing on nearby Rush Lake; Ophir, now a quiet village, which once had a big silver nugget exhibited at the 1904 St Louis World's Fair; and Mercur, a ghost town whose history you can trace at the Barrick Mercur Gold Mine Visitor Center off Route 73.
A few miles south is the ghost town of Fairfield, once an overnight stop on the old Pony Express and overland stage-coach routes across the Great Salt Desert to the west. The two-story adobe hotel at Stagecoach Inn State Park has been restored and refurnished and is open in season to visitors.

Above: view over Salt Lake City
Opposite: Salt Lake City's Capitol

Near by is the site of Camp Floyd, where US troops were billeted in the late 1850s during a minor spat with the Mormons.

▶ *Continue on **SR 73** to complete the Oquirrh Loop drive at Lehi.*

**3 Lehi,** Utah
Lehi was named after a character in the Book of Mormon. Don't miss the John Hutching's Museum of Natural History, which has displays of western Americana among its exhibits of pioneer and Indian artifacts and an extensive mineral collection. Highlights include Butch Cassidy's sawn-off shotgun.

---

### FOR CHILDREN

There are lots of outdoor adventures suitable for youngsters along this itinerary. But for kids who love the thrilling rides and boisterous fun of a family entertainment park, you can make an extra stop at the Saratoga Amusement Park off Route 68 on the northwest shore of Utah Lake near Lehi.

---

▶ Just north of Lehi pick up **SR 92** eastbound for the 20-mile (32km) Alpine Loop drive round Mt Timpanogos (if closed, use **US 189** north from Provo).

## ④ Timpanogos Cave National Monument, Utah

Although closed in winter to everyone except cross-country skiers and snowmobilers, the Alpine Loop is probably Utah's most popular scenic drive. It is noted for its spectacular fall foliage and magnificent mountain views as it winds around the slopes of impressive Mt Timpanogos. There is a 6-mile (10km) hiking trail up the mountain to the 11,750-foot (3,581m) summit via lovely Emerald Lake, but most visitors are content just to explore the underground wonderland of Timpanogos Cave National Monument. Even so, it is a fairly strenuous one-and-a-half mile (2.5km) walk from the Visitor Center up to the cave entrance, 1,065 feet (325m) above the canyon floor. Inside, there are three caves connected by man-made tunnels and filled with amazing, beautifully colored limestone formations and sparkling rock crystals. The guided tour takes you past such poetically named wonders as the Cavern of Sleep and Father Time's Jewel Box.

---

### RECOMMENDED WALKS

There are many opportunities for walking. Well worth the 12-mile (19km) round trip from the Alpine Loop is Cascade Springs, where a tree-lined walkway offers a pleasant stroll to the crystal-clear springs.

---

▶ Continue southeast on **SR 92** to Provo Canyon.

## ⑤ Provo Canyon, Utah

Near Provo Canyon is movie actor Robert Redford's year-round Sundance Resort, where you can stay in elegant cottage or mountain home accommodations and enjoy excellent winter

Mount Timpanogos

skiing facilities, fine dining in the Tree Room restaurant and outdoor musicals during the Sundance Summer Theater season.

One of the most popular visitor attractions is the aerial tramway that soars to 1,753 feet (534m) above Provo Canyon just south of Wildwood and provides magnificent views of lovely Bridal Veil Falls and the surrounding green countryside.

ℹ *2545 N Canyon Road, Provo*

---

### FOR CHILDREN

Children can enjoy the 45-minute musical shows specially written for them at the Sundance Children's Theatre.

---

▶ From Bridal Veil Falls follow **US 189** north up Provo Canyon and the Heber Valley for 15 miles (24km) to Heber City.

colorful Swiss Days festival held in early September. Midway is also known for the hot springs that supply the pools at the Homestead and Mountain Spaa resorts. It is also close to Wasatch Mountain State Park, just outside town on Route 224, a vast recreational area used for camping, hiking, picnicking, horse riding and golf in summer, and for cross-country skiing and snowmobiling in winter.

▶ *Return to Heber City and follow* **US 40/189** *north and* **SR 32** *east for 16 miles (26km) to Kamas, then take* **SR 150** *east to Mirror Lake.*

**8 Mirror Lake,** Utah
One of the most popular summer drives in Utah is to beautiful Mirror Lake, nestled amid the pine-clad 13,000-foot (3,962m) peaks of the Uinta Mountains, Utah's highest range. The lake offers excellent fishing, camping and boating and hiking and horsepacking trails into the surrounding mountains. No roads penetrate this remote unspoiled wild country, designated the High Uintas Wilderness Area, where you can unwind in breathtaking scenery encompassing spectacular peaks, dense forests, icy lakes, sparkling streams teeming with fish, lush wildflower meadows and an abundance of wildlife.

---

**SPECIAL TO...**

This part of Utah has two special adventures to offer bold outdoor types longing to escape to the wild. From trailheads at Mirror Lake you can take off into the Uinta wilderness on a guided horsepacking trip. Or, if you prefer a rugged four-wheel jeep adventure, you can follow the old Pony Express riders along the sagebrush trail they blazed years ago across the fearsome Great Salt Lake Desert, west of Fairfields.

---

▶ *Retrace* **SR 150** *and* **SR 32** *to the* **US 40/189** *junction, then turn north for 14 miles (23km) and west on* **SR 248** *for another 5 miles (8km) to Park City.*

**9 Park City,** Utah
Utah boasts 'The Greatest Snow on Earth' on the 10,000-foot (3,000m) peaks of the Wasatch Mountains, and the canyons carved into the slopes east of Salt Lake City provide rapid access to premier ski resorts at Alta, Snowbird, Brighton, Solitude and Park City.

Park City was once a booming mining town following a silver strike in 1868 but is now Utah's largest winter sports area, with more facilities at the nearby Park West and Deer Valley resorts.

Despite the accent on skiing, Park City doesn't close when the snow melts. During the rest of the year you can play tennis and golf, ride down the exciting 3,000-foot (914m) Alpine Slide and walk along pleasant woodland trails.

You can also browse along historic Main Street, with its restaurants and galleries, boutiques and antique stores, saloons and taverns and lively nightspots like the Claimjumper and Cisero's. There are also changing art shows at the Kimball Art Center and mining and skiing exhibits at the Park City Museum. A succession of festivals, summer concerts, theater productions and other cultural events also draw visitors throughout the year. Top annual events you might catch include the US Film Festival in January, and, in summer, the Park City Arts Festival and Autumn hot-air balloon competition.

ⓘ *528 Main Street (Park City Museum)*

▶ *Leave Park City via* **SR 224** *north. Pick up* **I–80** *eastbound for 11 miles (18km) to Wanship, then northbound for 12 miles (19km) to Echo. Continue on* **I–84** *northwest to Morgan.*

**6 Heber City,** Utah
The most pleasant way to see the green countryside and forested mountain slopes along the Heber Valley is from the famous Heber Valley Railroad train that chugs up Provo Canyon and along the valley between Vivian Park and Heber City. But if you drive, you will at least have the opportunity to stop at Deer Creek Reservoir, a 7-mile (11km) lake at the north end of Provo Canyon used for boating, sailing and fishing. In Heber City there is an opportunity to see the magnificent surrounding scenery from the air in a glider.

ⓘ *475 North Main Street*

▶ *Follow 100 South Street west to Midway.*

**7 Midway,** Utah
Midway lies at an altitude of 5,500 feet (1,676m) amid beautiful alpine scenery that reminded early Swiss settlers of home, so they stayed. Townsfolk remember their heritage during the

**⑩ Echo,** Utah

From Kimball Junction Route 80 descends the eastern slopes of the Wasatch Range and follows the north-flowing Weber River through Wanship down to the old stagecoach community of Echo. Good places to stop for a break along this stretch are Rockport State Park (at the reservoir) and Echo Reservoir, both popular for picnicking, swimming, boating and fishing.

A few miles north of Henefer, a small community that developed on the old Mormon Pioneer and Pony Express trails, you will arrive at the curious geological feature in Weber Canyon known as the Devil's Slide – a good name you will agree, when you see it. It consists of two 40-foot high (12m) limestone reefs, 20 feet (6m) apart, which plunge hundreds of feet down the steep mountainside to the Weber River just like a schoolyard slide. Further west, as you follow the Weber River through the Wasatch Range, you will pass between high mountain slopes blanketed in pine and aspen in the area around the county town of Morgan.

▶ *Continue northwest on I–84. towards Ogden, then turn south on US 89 to Farmington.*

**⑪ Farmington,** Utah

Farmington is one of the historic Mormon communities clustered along the Great Salt Lake between Ogden and Salt Lake City and the location of the old Farmington Rock Chapel and the Utah State University Botanical Gardens.

The town's best-known visitor attraction, though, is the Lagoon Amusement Park, which is the place to go in Utah for thrilling rides, Wild West shootouts and various other entertainments.

From Farmington, if you have a suitable vehicle, you can take the 24-mile (39km) rough gravel Bountiful Peak Scenic Drive, which winds south along the Wasatch Front to Bountiful, providing breathtaking views of the Great Salt Lake and its stunning sunsets.

▶ *From Farmington or Bountiful take I–15 southbound to Salt Lake City.*

Mirror Lake nestles among the peaks of the Uinta Mountains

# Encounter with
## Death Valley

Crossing the burning deserts of Nevada's Great Basin and California's Death Valley is an awesome experience that requires some precautions, especially in summer. But the rewards are unforgettable, with images of arid desert and mountain scenery, weird geological formations, amazingly tough desert plants, wild animals and, here and there, resilient little communities, comfortable resorts and ghost towns.

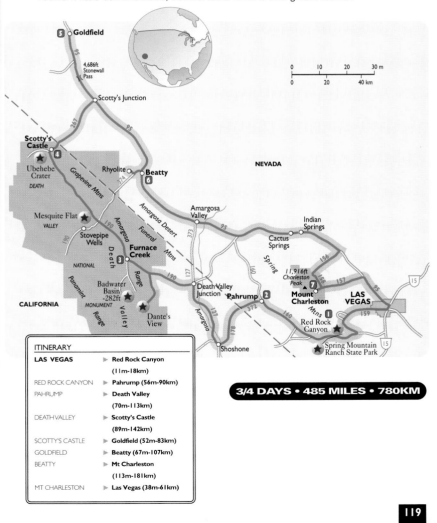

| ITINERARY | |
|---|---|
| **LAS VEGAS** | ▶ **Red Rock Canyon** |
| | **(11m-18km)** |
| RED ROCK CANYON | ▶ **Pahrump (56m-90km)** |
| PAHRUMP | ▶ **Death Valley** |
| | **(70m-113km)** |
| DEATH VALLEY | ▶ **Scotty's Castle** |
| | **(89m-142km)** |
| SCOTTY'S CASTLE | ▶ **Goldfield (52m-83km)** |
| GOLDFIELD | ▶ **Beatty (67m-107km)** |
| BEATTY | ▶ **Mt Charleston** |
| | **(113m-181km)** |
| MT CHARLESTON | ▶ **Las Vegas (38m-61km)** |

**3/4 DAYS • 485 MILES • 780KM**

i *3150 Paradise Road, Las Vegas*

▶ *Take Charleston Boulevard west out of Las Vegas and continue on SR 159 for about 11 miles (18km) to the Visitor Center at Red Rock Canyon.*

## ❶ Red Rock Canyon,
Nevada
Red Rock Canyon is a natural wonderland encompassing rugged scenery and unique desert vegetation. From the Visitor Center you can follow a self-guided 13-mile (21km) scenic drive along the multicolored rock escarpment, with its towering rock chimneys and boulder-strewn ravines. There is a pleasant spot for a break at Willow Springs picnic area, where, after rain, you may see temporary cascades of water tumbling from the high crags. Along the drive you may also catch a glimpse of the canyon's wild burros and desert bighorn sheep, the state animal.

Just south of Red Rock Canyon is Bonnie Springs Old Nevada, a re-created Old West town with various attractions, including a petting zoo. Not to be missed is a tour of the lovely old ranch home at nearby Spring Mountain Ranch State Park, which counted among its owners the millionaire recluse Howard Hughes.

---

### RECOMMENDED WALKS

Among Red Rock Canyon's many trails is the pleasant walk into the damp, cool recesses of Pine Creek Canyon, with its exotic vegetation at the foot of 3,000-foot (914m) cliffs.

---

▶ *Continue south on SR 159, then go west on SR 160 for another 42 miles (68km) to Pahrump.*

## ❷ Pahrump, Nevada
The first stretch of Route 160 follows the Old Spanish Trail to California blazed through the deserts of the Great Basin in the 1820s. Further north, what used to be the quiet old farming community of Pahrump has developed rapidly in recent years into a desirable residential and retirement area, with golf courses, a winery and gaming opportunities. If you are here in September you may catch the town's Harvest Festival, Fair and Rodeo. Before leaving for Death Valley, check your car for fuel and water and, in summer, take extra water for your own consumption.

▶ *From Pahrump follow SR 372/178 southwest for 26 miles (42km) to Shoshone, California, then take SR 127 north up the Amargosa River valley for 26 miles (42km) to Death Valley Junction (Amargosa). Take SR 190*

Death Valley's seemingly inhospitable environs actually support a rich diversity of life

*northwest and after 18 miles (29km) enter Death Valley National Monument.*

### 8 Death Valley and Furnace Creek, California

Walled in on three sides by high mountain ranges, the 140-mile (225km) desert cauldron of Death Valley National Monument contains the hottest, driest and lowest places in America. Temperatures are

Red Rock Canyon, near Las Vegas, Nevada

usually up to 126°F (52°C) in summer, but have reached 134°F (57°C); precipitation is normally less than 3 inches (76mm) a year; and the lowest point, at Bad Water, plunges to 282 feet (86m) below sea level.

The terrain encompasses rugged mountainsides and canyons of multicolored rocks, expanses of sand dunes left by prehistoric seas, and parched salt flats that shimmer in the searing heat. But there are also a few permanent streams, freshwater springs and even a small salty pool, and various wild creatures and plants that have adapted to these tough conditions. Here and there, abandoned gold, silver and borax mines indicate the puny incursions of humans into this unwelcoming land.

About 19 miles (31km) west of Death Valley Junction, follow the winding 12-mile (19km) side road off Route 190 to Dante's View, where you will get breathtaking panoramic views of the valley and the Panamint Mountains in the west. There is another famous viewpoint at

Zabriskie Point, off Route 190 on the way to Furnace Creek Inn and Ranch, a luxurious palm-fringed hotel resort with excellent facilities for golf, swimming, tennis and horseback riding. Drop by the Visitor Center nearby for information on Death Valley's history and natural wonders, before driving down to see Bad Water and the expanse of crusty salt formations known as the Devil's Golf Course.

### FOR HISTORY BUFFS

Many of the roads in Death Valley today follow the routes to the old borax mines that sprang up in the 1880s. They were carved out by the famed 20-mule wagon teams that shipped the mineral out in 20-ton loads. One of these roads traverses Twenty Mule Team Canyon, west of Death Valley Junction, from the old borax-mining town of Ryan. You can learn more about Death Valley's mining history at the Visitor Center near Furnace Creek and at the Borax Museum, Furnace Creek Ranch.

## BACK TO NATURE

As far as living things are concerned, Death Valley does not really live up to its name, as many animals and plants have adapted to the harsh conditions. Animals tend to be nocturnal and often wear camouflage to hide their presence, so you will be lucky to see the resident antelopes, kangaroo rats, kit foxes, bobcats, desert coyotes and lizards, except perhaps at dawn or dusk. Among the plants, saltbush, creosote bush, sage and various kinds of cacti are common, but if you are here in spring you will see spectacular displays of wildflowers like the lovely desert primrose and fivepoint, especially if there have been winter rains earlier in the year.

▶ Retrace the route back to Furnace Creek and continue north on **SR 190** to Scotty's Castle.

**4 Scotty's Castle,** California
Just north of the intersection where Route 190 turns west to Stovepipe Wells is Mesquite Flat, another curious geological phenomenon, a sea of great windblown sand dunes reminiscent of the Sahara Desert.

Continuing north, with the red-and-black slopes of the Grapevine Mountains coloring the horizon on the right, you will eventually arrive at the amazing desert mansion known as Scotty's Castle, a well-known Death Valley landmark since the 1920s that is open for tours. The 25-room house has a music room with a 1,600-pipe organ, and indoor waterfalls that acted as air-conditioners in summer. Another interesting sight a few miles west is the Ubehebe Crater, an 800-foot (244m) deep volcanic cone with brightly colored walls.

## SPECIAL TO...

The flamboyant Walter Scott, a cowboy-prospector who had once performed in Buffalo Bill's Wild West Show, claimed that Scotty's Castle, Death Valley's most famous landmark, was financed in the 1920s from the proceeds of a secret gold mine. In fact, it was built and owned by a Chicago businessman, Arthur M Johnson, who came to Death Valley for health reasons and befriended the old desert rat. The ornate, turreted castle is filled with luxurious furnishings and art treasures, which you will see on a fascinating guided tour.

▶ Continue northeast into Nevada and follow **SR 267** to Scotty's Junction. Take **I–95** northbound for 31 miles (50km) to Goldfield.

**5 Goldfield,** Nevada
Goldfield was one of those western Nevada mining towns that sprang to life around the turn of the century following the discovery of gold and silver. The strike promised to be, as the old rallying cry went, 'greater than the Comstock', Nevada's greatest-ever bonanza. By 1907 Goldfield grew to 20,000 hardy souls, making it Nevada's largest city, but the ores soon ran out and people drifted away, leaving only memories among the crumbling ruins.

Today, however, there are some signs of life, but the old Goldfield Hotel, once the finest hostelry between Salt Lake City and San Francisco, is only partly restored. You can visit the old Esmeralda County Courthouse, with its original Tiffany lamps, and look for treasures of your own in the town's quaint antique stores.

▶ From Goldfield retrace **I–95** to Scotty's Junction and continue south for another 36 miles (58km) to Beatty, then 29 miles (47km) to Amargosa Valley.

**6 Beatty and Amargosa Valley,** Nevada
Unlike many other old Nevada mining towns, Beatty has survived, and today offers hotel accommodations, restaurants, gaming facilities and other services. The town is a popular gateway to Death Valley, and about 4 miles (6km) west via Route 374 you can visit the atmospheric ghost town of Rhyolite, a flourishing silver-mining community from 1905 to 1910 and now one of the most photographed ruins in the state. In 1907 it had a population of

Built by a wealthy Chicagoan, Scottys' Castle, a fantasy palace in the Moorish style, is filled with art

Las Vegas by night is a dazzling spectacle of multi-colored neon lights. Casinos never close and the nights are spent in a non-stop merry-go-round of entertainment

12,000. Although Rhyolite's old opera house is now a silent memory, the one at Amargosa Valley, further south, still mounts theatrical and musical shows every year.

While in the area you can also see the famous Amargosa Sand Dunes, relics of a long-vanished inland sea.

▶ *From Amargosa Valley continue south on I–95 for 57 miles (92km), then turn right and follow SR 156 and SR 158 for 27 miles (48km) to Mount Charleston in the Spring Mountains.*

---

### RECOMMENDED WALKS

On Mount Charleston there are short, easy trails off the Deer Creek Cutoff (SR 158) to Robber's Roost and to Desert View, with its spectacular panoramas of the surrounding desert and distant mountain ranges.

---

### FOR CHILDREN

Except for Bonnie Springs, Old Nevada, places with attractions especially devised for kids are rare on this tour. Hopefully young companions will be fascinated by the scenic splendor and geological curiosities and the relics of Nevada's old mining towns. They will also have opportunities to see strange desert plants, walk among ancient sand dunes, picnic in the mountains, and perhaps even swim and ride horses at the Furnace Creek Inn and Ranch.

---

### ◳ Mount Charleston, Nevada

One way to escape Nevada's blistering summer heat is to drive up the forested slopes into the cool air of Mount Charleston, at 11,918 feet (3,633m) the highest peak in the Spring Mountains, just northwest of Las Vegas. The scenic road climbs to 8,000 feet (2,438m) through stands of pinyon juniper and pine, providing access to numerous campgrounds, picnic sites and walking trails.

In winter the area is popular with cross-country skiers, while the Lee Canyon resort has good facilities for downhill enthusiasts.

▶ *From Mount Charleston follow SR 157 east for 22 miles (35km) and pick up I–95 southbound for 16 miles (26km) to Las Vegas.*

---

### SCENIC ROUTES

Spectacular stretches of highway abound on this scenic desert tour, but the highlights are perhaps the 13-mile (21km) drive at Red Rock Canyon; Route 190 and the side road to Dante's View in Death Valley; and the loop drive to Mt Charleston via Routes 156, 158 and 157.

---

# THE DESERT SOUTHWEST

In 1912 New Mexico and Arizona became, respectively, the 47th and 48th states of the Union, the last of the contiguous territories to reach statehood. Won in the Mexican-American War of 1846–48, they had been part of Spain's, and later Mexico's, vast North American empire since the 16th century, when Spanish conquistadors passed through the area in a vain search for gold. As American settlers moved in, trouble with the indigenous Indians flared up, first with the Navajo, who were defeated by Kit Carson in 1864, and then, more devastatingly, with the Apache. Charismatic Apache leaders like Cochise and Geronimo waged a ferocious 25-year war.

Central Avenue divides Phoenix east–west

Eventually the Apache, like the Navajo and others, were rounded up and sent to the region's immense reservations. During these eventful frontier days, the town of Tombstone wrote itself into the history books with the famed gunfight at the OK Corral.

The Spanish, Mexican, Indian and Old West heritage of Arizona and New Mexico is still much in evidence. Everywhere you will encounter Spanish place names and hear Spanish spoken. You will also see ancient Indian archeological sites, thriving adobe pueblos, Spanish missions, frontier ghost towns, old military forts and traces of the old Santa Fe Trail.

The Southwest is a region of sunny skies and scenic splendor which draws large numbers of visitors each year. Dramatic canyons, rugged mesas, forested mountain ranges, and expanses of desert cactus form landscapes of breathtaking grandeur. Arizona is the land of the awesome Grand Canyon carved by the Colorado River, of the Painted Desert, Petrified Forest, Sunset and Meteor Craters, Monument Valley (often seen in old movie Westerns), the Canyon de Chelly and the magnificent Sonoran Desert.

New Mexico, the 'Land of Enchantment', has the southernmost ranges of the Rocky Mountains and their ski slopes, jagged Shiprock Butte, Carlsbad Caverns with their great swarms of bats, the gleaming dunes of White Sands National Monument and many other natural wonders.

## Phoenix

More than 2 million people live in metropolitan Phoenix, a cluster of 23 communities, including Phoenix itself, which sprawls across a great mountain basin in south-central Arizona. Often referred to as the 'Valley of the Sun', Phoenix has a dry, sunny climate – hot in summer, mild in winter – which helped make it one of the Sunbelt's fastest-growing cities in recent years.

Around 10 million visitors flock in every year to enjoy the area's excellent hotel resorts, shops and malls, performing arts, nightlife, and varied outdoor activities and events. In addition to spectator sports, there are golf, tennis, horseback riding, hot-air ballooning, desert four-wheeling, sailing, river rafting and tubing, fishing – and even covered-wagon trips that recapture the area's Old West atmosphere.

Phoenix began life here as a small frontier settlement back in 1860, but by 1889 it had grown enough to become Arizona's territorial and, in 1912, state capital. Today, it is a blend of the Old and New West, with a touch of Mexican and Indian flavor. The cultural mix is reflected in the city's main visitor attractions, which include the impressive State Capitol and Museum; the excellent Phoenix Art Museum and Heard Museum of Anthropology and Primitive Art; the Herberger Theater Center performing arts complex; the excavated Hohokam Indian ruins at Pueblo Grande; and beautiful Papago Park, location of the large Phoenix Zoo and the cacti collections of the Desert Botanical Garden.

## Albuquerque

Albuquerque, New Mexico's largest city, spreads across the broad Rio Grande valley, overlooked by the rugged 10,000-foot (3,048m) wall of the Sandia Mountains. A major

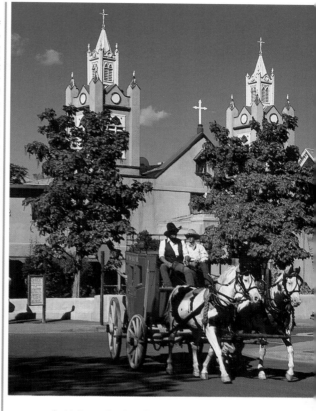

Old Town Square, Albuquerque

center of high technology industry and research, transportation and tourism, the city has a growing population that today stands at more than 480,000. Founded by Spanish colonists in 1706 and named for the Duke of Albuquerque, the town of Albuquerque has, over the years, acquired a distinct Spanish, Mexican and Indian flavor, which adds spice to the local architecture, art, music and cuisine.

The Old Town, near the Rio Grande, marks the site of the original Spanish settlement. The focal point is the Plaza, flanked by colorful shops, galleries and restaurants and the old church of San Felipe de Neri, on the northwest corner. Nearby are the Albuquerque Museum and New Mexico Museum of Natural History. Not far away are the delightful Rio Grande Nature Center and the Zoo, while scattered around the city there are many outstanding and unusual museums, such as the Indian Pueblo Cultural Center, the Maxwell Museum of Anthropology and the National Atomic Museum.

Not to be missed while in Albuquerque are an exciting cable car ride up the Sandia Mountains on the Sandia Peak Tramway and a trip to Coronado State Park and Monument, where the first Spaniards in the area over-wintered in 1540. Special events worth catching in Albuquerque include the famous nine-day International Balloon Fiesta held in October.

# Apache &
## Saguaro Trails

Southeast of Phoenix is a natural wonderland of dry, rugged mountains and unique cactus desert where Indian peoples long ago learned to scratch a living. Here Spanish conquistadors searched in vain for the fabled Seven Cities of Cibola, doughty missionaries hunted for souls, and rough mining prospectors, mean gunfighters and determined settlers gathered in frontier towns constantly harried by the Apaches.

ITINERARY

| PHOENIX | ▶ | **Apache Junction** |
| | | **(31m-50km)** |
| APACHE JUNCTION | ▶ | **Globe (76m-122km)** |
| GLOBE | ▶ | **Superior (23m-37km)** |
| SUPERIOR | ▶ | **Casa Grande (41m-66km)** |
| CASA GRANDE | ▶ | **Tucson (82m-131km)** |
| TUCSON | ▶ | **Tucson Mountain Park** |
| | | **(48m-77km)** |
| TUCSON MOUNTAIN | ▶ | **Phoenix (102m-163km)** |
| PARK | | |

**4 DAYS • 403 MILES • 646KM**

ⓘ *1100 West Washington, Phoenix*

▶ *Drive east from downtown Phoenix on I–10 and US 60, or East Van Buren Street and Apache Boulevard, through Tempe and Mesa to Apache Junction.*

### ❶ Apache Junction and the Apache Trail, Arizona

This famous scenic road, unpaved in part, winds along the north side of the Superstition Mountains past towering rock buttes, rugged canyons, mountainsides dotted with saguaro cactus and blue man-made lakes. Just north of Apache Junction you can eat your fill at the Mining Camp Restaurant and Trading Post before exploring the old ghost town of Goldfield, which offers mine tours, gold-panning and a museum.

Beyond Lost Dutchman State Park, with its hiking trails and fine views, you come to Canyon Lake, one of the four great reservoirs created by dams along the Salt River at the beginning of the century to provide water for Phoenix. All have campgrounds, picnic areas and facilities for boating, fishing and water-skiing. Canyon Lake also offers cruises aboard *Dolly's Steamboat*. Among the attractions at the nearby quaint old stage-coach town of Tortilla Flat is a unique opportunity to sample prickly pear ice cream. A few miles past the town there is a 20-mile (32km) stretch of unpaved

*The Apache Trail climbs past the famed Superstitition Mountains*

road and a scary descent into Fish Creek Canyon down a sheer cliff face.

Beyond tranquil Apache Lake you will see the 275-foot (84m) Theodore Roosevelt Dam, completed in 1911, and its 25-mile (40km) lake. At this point paved again, the road turns southeast through Roosevelt to Tonto National Monument, the site of prehistoric cliff dwellings. A foot trail leads to a well-preserved complex inhabited by Salado Indians in the 14th century. From mid-October through April there are three-hour ranger-led tours to a 40-room dwelling in the upper ruin.

> **FOR HISTORY BUFFS**
>
> The appropriately named Superstition Mountains, which overlook the Apache Trail, are the source of many old tales about hoards of gold hidden in the wilderness. The best known is the legend of the Lost Dutchman Mine, the supposed secret cache of a German prospector (the so-called 'Dutchman', named Jacob Waltz, which no one has ever been able to find since his death in 1891. You could take a look yourself if you stop by Lost Dutchman State Park just north of Apache Junction.

▶ *Turn northeast and follow the scenic Apache Trail (SR 88) to Globe and Miami.*

### ❷ Globe and Miami, Arizona

Globe is an old mining town said to have been named after a large round nugget of almost pure silver found here. Among its attractions are the restored 1906 Courthouse, which houses the community's art gallery, and the Gila County Historical Museum, which displays pioneer memorabilia and items relating to the area's early mining history. South of town, on Jesse Hays Road, is the site of excavated Indian ruins at Besh-Ba-Gowah (Metal Camp) Archeological Park, where craftspeople have re-created what are probably the most realistic Indian dwellings in the state.

A few miles west you can tour the copper-mining operations and open pit at Miami. On the edge of town you will also see a marker indicating the site of the Bloody Tanks Massacre perpetrated by local settlers against the Indians in 1864.

ⓘ *1360 North Broad Street, Globe*

▶ *From Miami continue west on US 60 to Superior.*

### ❸ Superior, Arizona

There is an especially scenic stretch of highway along Queen Creek Canyon and through the tunnel into the copper-mining town of Superior. A few miles beyond town along US 60 don't miss the Boyce Thompson Arboretum, where you can see excellent displays of desert plants, animals and birds.

[i] 151 Main Street

▶ *Continue west on* **US 60** *to Florence Junction. Turn south on* **SR 79** *for Florence, then west on* **SR 287** *to Casa Grande Ruins National Monument.*

**4 Florence and Casa Grande Ruins National Monument,** Arizona

The desert community of Florence, the seat of Pinal County, lies on the old main road (Highway 79) between Phoenix and Tucson. Some of its original adobe buildings are preserved in downtown McFarland State Historic Park, where the restored Pinal County Courthouse (circa 1878) serves as a museum of local history and law. West of Florence, at

Casa Grande (Big House) Ruins National Monument

Coolidge, is Casa Grande Ruins National Monument, one of Arizona's most mysterious sites. There has been much speculation about the purpose of this four-story structure, built by Hohokam Indians around 1350 and now protected beneath a steel 'umbrella'. House, temple, watchtower, astronomical observatory – who knows?

[i] Jacob Souter House, 270 Bailey Street, Florence

▶ *From Florence follow* **US 79** *southeast across the Sonoran Desert through Oracle Junction to Tucson.*

**5 Tucson,** Arizona

Around 700,000 people live in Tucson, which sprawls over a broad desert valley surrounded by mountains. The home of the University of Arizona, Tucson is a vibrant business and cultural center, with many museums, galleries, performing arts events and festivals. Known affectionately as the 'Old Pueblo', the city grew around the Spanish *presidio* (garrison) built at the foot of Sentinel Peak in 1776. Now called 'A' Mountain for the huge letter 'A' set into its slopes, the peak offers spectacular views of the city and mountains beyond and is a good place to get your bearings.

The original *presidio* is now gone, but a walking tour of the historic downtown area reveals many other old adobe structures among the government buildings, offices and shops. Also here is the Tucson Museum of Art, with pre-Columbian artifacts.

Of interest to visitors on the university campus are the Flandrau Science Center and Planetarium, and fine museums of history, art and photography. On the north side of town you can see desert plants at the Tucson Botanical Gardens and the delightful Tohono Chul Park, with its popular restaurant, and enjoy a trolley ride up rugged Sabino Canyon. A drive south takes you to the impressive display of historic aircraft at the Pima Air and Space Museum. But not to be missed south of town is the San Xavier del Bac Mission of 1797, Tucson's beautiful 'White Dove of the Desert'.

[i] 130 S Scott Avenue, Tucson

Golden poppies clothe the slopes of Tonto National Monument

▶ *From Mission San Xavier del Bac go north on Mission Road, west on Ajo Way, and north on Kinney Road, to the desert attractions of Tucson Mountain Park.*

## ❽ Tucson Mountain Park,
Arizona

Many Western movies, TV series and commercials have been filmed on the permanent set of adobe-and-wood buildings at Old Tucson Studios, a 1939 re-created Old West Town known as Arizona's 'Hollywood in the Desert'. Along streets once trodden by stars like John Wayne, you can, if you are lucky, watch scenes being shot or enjoy stunt shows, make-believe shoot-outs and saloon brawls, and ride on a stagecoach or narrow-gauge railroad. Not far away you will see desert life at close quarters at the superb Arizona-Sonora Desert Museum. It is a sort of combined zoo, aquarium, botanical garden, museum and information center, with fascinating geological exhibits and displays of living

animals, birds and plants native to the American Southwest in their natural habitats.

Continuing north, you will then see nature for real: the western section of Saguaro National Monument, a protected expanse of the Sonoran Desert that has especially fine stands of saguaro cactus and other desert vegetation, an unforgettable sight at sunset.

---

### BACK TO NATURE

Of all the desert plants you will learn to identify on this tour of the Sonoran Desert, you cannot mistake the distinctive saguaro cactus. But can you recognize Arizona's state tree, the beautiful palo verde, which splashes the desert with yellow flowers in spring? Keep your eyes open, too, for the desert's special wild creatures, like the cactus wren, exotic hummingbirds, the comical roadrunner and the venomous Gila monster and its potential dinner, the leaping kangaroo rat.

---

i̅ *130 S Scott Avenue Tucson*

▶ *At Cortaro, northeast of Saguaro National Monument, pick up I–10 northbound for the 92-mile (147km) drive back to Phoenix.*

---

### RECOMMENDED WALKS

There are beautiful walking trails through spring wildflowers in Lost Dutchman State Park, near Apache Junction, and Picacho Peak State Park, along I–10 north of Tucson.

When visiting the Boyce Thompson Arboretum, near Superior, don't miss a walk along the 1¼-mile (2km) Picket Post Trail into the wilder desert area.

There are also enthralling walks along trails in Saguaro National Monument. A special treat is the 35-mile (56km) drive up the winding Catalina Highway northeast of Tucson to the 9,157-foot (2,791m) summit of Mount Lemmon and its spectacular panorama.

# The Enchanted
## Circle

Drive north out of Albuquerque and you enter a land that reflects those eternal images of the Old West: gorgeous forest-clad mountains, scrubby mesas gashed by deep river gorges, vast open prairies, ancient Indian pueblos and ruins, historic Spanish towns, old frontier forts and rough mining and ranching communities. It is a scenario where names like Kit Carson, Billy the Kid and the Santa Fe Trail seem to fit easily.

**4 DAYS • 435 MILES • 695KM**

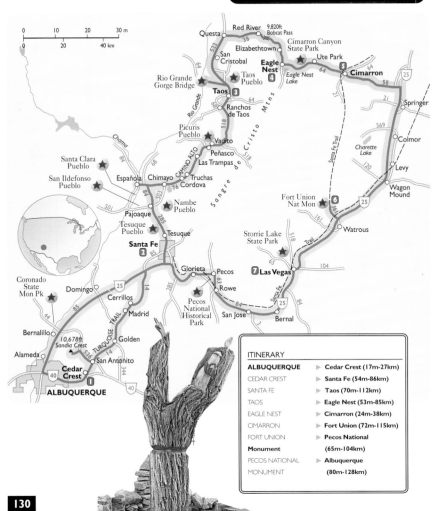

| ITINERARY | | |
|---|---|---|
| **ALBUQUERQUE** | ▶ | **Cedar Crest (17m-27km)** |
| CEDAR CREST | ▶ | **Santa Fe (54m-86km)** |
| SANTA FE | ▶ | **Taos (70m-112km)** |
| TAOS | ▶ | **Eagle Nest (53m-85km)** |
| EAGLE NEST | ▶ | **Cimarron (24m-38km)** |
| CIMARRON | ▶ | **Fort Union (72m-115km)** |
| FORT UNION | ▶ | **Pecos National** |
| **Monument** | | **(65m-104km)** |
| PECOS NATIONAL | ▶ | **Albuquerque** |
| MONUMENT | | **(80m-128km)** |

*i 121 Tijeras Avenue NE, Albuquerque*

▶ *Head east on I-40 from downtown Albuquerque through Tijeras Canyon, and at Exit 775 turn north on to SR 14, the Turquoise Trail, through Cedar Crest.*

## ❶ Cedar Crest and the Turquoise Trail, New Mexico

This fascinating road winds through mesa country east of the Sandia Mountains and is the most scenic route between Albuquerque and Santa Fe. But don't miss the side trip on the Scenic Byway (SR 536) which takes you up the wooded slopes past the Sandia Ski Area to Sandia Crest, the area's highest peak. From the 10,678-foot (3,255m) summit there are breathtaking views of Albuquerque and for miles around.

Back on Route 14, continue north through the quiet old mining towns of Golden (gold), Madrid (coal) and Cerrillos (gold, silver and turquoise), now recovering from decline as artists' communities, with galleries, mining museums, boutiques, fine restaurants and music festivals.

▶ *From Cerrillos continue north on SR 14 and I-25 to Santa Fe.*

---

### FOR CHILDREN

It is a pretty safe bet that children on this tour will be enthralled by the exciting tales they hear about northeast New Mexico's eventful past. They will also enjoy special attractions like the Tinkertown Museum, an animated Old West town hand-carved in miniature, on the Sandia Crest road; living history demonstrations at Fort Union; Indian dances at the pueblos; and events such as the colorful Rails 'n' Trails Days in June at Las Vegas.

---

## ❷ Santa Fe, New Mexico

New Mexico's old Spanish capital, founded in 1609, lies at 7,000 feet (2,134m) near the southern end of the Sangre de Cristo Mountains. Its Spanish Colonial and Pueblo Indian heritage is plain to see as you wander around its historic center, with its adobe architecture, tree-shaded plaza and cool courtyards. Be sure to see the Palace of the Governors, Museum of Fine Arts, Institute of American Indian Arts Museum, San Miguel Mission, St Francis Cathedral and pretty Loretto Chapel. Browse through the fine shops and galleries along Canyon Road and take a look inside one or more of the museums clustered together south of the downtown area: the Museum of Indian Arts and Culture, the Museum of International Folk Art and the Wheelwright Museum, which has an especially impressive collection of Navajo arts and crafts.

Among the many cultural and other events you might catch are the Indian Market on the plaza in August and the summer season of the world-renowned Santa Fe Opera north of town.

*i 491 Santa Fe Trail*

▶ *From Santa Fe take US 84–285 north to Española, then follow the old Camino Alto (SR 76, 75, 518 and 68) north for about 46 miles (74km) to Taos.*

---

### SCENIC ROUTES

Splendid scenery awaits you all along this tour, but special highlights include the sections on the Turquoise Trail (SR 14) and Sandia Crest road (SR 536); the Camino Alto between Chimayo and Taos; Route 38 up the Red River Valley and over the Bobcat Pass to Eagle Nest; and Highway 64 down the eastern slopes of the Sangre de Cristo Mountains to Cimarron.

---

## ❸ Taos, New Mexico

Worth visiting north of Santa Fe are the Santa Fe vineyards and the Pueblo Indian settlements, including the San Ildefonso and Santa Clara pueblos, where you can see beautiful handmade crafts, colorful dances and various other attractions.

On the scenic Camino Alto, the high road that winds along the western slopes of the Sangre de Cristo Mountains, you will pass through picturesque old Spanish villages, including Chimayo, Cordova, Truchas and Las Trampas, where skilled woodcarvers and weavers practise their craft. Worth a stop along the way are the famous Santuario de Chimayo and the

*San Francisco de Asís, Taos, is one of the southwest's most splendid Spanish churches*

sturdy old church of San Francisco de Asís at Ranchos de Taos, a popular subject for New Mexican artists.

Picturesque Taos, founded by the Spaniards around 1617, has

been a thriving writers' and artists' colony since the late 1800s. When you have browsed through the boutiques and galleries around the historic little plaza, visit the homes and studios of artists Nicolai Fechin or Ernest L Blumenschein and tour the superb art exhibits at the Millicent A Rogers Museum north of town. But don't miss the historic places, like the impressive Colonial hacienda of landowner Don Antonio Severino Martínez; the home of New Mexico's first territorial governor, Charles Bent; and the house and grave of the legendary frontiersman Kit Carson.

North of town be sure to visit famed Taos Pueblo, the 900-year-old Indian community noted for the multistory adobe architecture that has so impressed artists and visitors over the years. You will also be captivated by the beautiful crafts and the dance ceremonials.

**4 Eagle Nest,** New Mexico
Your only glimpse of the famed Rio Grande on this tour is a spectacular one. Stay on US 64 as you leave Taos and you will enjoy a breathtaking view of its colossal gorge from the road bridge 660ft (201m) above the turbulent water. Continuing north on Route 522, you can take a long, unpaved side road at San Cristobal to see writer D H Lawrence's Ranch and Shrine before following the Red River Valley into the mountains. Nestled in the gorgeous scenery is the old mining community of Red River, now a popular family vacation center and winter ski resort. Summer activities on offer include hiking, fishing, Jeep trips, horseback riding, square dancing and hissing the villain at the Red River Inn melodrama. The scenic drive over 9,820-foot (2,993m) Bobcat pass and through the old gold-mining ghost town of

Elizabethtown eventually brings you to the all-year recreation center of Eagle Nest, where the beautiful lake is popular for fishing, boating and windsurfing.

▶ *From Eagle Nest follow* **US 64** *east for about 24 miles (38km) to Cimarron.*

**5 Cimarron,** New Mexico
The 400-foot (122m) cliffs of Cimarron Canyon are a memorable sight along the scenic drive to Cimarron. This quiet little town, set in verdant ranch country, was once one of the wildest places on the old Santa Fe Trail. Many Old West notables, and gunslingers like Wyatt Earp and Jesse James, checked in at the St James Hotel, where bullet holes still ventilate the dining-room ceiling. For more about Cimarron's colorful past, drop by

Fort Union National Monument, near Watrous

▶ *Follow* **US 64** *and* **SR 522** *north to Questa, then* **SR 38** *east for about 29 miles (46km) through Red River and Sangre de Cristo Mountains to Eagle Nest.*

---

### SPECIAL TO...

Long before the Spanish explorer Francisco de Coronado wandered through the area in 1540, the many-skilled Pueblo Indians of the Rio Grande valley had become exceptionally adept at making beautiful decorated clay pots and figurines. Among their finest achievements are the polished black pottery developed this century at the San Ildefonso pueblo and the polished red-and-black ware made at the Santa Clara pueblo. Other pueblo crafts include exquisite jewelry, bead-work, wood carvings, woven belts and handmade quilts – all of which, like the pottery, make wonderful souvenirs of a visit to New Mexico.

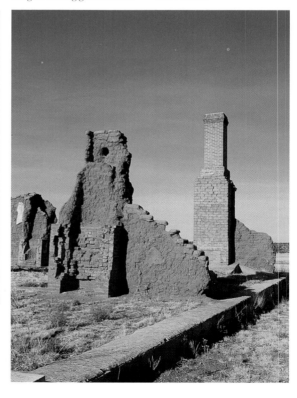

The town of Springer is a trading center for the surrounding ranches the Old Mill Museum. Be sure, too, to visit the Philmont Scout Ranch, where you will see a vast herd of buffalo, Kit Carson's house and museum, the Villa Philmonte and the museum and library of Ernest Thompson Seton, co-founder of the Boy Scouts of America.

▶ Take **SR 58** east for 19 miles (31km) to join **I–25** south-bound for 53 miles (85km) through Springer to Watrous and nearby Fort Union National Monument.

### ⑥ **Fort Union National Monument,** New Mexico

On the prairies east of Cimarron, don't miss the Santa Fe Trail Museum in the old courthouse at Springer. Its exhibits depict the everyday life of residents at the turn of the century.

Further south, near Watrous, are the stark ruins of Fort Union, the chief quartermaster depot built in the mid-1800s to protect settlers and travelers on the trail from marauding Indians.

▶ From Watrous continue south on **I–25** to Las Vegas, then on to Pecos National Monument.

### ⑦ **Las Vegas and Pecos National Monument,** New Mexico

Settled near hot springs by Spanish families in 1835, the little adobe-built prairie community of Las Vegas soon found itself hosting not only respectable traders and travelers on the Santa Fe Trail but also less salubrious characters such as Doc Holliday and Billy the Kid.

But with the coming of the railroad in 1879, the 'New Town' district sprang up east of town, and Las Vegas blossomed for a time as New Mexico's largest and wealthiest city and a silent movie capital. Today, walking tours of the town's nine historic districts take you past hundreds of architectural treasures, including grand Victorian hotels, like the Plaza and Casteñada.

Another sightseeing must along the drive back to Albuquerque is Pecos National Monument, with its haunting ruins of an ancient Indian pueblo and two missions built by Spanish Franciscans. Visitors can wander through the ruins on a self-guided trail.

ℹ️ *727 Grand Avenue, Las Vegas*

▶ From Pecos National Monument continue south-west on **I–25** for about 80 miles (128km) to Albuquerque.

---

### BACK TO NATURE

With terrain ranging from dry mesas to lush mountain pastures and grasslands, this corner of New Mexico has been blessed with a whole Noah's Ark of wild creatures and plants. Among the wild animals you might see in the mountains are black bear, cougar, elk, bobcat, bighorn sheep and even porcupines. Birds range from ravens and wild turkeys to falcons and exotic hummingbirds. Wildflowers too numerous to list brighten the mountains in summer, while fall splashes the dark-green forests with patches of golden aspen.

---

### RECOMMENDED WALKS

In addition to walking around the various historic towns and other sites on this tour, you can enjoy New Mexico's great outdoors by following off-highway trails in the Sandia and Sangre de Cristo Mountains. Of special interest are scenic trails at Sandia Crest; in the Wild Rivers Recreation Area by the Rio Grande west of Questa; around Red River; and in Cimarron Canyon State Park.

---

### FOR HISTORY BUFFS

The fabled Santa Fe Trail entered history in 1821, after Mexico declared independence from Spain and trader William Becknell found he could get through unchallenged from Missouri to the old Spanish Colonial capital.

Two branches of the trail crossed northeast New Mexico's grasslands, joined at Watrous and followed the route of today's I–25 to Santa Fe. You can still see old wagon ruts and historic buildings on the trail at Cimarron, Fort Union and Las Vegas.

# THE WEST COAST

In 1845, America's western boundary lay along the edge of the Rocky Mountains, but a year later, within months of taking office, President James K Polk had pushed it westward to the Pacific coast by winning Washington and Oregon from Britain, and California from Mexico. With the discovery of gold in California's Sierra Nevada in 1848, thousands of people flocked overland or by sea to the Far West to seek their fortune.

Today the West Coast is a major vacation destination offering countless sightseeing attractions and outdoor adventures. There are the fascinating large cities of Seattle, Sacramento, Portland, San Francisco, Los Angeles and San Diego. There are also natural wonders – magnificent stretches of shoreline, superb beaches, shimmering bays, fertile valleys, spectacular mountain ranges, thundering waterfalls, impressive forests of redwood and sequoia, and awesome deserts. The backbone of the region is the north-south mountain barrier formed by the Cascade Range, which separates a mild coastal climate from the interior continental one, and the Sierra Nevada. In the north spectacular snow-capped volcanoes like Mount Rainier and Mount Baker soar above the forested slopes of the Cascades in Washington and Oregon.

Further south, in California's Sierra Nevada, are the majestic granite landscapes of Yosemite National Park, and the great sequoia trees (*Sequoiadendron giganteum*) of Kings Canyon and Sequoia National Parks. To the east and south are dry plateau and desert regions, at their most awesome in the arid expanses of California's Mojave Desert and the blazing cauldron of Death Valley, one of the hottest and driest regions in the world.

West of the flat, cultivated lands of Puget Sound, Oregon's Willamette Valley and the immense Central Valley of California, the Coast Ranges look out over the Pacific Ocean behind the region's magnificent 1,400-mile (2,250km) shoreline. Here the land meets the sea at the wild headlands and coves of Washington and Oregon, the rugged Big Sur coast and the golden, sun-drenched beaches of southern California.

The Space Needle, a prominent landmark on the Seattle skyline

## Seattle

The futuristic 605-foot (184m) Space Needle that dominates Seattle's skyline affords magnificent panoramas of this busy port city's fine waterfront setting beside Puget Sound. At its foot is the Seattle Center, an entertainment and cultural complex that includes the fascinating Pacific Science Center. A ride on the Monorail and a short walk will bring you to bustling Pike Place Market and the ferry terminals, shops, restaurants and visitor attractions along the waterfront. Among these is the Seattle Aquarium and Omnidome film experience on Pier 59. At historic Pioneer Square there are underground tours of the original downtown district destroyed by fire in 1889 and now lying beneath the boutiques, restaurants and night spots of the restored and raised area. Nearby are the landmark Kingdome Stadium and the 48-block Asian neighborhood known as the International District. Also worth visiting are the Seattle Art Museum in Volunteer Park and the Seattle Zoo in Woodland Park.

## San Francisco

Often shrouded in sea fog, the majestic Golden Gate Bridge sweeps across the entrance to San Francisco Bay, where one of the world's best-loved cities rolls over its hills behind the bustling waterfront. Here the bayside Embarcadero is a major visitor attraction, with its bay cruises, maritime museum and shopping complexes, and the seafood restaurants of Fisherman's Wharf. Ferries transport visitors to the grim former Alcatraz penitentiary out in the bay, while clanging cable cars hurtle up and down the city's hills to other sightseeing highlights. Most of these are also on the designated 49-mile (79km) Scenic Drive recommended for visitors. However you get around, be sure to visit the Civic Center complex, Union Square, colorful Chinatown, the Coit Tower on Telegraph Hill, lovely Golden Gate Park with its excellent museums, the fine city Zoo, and Mission Dolores, which recalls the founding of the city by Spaniards in 1776. A sophisticated, liveable city of around 752,000 people, San Francisco also has an excellent performing arts scene, superb restaurants and lively nightlife.

## Los Angeles

America's second city is part of a vast megalopolis of more than 12 million people that sprawls across the broad plain between the Pacific Ocean beaches and the San Gabriel Mountains. Crisscrossed by a network of busy freeways, this colossal maelstrom of a city is packed with places of interest. Most visitors make straight for Hollywood, home of the movies; and to marvel at the palatial homes built by the stars in nearby Beverly Hills.

Los Angeles also has countless other attractions, including fine museums, like the J Paul Getty Museum in Malibu, performing arts venues, such as the famous Hollywood Bowl and the downtown Music Center, lively night spots, fine restaurants, and shopping highlights like the famed Rodeo Drive boutiques in Beverly Hills. Out of town are big theme parks, such as Disneyland.

## San Diego

California's second largest city, the naval base and port of San Diego, nestles beside its magnificent sheltered bay near the Mexican border. With its warm, dry, sunny climate, its superb beaches, its outdoor recreational opportunities and its numerous cultural, entertainment and sightseeing attractions, the city has much to offer visitors. Downtown are the shops, galleries and restaurants of the revitalized 19th-century Gaslamp Quarter, the Seaport Village shopping complex, and the historic ships of the waterfront Maritime Museum. In immense Balboa Park are the impressive San Diego Zoo, several fine museums and the Old Globe Theater. At Old Town you can tour the historic Mexican district that grew below the original Spanish hilltop settlement of 1769. The old Spanish mission, San Diego de Alcalá, is now relocated further east. Another major city attraction is Sea World marine entertainment park in the huge Mission Bay aquatic playground north of town.

Cable cars are a fun way to travel around San Francisco

# The Evergreen
## State

This challenging tour offers a rewarding adventure. It starts with a ferry crossing from Seattle and a pleasant drive through the islands, fishing ports and logging towns of Puget Sound. As you cross to the Olympic Peninsula you enter a wilderness of rugged mountains and glaciers, dense rain forests, rivers teeming with salmon and steelhead, lonely windswept beaches and headlands and remote Indian reservations.

**4 DAYS • 510 MILES • 816KM**

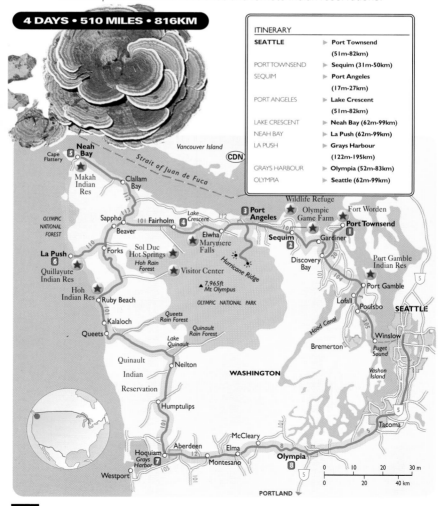

| ITINERARY | | |
|---|---|---|
| **SEATTLE** | ▶ | **Port Townsend** (51m-82km) |
| PORT TOWNSEND | ▶ | **Sequim** (31m-50km) |
| SEQUIM | ▶ | **Port Angeles** (17m-27km) |
| PORT ANGELES | ▶ | **Lake Crescent** (51m-82km) |
| LAKE CRESCENT | ▶ | **Neah Bay** (62m-99km) |
| NEAH BAY | ▶ | **La Push** (62m-99km) |
| LA PUSH | ▶ | **Grays Harbour** (122m-195km) |
| GRAYS HARBOUR | ▶ | **Olympia** (52m-83km) |
| OLYMPIA | ▶ | **Seattle** (62m-99km) |

*i* *800 Convention Place, Seattle*

▶ *Take the ferry from Seattle's Pier 52 across Puget Sound to Winslow. Follow **SR 305** and **SR 3** north for 20 miles (32km) to Port Gamble. Cross the Hood Canal Floating Bridge on **SR 104** and after 16 miles (26km) turn north on **US 101** and **SR 20** for 15 miles (24km) to Port Townsend.*

---

### FOR HISTORY BUFFS

Port Gamble was founded as a logging village in 1853 and is now a National Historic Site. It is a picturesque town with an old working lumber mill, gas street lamps, many Victorian buildings and a famous General Store housing two museums. One of these, the Pope and Talbot Historical Museum, features life in a 19th-century lumber town.

---

### ❶ Port Townsend,
Washington

This fascinating old seaport at the entrance to Puget Sound is a favorite spot for artists and culture buffs, who throng here to enjoy its many arts festivals. As a

Black-tailed deer in the Olympic National Park

National Historic District, Port Townsend boasts it has the best collection of Victorian architecture north of San Francisco. Examples are the James House and Starrett House, which are open to the public during the semiannual Historic Home Tour festival in May and September. Don't miss the Rothschild House, another gracious 19th-century home, complete with period furnishings, and the century-old 'Tree of Heaven', said to have been a gift to the town from a Chinese emperor and now its most unusual attraction.

A short drive north out of town will take you to old Fort Worden, one of the historic coastal fortresses built in the area to guard the entrance to Puget Sound during Theodore Roosevelt's presidency. Here you will see the restored officers' quarters and the original large, grassy parade ground.

*i* *2437 E Simms Way*

▶ *Return to Discovery Bay on **SR 20**, then turn west on **US 101** for 18 miles (29km) through Gardiner to Sequim.*

### ❷ Sequim, Washington

Pronounced '*Skwim*', this small town is the gateway to a popular retirement area which lies in irrigated farm country on the sheltered northeast side of the Olympic Mountains.

Recreational activities include camping, hiking, bicycling, golf, hunting, fishing, boating and windsurfing. Equally varied are the area's attractions, which include the Neuharth Winery, and the Olympic Game Farm, a 90-acre (36-hectare) preserve of trained lions, bears and other wild animals used in movies and TV programs. If you are lucky you might see a training session or even a scene being shot.

*i* *1210 E Washington*

▶ *From Sequim continue west on **SR 101** to Port Angeles and Olympic National Park.*

### ❸ Port Angeles and Olympic National Park,
Washington

Port Angeles is the largest town on the Olympic Peninsula, a major fishing port, and a ferry terminal providing a year-round service to Victoria, British Columbia. It is also the entry point to the mountain section of the 1,400-square-mile (3,626sq

km) Olympic National Park, a scenic wilderness of snow-capped peaks, great glaciers, rushing torrents and flower-speckled meadows, teeming with wildlife and dominated by 7,965-foot (2,428m) Mount Olympus. The lower slopes are clothed in the vast tracts of coniferous trees that form the Olympic National Forest. Follow the popular Heart o' the Hills Highway south for 18 miles (29km) up to 5,228-foot (1,593m) Hurricane Ridge or even further to Obstruction Point. The viewpoints here offer spectacular panoramas of the mountain peaks and glaciers and of the Strait of Juan de Fuca and distant Vancouver Island.

*i* *121 East Railroad; also 3002 Mount Angeles Road (park)*

▶ *Rejoin* **US 101** *at Port Angeles and continue west for 15 miles (24km) to Lake Crescent.*

## ❹ Lake Crescent,
Washington

Ten miles (16km) long and 1½ miles (2km) wide, this crescent-shaped stretch of deep, ice-cold water is the largest of the three

### BACK TO NATURE

A paradise for nature lovers, the Olympic Peninsula supports a wide range of flora and fauna, from the rich marine life around its shores to the wild animals and plants of its forests and mountains. On the high slopes of the Olympic National Park you will see colorful wildflower meadows and perhaps deer, elk, mountain goats and marmots and such birds as the majestic bald eagle. In the eerie stillness beneath the giant trees of the rainforests you might also glimpse deer, raccoons, the rare Roosevelt elk and various birds as they flit through the damp undergrowth of moss, ferns and fungi.

lakes along US 101 west of Port Angeles. Cradled in a magnificent mountain setting, it is a pleasant spot to stretch your legs and admire the scenery. Just beyond Fairholm, a 16-mile (26km) spur road off US 101 offers an interesting detour to see (and perhaps make use of)

One of the many trails in the Hoh Rain Forest, Olympic National Park

the mineral pools at the old resort at Sol Duc Hot Springs.

*i* *Storm King, Lake Crescent*

### RECOMMENDED WALKS

Pleasant walks of varying lengths which are not too strenuous can be found at the wildlife refuge on Dungeness Split, north of Sequim; at Hurricane Ridge, south of Port Angeles, where there is a guided nature walk; at Lake Crescent, where there is a ¾-mile (1km) trail from Storm King Visitor Center to pretty Marymere Falls; at La Push, where trails through the woods take you to scenic beaches; and at the end of the side roads into the rainforest up the Hoh, Queets and Quinault rivers.

▶ *Continue west on* **US 101** *to Sappho. Take the Burnt Mountain Cutoff (SR 113)*

the cultural heritage and lifestyle of the area's Indian community, especially if you are here for the annual Makah Days celebration in August. Go and see the exhibits recording their 2,500-year history at the Makah Cultural and Research Center, then walk around the town, with its Indian-owned, charter-fishing businesses, retail outlets and motels. Browse through the craft shops for a souvenir of your visit, and sample the Indian-style smoked salmon, a Washington specialty. For a sightseeing treat take the 7-mile (11km) drive and trail west out of town to Cape Flattery, where the cliffs afford marvelous views of rocky Tatoosh Island and its lighthouse across the pounding surf.

▶ *Retrace the route to Sappho, then follow* **US 101** *south through Forks and Queets to Lake Quinault, with trips to the Pacific Shoreline, starting at La Push, and the Olympic National Forest and Park.*

## ⑥ La Push, the Pacific Shoreline and Rain Forest, Washington

A narrow 60-mile (96km) strip of the Pacific shoreline between Neah Bay and Queets, in the south, forms a separate, smaller section of Olympic National Park. It is a wild, deserted coastline of rocky headlands, boulder-strewn coves, sandy beaches and rugged offshore islets populated by seabirds and marine animals. But be warned: there is often no escape if you get trapped at the water's edge by the incoming tide. Much safer are the long sandy beaches, where you can take a brisk walk or hunt for driftwood and agates. To get to the shoreline, either take the spur road from US 101 just north of Forks to the oceanfront village of La Push or stay on US 101 until you reach the coast at Ruby and Kalaloch beaches.

Drenched in heavy rainfall throughout the year (about 140 inches [350cm] annually), the western slopes of the Olympic Mountains are covered with a thick blanket of moss-draped rainforest that is unique in North America. Between Forks and Lake Quinault spur roads and trails enter the forest from US 101 and follow the Hoh, Queets and Quinault river valleys. The Hoh section of the forest is especially recommended. Its visitor center has informative displays and is a departure point for several nature trails, including the 'Hall of Mosses' trail.

*i* *Visitor Center at Kalaloch (summer) and Hoh Rain Forest, Olympic National Park*

▶ *From Lake Quinault continue south on* **US 101** *for 39 miles (62km) to Grays Harbor.*

*north for 10 miles (16km) and join* **SR 112** *westbound along the coast for about 27 miles (43km) through Clallam Bay to Neah Bay.*

## ⑤ Neah Bay, Washington

This small fishing village, located in the Makah Indian Reservation at the northwest tip of the Olympic Peninsula, provides an opportunity to see

The tranquility of Second Beach, Olympic National Park

## FOR CHILDREN

There are many things for kids on this tour. Extra sightseeing treats include the collection of seashells at the Of Sea and Shore Museum in the General Store at Port Gamble and exhibits of life in the sea at the Arthur D Feiro Marine Laboratory, Port Angeles. Kids will also enjoy hunting for the famous crabs at Dungeness Bay; beachcombing for driftwood, agates and Japanese glass fishing floats along the Pacific shoreline; and canoeing in Indian dugouts at Lake Quinault.

## 7 Grays Harbor, Washington

This immense natural inlet is the location of the twin industrial ports of Hoquiam and Aberdeen, which are often ignored by visitors passing through to the Pacific beaches. Well worth a stop is Hoquiam Castle, a turreted 20-room mansion once owned by a lumber magnate, now restored to its former elegance. Another attraction is Grays Harbor Historical Seaport, just outside Aberdeen on US 12, which features a maritime museum,

## SCENIC ROUTES

The most spectacular sections of highway on this scenic tour offer fine views of the Olympic Peninsula's forests, mountains and shoreline. They include the Heart o' the Hills Highway to the mountaintop vistas in Olympic National Park; US 101 along the shores of Lake Crescent; the spur road through the forest to Sol Duc Hot Springs; the coast road (SR 112) between Clallam Bay and Neah Bay; and US 101 between Ruby Beach and Kalaloch.

two full-scale replica 18th-century ships and other exhibits.

[i] *5–6 Duffy Street*

▶ *From Aberdeen follow* **US 12** *to Elma, then take* **SR 8** *and* **US 101** *to Olympia.*

## BACK TO NATURE

In spring, Grays Harbor National Wildlife Refuge has the largest gathering of migrating shorebirds in the country.

## 8 Olympia, Washington

With a population of around 33,000, Washington's capital is small compared to other major cities in the state. But what it lacks in size it makes up for in the grandeur of its public buildings, which are set in magnificent landscaped grounds around the Legislative Building. Many, however, are closed at weekends. At the State Capitol Museum, in a Spanish-style mansion you will see exhibits relating to Washington's history and government and a gallery with changing displays of art.

[i] *1000 Plum Street*

▶ *From Olympia pick up* **I–5** *northbound for 62 miles (99km) to return to downtown Seattle.*

## SPECIAL TO...

The Pacific Northwest is famed for the rich harvest of seafood fished from its waters, notably salmon, trout, clams, oysters and the renowned Dungeness crab.

The waterfront at Port Townsend

# Monterey &
## Big Sur

**4 DAYS • 495 MILES • 792KM**

This tour takes you from San Francisco down one of the country's most spectacular shorelines where you will experience breathtaking scenery (sometimes shrouded in eerie sea fog), quaint art colonies and fishing communities, teeming marine life, the roar of the surf and the tangy smell of the Pacific breezes.

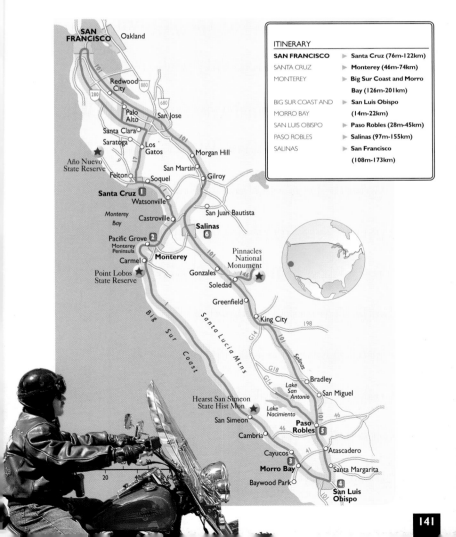

| ITINERARY | | |
|---|---|---|
| **SAN FRANCISCO** | ► | **Santa Cruz (76m-122km)** |
| SANTA CRUZ | ► | Monterey (46m-74km) |
| MONTEREY | ► | **Big Sur Coast and Morro Bay (126m-201km)** |
| BIG SUR COAST AND MORRO BAY | ► | San Luis Obispo (14m-22km) |
| SAN LUIS OBISPO | ► | **Paso Robles (28m-45km)** |
| PASO ROBLES | ► | Salinas (97m-155km) |
| SALINAS | ► | **San Francisco (108m-173km)** |

▶ *Take either the Bayshore Freeway (US 101) or I–280 south from downtown San Francisco through Santa Clara, then SR 17 south for about 31 miles (50km) to Santa Cruz.*

---

### SPECIAL TO...

Santa Clara and neighboring San Jose have enough visitor attractions between them to justify a completely separate tour. But try not to miss a guided tour of the weird 160-room Winchester Mystery House in San Jose, which has doors opening onto blank walls and stairs that lead nowhere. It is a product of the irrational fears of rifle heiress Sarah Winchester. She thought malevolent spirits would harm her if work on the house stopped, so she kept carpenters busy on it for 38 years.

---

**❶ Santa Cruz,** California
Just before Santa Cruz take a detour to Felton, where the Roaring Camp and Big Trees Railroad has steam train rides, chuck-wagon barbecues and Western music at the 1880s log camp in the redwoods. A few miles south, the resort town of Santa Cruz fronts onto fine swimming and surfing beaches at the north end of Monterey Bay. Take a stroll along the historic Boardwalk, with its 1911 carousel and 1924 rollercoaster, its busy amusement arcades, eateries and other attractions, and wander around the yacht harbor, the fish market, shops and seafood restaurants on the Municipal Wharf. The present Mission Santa Cruz is only a 1931 replica of the original one destroyed in 1857, but the nearby Casa Adobe is the genuine article and is Santa Cruz's oldest house. The town's most puzzling visitor attraction is the Mystery Spot, a 150-foot (46m) circle where the laws of gravity seem to go crazy.

The roller-coaster on Santa Cruz's historic boardwalk

*i* *701 Front Street*

---

### FOR CHILDREN

Treats for children include a trip to see the elephant seals at Año Nuevo State Reserve near Santa Cruz and rides and other fun attractions at the Paramount's Great America theme park in Santa Clara; beachcombing for semi-precious stones, shells and driftwood at Cambria; and a tour of Helen Moe's Antique Doll Museum, just north of Paso Robles.

---

▶ *Follow SR 1 south along Monterey Bay to Monterey.*

**❷ Monterey and the 17-Mile Drive,** California
At the south end of Monterey Bay is the historic town of Monterey, the old Spanish and

Lone Pine Rock is one of the highlights on the scenic 17-mile Drive which is famous for its seascapes

Mexican capital of Alta California. Collect a map from the Chamber of Commerce and follow the self-guided 'Path of History' tour of the old buildings preserved in the Monterey State Historic Park and explore the lively scene down at Fisherman's Wharf. There are fish stands, curio shops and restaurants, boat trips and whale-watching cruises around Monterey Bay. Marine life is also on show at the superb Monterey Bay Aquarium at Cannery Row, the former fish-canning factory area on the waterfront immortalized by the author John Steinbeck.

From nearby Pacific Grove you can follow the famed '17-Mile Drive' around the craggy shoreline of the Monterey Peninsula, with its golf courses, windswept cypresses and white-sand beaches, and its offshore rocks and kelp beds teeming with seabirds and marine

mammals. Parts of this coast are too dangerous for swimming. But don't miss the walk to the famous – and much photographed – 'Lone Cypress'.

At Carmel, a picturesque artists' and writers' community lying beside a silvery curve of beach, encircled by mountains and rolling hills, you will be tempted to linger in the smart boutiques, galleries and shops along the pretty tree-shaded streets. But leave enough time to visit beautiful Mission San Carlos Borromeo, the last resting

place of Father Junipero Serra, the founder of California's chain of missions, and to walk through Point Lobos State Reserve, with its grove of cypresses and marine life just south of town.

[i] *380 Alvarado Street, Monterey*

▶ *From Carmel follow* **SR 1** *south for about 126 miles (201m) along the Big Sur coast through San Simeon to Morro Bay.*

Sealions at Monterey

## 8 Big Sur Coast and Morro Bay, California

South of Carmel, Route 1 follows the spectacular Big Sur coast below the Santa Lucia Mountains, a wild shoreline of rugged headlands, rocky bays and crashing surf almost uninhabited except for seabirds, sealions and other marine life.

At San Simeon you will find the coast's most famous manmade wonder: amazing Hearst Castle, officially Hearst San Simeon State Historical Monument. Created between 1919 and 1947 by the publishing magnate William Randolph Hearst, this luxurious hilltop mansion – a huge complex in Hispano-Moorish style called La Cuesta Encantada (The Enchanted Hill) – is packed with art treasures and surrounded by opulently landscaped grounds. You will need an advance reservation for a 1¾-hour tour.

South of the quaint art colony of Cambria and the port of Cayucos, a favorite of antique hunters, the 576-foot (176m) extinct volcanic peak of Morro Rock comes into view, dominating the vast harbor of Morro Bay. Evening dinner cruises around the bay are available aboard the

*Tiger's Folly II.* You can also explore the fish markets, tempting seafood restaurants, aquarium and gift shops along the waterfront Embarcadero, and, if you are a chess-player, try a game on the gigantic chessboard below the Centennial Stairway on Harbor Street.

---

### BACK TO NATURE

There are few sights on this tour more thrilling than a sea otter lolling on its back in the waves, busily breaking open a clam on a stone carefully placed on its stomach. The Monterey Bay and Peninsula and the coast down to Morro Bay offer more wildlife wonders, with sightings of brown pelicans, cormorants and other seabirds, sealions, elephant seals, dolphins and whales. There are also special seasonal delights, such as the gathering of monarch butterflies at Natural Bridges State Beach near Santa Cruz in March or of eagles at Lake San Antonio near Paso Robles every winter. There are also the California poppies, the eternal redwoods and much, much more.

---

[i] *9511 Hearst Drive, San Simeon; also 895 Napa Street, Morro Bay*

▶ *From Morro Bay follow* **SR 1** *inland to San Luis Obispo.*

## 4 San Luis Obispo, California

This pleasant old college town and county seat grew by the creek where the Spaniards established Mission San Luis Obispo de Tolosa in 1772. When you have explored the shops and cafés that today line the old Mission Plaza, take a short walk to the San Luis Obispo County Historical Museum, where you will discover more about the area's original Indian inhabitants. As you wander around the streets you will discover many fine 19th-century homes, such as the restored Dallidet Adobe and the Victorian Jack House and garden. May is a good time to visit San Luis Obispo, when the town comes to life with parades, a rodeo, a Spanish Market and lots of entertainment during the annual Fiesta.

[i] *1041 Chorro Street*

▶ *Take* **US 101** *north for about 28 miles (45km) to Paso Robles.*

Steinbeck House, on Central Avenue, Salinas, was the birthplace and boyhood home of novelist John Steinbeck (1902–68)

### 5 Paso Robles and the Upper Salinas Valley, California

North of San Luis Obispo, US 101 roughly follows the route of the old Camino Real, or Royal Highway, that linked the missions and towns established by the Spaniards along the Salinas River valley.

Around Paso Robles, named for its oak groves, is a large wine-growing region where you can visit wineries for free tastings and tours. A wine festival in May highlighs local wineries.

In the mountains north of town via scenic Route G14, Lake Nacimiento offers relaxation and recreation with a range of facilities for camping, picnicking, hiking, boating and fishing.

Back on US 101, make a stop at San Miguel to see the lovely Mission San Miguel Arcangel of 1797, still in good repair; the restored 1846 Rios-Caledonia Adobe, which once served as an inn and stage stop; and the nearby Estrella Adobe Church, built by Protestant pioneers in 1878.

At Soledad, a detour east on Route 146 brings you to Pinnacles National Monument, 16,000 rugged acres (6,474 hectares) of volcanic rock spires, cliffs, canyons and caves.

[i] *548 Spring Street, Paso Robles*

▶ *From Paso Robles continue north on* **US 101** *for 97 miles (155km) to Salinas.*

### 6 Salinas, California

This manufacturing city, the seat of Monterey County, is the hub of the fertile agricultural region of the lower Salinas Valley. It is also the birthplace of author John Steinbeck. The Steinbeck House, now a restaurant and gift

Hearst Castle, the fabulous estate of the late newspaper tycoon William Randolph Hearst

---

### FOR HISTORY BUFFS

Just off US 101, 19 miles (31km) north of Salinas, the old town of San Juan Bautista spans three centuries of California history. Next to the well-preserved Spanish Mission San Juan Bautista, founded in 1797, is the 6-acre (2.5 hectare) section of town designated as the San Juan Bautista State Historic Park. It contains a number of restored historic buildings, including the Plaza Hotel (1858), the Castro Adobe (1840) where officials of the Mexican government stayed, and the Zanetta House (1868).

### RECOMMENDED WALKS

You will have plenty of exciting opportunities for bracing walks along miles of unspoiled beaches between Carmel and Morro Bay and for strolls among the art galleries and shops in little oceanside communities like Carmel, Big Sur and Cambria.
If you prefer something more strenuous, there are rugged trails at Pinnacles National Monument, where sturdy shoes are advisable.

### SCENIC ROUTES

Wherever you are in sight of the Pacific Ocean on this tour you will find something interesting to look at. But the most spectacular sections of the itinerary are the 17-Mile Drive off Route 1 around the Monterey Peninsula, with its views of the film star and celebrity homes and wildlife along the rugged shoreline; and the Big Sur coast, also on Route 1, between Carmel and San Simeon.
There is also a beautiful drive through green mountain scenery to Lakes Nacimiento and San Antonio on Route G14 north of Paso Robles.

---

shop, is one of the historic buildings preserved in the original downtown shopping district, a nine-block area known as Oldtown. Two other historic buildings, the Boronda Adobe and the 1868 Harvey-Baker House, now form the Monterey County Historical Museums; their exhibits document the area's history. If you time your visit to Salinas right, you can enjoy the thrills and spills of the big four-day Annual California Rodeo that draws thousands to the town every July.

[i] *119 E Alisal Street*

▶ *Continue north on* **US 101** *to San Francisco.*

# California
## Gold

On this tour from San Francisco you will step back in time to the heady days of California's 1849 gold rush as you explore the picturesque and revitalized old mining towns in the foothills of the Sierra Nevada. In these forested mountains you will also discover the awesome grandeur of Yosemite National Park, one of California's greatest scenic gems. The return drive then takes you through the irrigated farmlands of the Central Valley where, in addition to the varied local attractions, you can sample the region's agricultural riches.

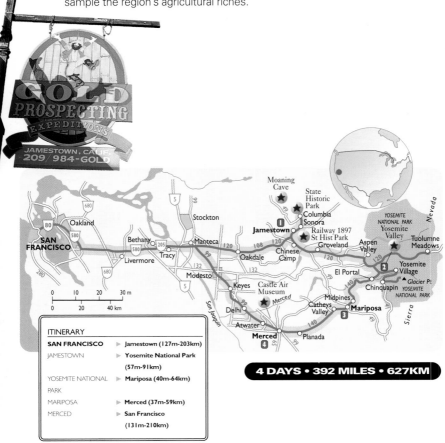

### ITINERARY

| | |
|---|---|
| **SAN FRANCISCO** | ▶ **Jamestown** (127m-203km) |
| JAMESTOWN | ▶ **Yosemite National Park** (57m-91km) |
| YOSEMITE NATIONAL PARK | ▶ **Mariposa** (40m-64km) |
| MARIPOSA | ▶ **Merced** (37m-59km) |
| MERCED | ▶ **San Francisco** (131m-210km) |

**4 DAYS • 392 MILES • 627KM**

ℹ 900 Market Street, San Francisco

▶ Cross the Bay Bridge from downtown San Francisco to Oakland and follow I–580, I–205, SR 120 and SR 108 east for about 127 miles (203km) via Livermore, Manteca and Oakdale to Jamestown and California's Gold Country.

### FOR CHILDREN

There are many attractions children can enjoy on this tour. Possibilities include a tour of the candy-making process (and samples) at Hershey Chocolate USA at Oakdale; a gold-panning bus tour and steam train ride at Jamestown; or a stage-coach ride at Columbia; and a visit to Applegate Park and Zoo at Merced, which has displays of wild animals and birds and rides for the youngsters.

### FOR HISTORY BUFFS

As you cross the bridge over Woods Creek coming into Jamestown on Route 49, you are right at the spot where prospectors led by the Reverend James Woods discovered a 75-pound (34kg) gold nugget and sparked off the rush to the area in the summer of 1848. Gold is still being found in Jamestown, but if you are not successful panning for it you can buy souvenir bags of it in local shops.

**❶ Jamestown and the Gold Country,** California
The wooded foothills of the Sierra Nevada are the scene of the great California gold rush of 1849. Here the highway crosses

The first discovery of gold in Tuolumne County was made near Jamestown in 1848

Completed in 1937, Golden Gate Bridge, which spans the entrance to San Francisco's harbor, has become one of the world's most famous landmarks

Route 49, the Golden Chain Highway linking the old mining camps on the rich gold-bearing vein, or Mother Lode, that runs north to south along the hills. In this southern section, immortalized in the stories of Mark Twain and Bret Harte, are Jamestown, Sonora and Columbia.

These picturesque, restored old mining communities now lure visitors with quaint antique stores, restaurants, boutiques, old abandoned mines, gold-panning trips and many other attractions that evoke the gold rush era. A special attraction at Jamestown, the location for hundreds of movies and TV features, is a ride on an old steam train at the Railtown 1897 State Historic Park.

At Sonora, 'Queen of the Southern Mines', you will see fascinating gold rush artifacts at the Tuolumne County Museum and History Center, housed in the old county jail.

And at Columbia, so well restored that the entire town is now a designated State Historic Park, there are guided walking tours and stagecoach rides along the tree-shaded streets, and regular performances of plays at the restored Fallon House Theater.

ℹ 55 West Stockton Road, Sonora

miles (80km) through Groveland to Yosemite National Park.

## SPECIAL TO...

A few miles north of Columbia is Moaning Cave. It is California's largest public cavern and has a main chamber big enough to hold the Statue of Liberty. Three tours, lasting between 45 minutes and 3 hours, are available, one of them involving a 180-foot (55m) rope descent into the main chamber.

▶ From Jamestown drive south to Chinese Camp. Continue east on **SR 120** for about 50

## RECOMMENDED WALKS

The guided walking tours of Jamestown, Sonora and Columbia take you around the historic treasures at an easy pace.
At Yosemite National Park you can follow more strenuous foot trails through the majestic scenery or enjoy gentler strolls by the Merced River.

**2 Yosemite National Park,** California

One of the greatest gems in America's national park system, Yosemite is a natural wonderland of forests, lakes, waterfalls and 10,000-foot (3,048m) peaks covering more than 1,200 square miles (3,108sq km) on the western slopes of the Sierra Nevada. If you have plenty of time, start your visit with the spectacular 80-mile (129km) round-trip drive up the scenic Tioga Pass road (Route 120) into the high country to Tuolumne Meadows. Return the same way, then make for Yosemite Valley, the most popular of the park's attractions. This 7-mile (11km) flat-bottomed gorge, carved by glaciers long ago and now drained by the beautiful Merced River, contains Yosemite's most impressive natural wonders. Turn a blind eye to the tourist facilities and the summer traffic congestion and you will be spellbound by the sheer grandeur of its towering rock walls, colossal granite domes and many thundering, snow-fed waterfalls, among them the 2,425-foot (739m) Yosemite Falls, America's highest waterfall.

Another scenic drive, a 32-mile (51km) round-trip, will take you from Chinquapin, south of the valley, past the Badger Pass ski area and up to Glacier Point. Here you will get stunning views of Yosemite Falls and the valley 3,214 feet (980m) below.

⟨i⟩ *Yosemite Village, in Yosemite National Park*

▶ *From Yosemite Valley take* **SR 140** *southwest through El Portal for 40 miles (64km) to Mariposa.*

**3 Mariposa,** California
West of Yosemite you pass through the forested Merced River Canyon, a popular spot for white-water rafting and trout fishing, before reaching the old gold-mining town of Mariposa.

The sheer, near-vertical face of El Capitan, in Yosemite

The main visitor attractions here are the timber Country Courthouse built in 1854, the oldest still in use in California; the California State Mining and Mineral Exhibit, which has excellent gold-mining, mineral and gem displays; and the Mariposa Museum and History Center, which houses old gold-mining equipment and artifacts of pioneer family life. You can also take a one-hour narrated air tour of the Yosemite area.

*i* *5158 Highway 140*

▶ *Continue west on SR 140 for 37 miles (59km) to Merced. Then follow SR 99 north for about 55 miles (88km) along the San Joaquin Valley via Modesto to Manteca.*

**4 Merced and the San Joaquin Valley,** California
Merced and Modesto are important processing and distribution centers for the agricultural produce of the San Joaquin Valley. Of interest to visitors at Merced are the fine county courthouse of 1875, which houses a local history museum, and the Yosemite Wildlife Museum, with dioramas of California's wild creatures in their natural habitats. Other varied attractions then beckon as you follow Route 99 north. They include the fine displays of historic aircraft at the Castle Air Museum near Atwater and tours of the restored 19th-century McHenry Mansion and the nearby McHenry Museum, with its local history exhibits, at Modesto. And if you want to try some of the area's produce, you can sample the almonds at Blue Diamond Growers in Salida and taste the various wines at Delicato Vineyards in Manteca.

Bridal Veil Falls, on the Merced River, Yosemite

*i* *690 W 16th Street, Merced; also 1114 J Street, Modesto*

▶ *From Manteca head west to pick up I–205 and I–580 westbound for the 76-mile (122km) drive back to San Francisco via Oakland and the Bay Bridge.*

---

### SCENIC ROUTES

Many stretches of highway in the Sierras will captivate you with their scenic surroundings, but one of the highlights is certainly the Tioga Pass road (SR 120), which affords spectacular views of high-country scenery, with its bare rock expanses, glacial boulders, crystal lakes, pine thickets, twisted junipers and wildflower meadows.

---

### BACK TO NATURE

The High Sierra is home to such wild animals as mountain lion, bighorn sheep and black bear, though you will have to be lucky to catch a glimpse of them. Most likely to catch your eye are the magnificent forest trees, perhaps even giant sequoias. For more about California's plants and animals check out the Yosemite Wildlife Museum at Merced and the Great Valley Museum of Natural History at Modesto, which concentrates on the flora and fauna of the Central Valley.

# Mountain &
## Desert Resorts

An hour's drive east along the freeway from Los Angeles brings you to the historic heartland of California's famed citrus industry, where you will begin a scenic drive up into the cool pine forests of the San Jacinto Mountains. Below the rugged east face you can explore fabulous Palm Springs, one of the lush, air-conditioned resort communities of the Coachella Valley, where the irrigated desert is patterned with regimented rows of date palms and grapefruit. You will then see the desert as nature intended – hot, dry and hostile – as you drive through the wild grandeur of Joshua Tree National Monument, not without its own hardy residents, of the plant and animal variety.

### 3/4 DAYS • 406 MILES • 650KM

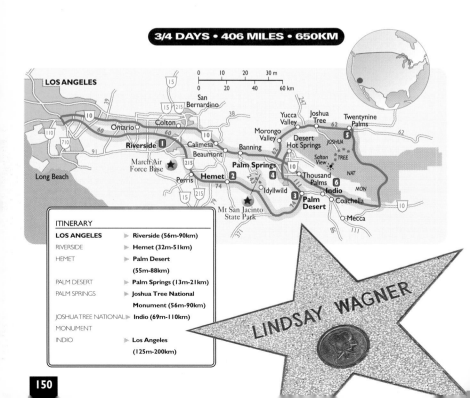

| ITINERARY | |
|---|---|
| **LOS ANGELES** | ▶ **Riverside (56m-90km)** |
| RIVERSIDE | ▶ **Hemet (32m-51km)** |
| HEMET | ▶ **Palm Desert** |
| | **(55m-88km)** |
| PALM DESERT | ▶ **Palm Springs (13m-21km)** |
| PALM SPRINGS | ▶ **Joshua Tree National** |
| | **Monument (56m-90km)** |
| JOSHUA TREE NATIONAL ▶ | **Indio (69m-110km)** |
| MONUMENT | |
| INDIO | ▶ **Los Angeles** |
| | **(125m-200km)** |

LINDSAY WAGNER

*i* 685 South Figueroa Street, Los Angeles

▶ Follow the Pomona Freeway (SR 60) east from Los Angeles for 56 miles (90km) to Riverside.

**❶ Riverside,** California

An attractive, historic residential city, Riverside is the birthplace of California's billion-dollar citrus industry, which began when two navel orange trees sent from Brazil were planted here in 1873. It is also the site of the Riverside campus of the University of California and is known for its cultural attractions and 19th-century architecture. Driving around, you will see pleasant tree-lined boulevards, Victorian-fronted stores and gracious 19th-century homes, such as the beautifully restored Heritage House, built in 1891 on Magnolia Avenue and open some days for tours. A famous city landmark near the center of town is the recently renovated Mission Inn, a prestigious, rambling old hotel with patios and gardens, a chapel, 900-bell carillon and Tiffany windows. Its guest list over the decades has included such notables as Theodore Roosevelt, Humphrey Bogart and the honeymooning Reagans.

Other visitor attractions include the mission-style Art Museum and the Botanic Garden, with its collection of dry-climate plants, on the east side of the university campus. South of town at March Air Force Base, you will see displays of vintage aircraft and other aviation exhibits at the March Field Museum.

*i* 3443 Orange Street

> **FOR HISTORY BUFFS**
>
> If you wish to know more about the development of California's citrus industry, visit the Riverside Municipal Museum on Orange Street. Here you will find exhibits documenting the industry's early days in this area. Down the street you can also see the Japanese Memorial Pavilion, built in 1987 to commemorate the workers who helped to establish the citrus industry here.

> **FOR CHILDREN**
>
> If you linger at all the attractions of interest to children at Riverside, you may not get much further along the itinerary planned.
> Limit the choice to the fun on offer at Castle Park, which includes lots of rides, miniature golf and a video arcade; a tour of the full-size and scale locomotives (with rides some Sundays) at Hunter Park Live Steamers; or a visit to the Earth Science Museum at the Jurupa Cultural Center, where kids can enjoy Dinosaur Day and the Fossil Shack every Saturday morning.

▶ From Riverside follow I–215 south for about 18 miles (29km) through Perris, then take SR 74 to Hemet.

**❷ Hemet,** California

For anyone interested in railroads, there is a worthwhile stop at Perris, off Highway 215, to see the railroad equipment and trolleys on display at the free Orange Empire Railway Museum. Then drive on to Hemet, on Route 74, where a pageant based on Helen Hunt Jackson's 1884 love story *Ramona* is performed every spring in the mountainside amphitheater.

About 18 miles (29km) east, make a detour north on Route 243 into the San Jacinto Mountains to explore the little artists' community of Idyllwild and the forested wilderness of Mt San Jacinto State Park, where you will find many recreation facilities as well as campgrounds, hiking trails and a variety of wildlife above 5,500 feet (1,676m).

*i* 395 East Latham Avenue

> **SPECIAL TO...**
>
> Special attractions in this part of California are the colorful and unusual annual festivals and events. Highlights include the Easter Sunrise Service atop 1,337-foot (408m) Mt Rubidoux west of Riverside; Hemet's springtime Ramona pageant; January sled-dog races on Mt San Jacinto; and even turtle races during the Turtle Days celebration at Joshua Tree in May.

Date cultivation near Palm Desert, a center for dates and citrus fruits

Palm Springs Aerial Tram transports
passengers to Mountain Station

▶ *Return to SR 74 and follow
the scenic 36-mile (58km)
Palms to Pines Highway to
Palm Desert and the
Coachella Valley.*

## ❽ Palm Desert, California

Palm Desert is one of a cluster of
desert resort communities that
have developed in the dry,
sunny climate of the Coachella
Valley. Originally desert, the
valley is now a vast irrigated
garden producing huge quanti-
ties of dates and citrus fruit. To
get an idea of the original vegetation, stop by the 1,200-acre
(485-hectare) Living Desert
park when you arrive at Palm
Desert. Here you will see not
only marvelous displays of
desert plants but also the
wildlife that inhabits the region.
While in town also check out the
McCallum Theater for the
Performing Arts at the prestigious Bob Hope Cultural Center
on Fred Waring Drive, where
you might catch a show, play,
movie or other suitable entertainment to round off the day.

---

### BACK TO NATURE

Nature adopts various guises
on this tour, from cool, forested mountains to searing scrub
deserts. Keep your binoculars
handy for a sight of soaring
birds of prey, though for shy
desert creatures you will get
better close-up views at the
man-made preserves, such as
The Living Desert at Palm
Desert. A special bonus for
plant-lovers is the dazzling display of waxy, greenish-white
flowers put on by the Joshua
trees every March and April.

---

ℹ️ *69–930 Highway 111*

▶ *Follow SR 111 west to the
center of Palm Springs.*

## ❹ Palm Springs, California

The best known of the desert
resort communities, Palm
Springs grew around the natural
hot springs owned by the Agua
Caliente Indians at the foot of
10,831-foot (3,301m) Mount San
Jacinto. Since the 1920s the
town has enjoyed an undimin-
ished reputation as a glamorous
playground retreat for
Hollywood stars and the rich.
The place is certainly packed
with big, gorgeous homes and
swimming pools, exclusive
shops, fine restaurants, vibrant
night spots, dozens of well-
manicured golf courses and
hundreds of tennis courts. But
there are also many other attractions to lure passing visitors,
although some are closed during
the hottest summer months.

Apart from hot-air balloon
trips, an ever popular attraction
is the breathtaking 2½-mile
(4km) ride on the Aerial
Tramway to the cool terraces
among the pine trees 8,516 feet
(2,596m) up the sheer face of
Mount San Jacinto. Drive south
on Palm Canyon Drive to visit
the Palm Springs Desert
Museum, a cultural center
featuring natural history
displays, art exhibits and a
theater; to sample the 1930s and
'40s shopping experience at
Ruddy's General Store Museum
in the Village Green Heritage
Center complex; and to see the
palm oasis and desert plants at
Moorten's Botanical Garden.
Continue to the spectacular
Indian Canyons carved into the
east face of the San Jacinto
Mountains. Here you can walk
or ride on horseback along trails
past bubbling hot springs, spectacular cascades, Indian cliff
dwellings and stands of imposing palm trees. Then drive back
to town to enjoy some refreshing
aquatic fun at the Oasis
Waterpark.

Twelve miles (19km) north
along Gene Autry Trail is the spa
town of Desert Hot Springs,
with Cabot's Old Indian Pueblo
Museum, a replica four-story
Hopi Indian-style building with
an art gallery.

ⓘ *2781 N Palm Canyon Drive, Palm Springs*

▶ *Pick up **SR 62** west of Desert Hot Springs and continue north and east for about 43 miles (69km) to Twentynine Palms and Joshua Tree National Monument.*

## ❽ Joshua Tree National Monument, California

More than 870 square miles (2,253sq km) of rugged desert and mountain country are encompassed in Joshua Tree National Monument, a spectacular preserve of desert flora and fauna named for its strange-looking Joshua trees, with their greenish white flowers.

Stop by the Visitor Center at the Twentynine Palms entrance for information and a map before starting your tour. Take plenty of drinking water and plan to leave by the south (Cottonwood Spring) entrance.

On the way, don't miss the side trip to Salton View, a 5,185-foot (1,580m) overlook in the Little San Bernardino Mountains affording majestic views of the entire Coachella Valley. Other monument landmarks include the giant Split Rock and cave near Pinto Wye, the Cholla Cactus Garden and the rock formations at the Wonderland of Rocks in Hidden Valley.

▶ *Just beyond the south entrance of Joshua Tree National Monument pick up **I–10** westbound for 69 miles (110km) to Indio.*

## ❾ Indio, California

If you enjoy dates this Coachella Valley city has plenty of packing plants and wayside establishments where you can buy them in cookies, cakes, puddings or even just as they are.

Indio is known as the 'Date Capital of America', a bit of Arabia transported to California. Vast groves, or 'gardens', of date palms and grapefruit trees encircle the town, irrigated by water drawn from the Colorado River. Several in the Coachella Valley, including the Shields Date Gardens in Indio, are open to visitors. Polo is a popular sport in Indio. But if you are here in mid-February you can watch the unique, zany spectacle of camel and ostrich races during the lively annual National Date Festival.

ⓘ *82–503 Highway 111*

▶ *Follow **I–10** westbound for 125 miles (200km) to downtown Los Angeles.*

The rare and beautiful Joshua tree, a species of the lily family, grows 20 to 40 feet high and can live for up to 300 years

### RECOMMENDED WALKS

Places to stretch your legs on the tour include the hilly, 37-acre (15-hectare) Botanic Garden at Riverside; the little artists' community of Idyllwild; the mountainside forest trails in San Jacinto State Park; the Indian Canyons near Palm Springs; and the area's commercial nature parks and gardens. Follow sensible precautions when walking trails in Joshua Tree National Monument. In particular, don't get too close to the painful spines of the jumping cholla cactus when walking through the Cholla Cactus Garden.

### SCENIC ROUTES

Once you leave Hemet the road starts to get interesting as you follow the scenic Palms to Pines Highway (Route 74) around the San Jacinto Mountains, with its changing views of pine- and oak-covered slopes and painted rock desert and distant panoramas of the Coachella Valley. You will also enjoy the drive through wild desert scenery in Joshua Tree National Monument.

# Beaches &
## Back Country

A kaleidoscope of changing scenes awaits you on this tour of San Diego County's north shoreline and inland back country. After leaving San Diego you will explore the coast's long beaches and delightful resort communities, pass through miles of citrus and avocado groves, climb pine-clad mountains, cross vast expanses of arid desert and descend to an inland sea saltier than the ocean. This is Southern California without the glitzy theme parks but every bit as rewarding.

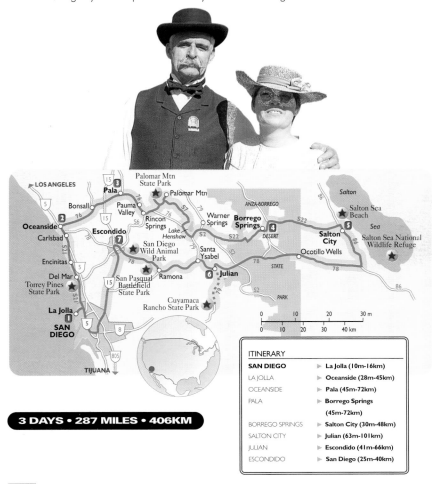

**3 DAYS • 287 MILES • 406KM**

| ITINERARY | |
|---|---|
| **SAN DIEGO** | ▶ La Jolla (10m-16km) |
| LA JOLLA | ▶ **Oceanside (28m-45km)** |
| OCEANSIDE | ▶ **Pala (45m-72km)** |
| PALA | ▶ **Borrego Springs (45m-72km)** |
| BORREGO SPRINGS | ▶ **Salton City (30m-48km)** |
| SALTON CITY | ▶ **Julian (63m-101km)** |
| JULIAN | ▶ **Escondido (41m-66km)** |
| ESCONDIDO | ▶ **San Diego (25m-40km)** |

*i* *Horton Plaza, San Diego*

▶ *Take I–5 north from downtown San Diego for about 10 miles (16km) to the Ardath Road turnoff to La Jolla.*

## ❶ La Jolla, California

Keep for another occasion a tour of Mission Bay's fabulous Sea World marine park and make straight for La Jolla (pronounced '*Hoy-a*'), a sophisticated little seaside town that boasts fine museums, galleries and cultural events. It stands on a rocky promontory below 822-foot (251m) Mount Soledad, from the summit of which there are fine views of the town and its rugged shoreline. Seafront landmarks to explore include Alligator Head, La Jolla Cove (a favorite of scuba divers), Whale Point and the caves in the cliffs below the town. Down by the shore you will also find the Museum of Contemporary Art, which displays paintings and sculptures from around the world. Around the bay north of town is another

*Mission San Luis Rey, northeast of Oceanside, dates from 1798*

major attraction, the Stephen Birch Aquarium-Museum at the magnificent marine aquarium at the Scripps Institution of Oceanography.

---

### FOR CHILDREN

Additional things for kids on the tour to see and do include the Mingei International Museum of World Folk Art in La Jolla, where toys feature among the many objects on display; and hunting for hermit crabs at La Jolla Cove; watching weekend hang gliders at Torrey Pines State Park; a desert trip from Borrego Springs; swimming in the Salton Sea; a monorail ride over the enclosures at San Diego Wild Animal Park; and rides and other activities at the Family Fun Center on Danway at Escondido.

---

▶ *Head north from La Jolla along the coast road (county road S 21) or I–5 through the beach communities as far as Oceanside.*

## ❷ Oceanside and San Diego's North Coast, California

Along the shoreline north of La Jolla is a series of pleasant resort communities and flat sandy beaches backed by high, windswept bluffs, marshy lagoons and meandering golf courses. The beaches are ideal not only for swimming but also for surfing and surf fishing.

At Torrey Pines State Park, named for its unique grove of gnarled Torrey pines, golf and hang gliding are the major sporting activities.

Further north, Del Mar is known for hot-air ballooning, the July County Fair and horseracing at the famed Del Mar Thoroughbred Club founded by Bing Crosby and Pat O'Brien in 1937.

Encinitas has the Quail Botanical Gardens and countless acres of commercially grown flowers on the way to Carlsbad, named after the famous Czechoslovakian spa, a growing resort town with good beaches and two lagoons. The 1,900-foot (579m) pier jutting into the Pacific is a famous landmark at

Oceanside, a popular destination for surfers. There is also a fine harbor with moorings for yachts, pleasure boats and sportfishing boats and waterfront shops and restaurants at Cape Cod Village.

*i* *210 West Plaza, Solano Beach; 929 N Hill Street, Oceanside*

### RECOMMENDED WALKS

There are especially enjoyable walks along the rugged shoreline at La Jolla, including the Coast Walk by the sea caves; along the pier and through Cape Cod Village at Oceanside; along the quiet trails in the area's state parks; down historic Main Street at Julian; and along the Kilimanjaro Hiking Trail at the San Diego Wild Animal Park, near Escondido.

▶ *From Oceanside turn inland on SR 76 for 34 miles (54km) through Pala and then turn left (northeast) on to county road S6 for 11 miles (18km) to Palomar Mountain and Palomar Observatory.*

### **3** Pala and Palomar Observatory, California

Two interesting places to visit on the route inland from Oceanside

are the restored Mission San Luis Rey, California's largest and richest mission, founded in 1798, and its much smaller branch Mission San Antonio de Pala. Built in 1816, the restored mission at Pala is still being used as a place of worship and school for Indian reservations in the area. It has a freestanding bell tower and a museum housing Indian artifacts.

Further east, county road S6, the 'Highway to the Stars', winds up the pine-studded slopes of 6,126-foot (1,867m) Palomar Mountain, where you can walk the forested trails in Palomar Mountain State Park before driving on to the famous Palomar Observatory, with its impressive 200-inch (5m) telescope and exhibit of astronomical photographs, at the crest.

▶ *Return to SR 76 via county road S7. South of Lake Henshaw turn left (northeast) on SR 79 for about 4 miles (6km), right (southeast) on county road S2 for 4 miles (6km), and left (east) on county road S22 for about 16 miles (26km) to Borrego Springs.*

### **4** Borrego Springs, California

The desert resort community of Borrego Springs lies amid the arid wilderness of Anza-Borrego

Desert State Park, its golf courses kept green by irrigation water from underground sources. The park encompasses some half a million acres (202,350 hectares) of rugged desert and mountain terrain, which supports a variety of wildlife, desert plants and colorful winter- and spring-blooming wildflowers. You can see an audio-visual presentation and get information on suitable self-guided car trips. Jeep trails and guided walks in the park are available from the Visitor Center just west of Borrego Springs.

*i* *Anza-Borrego Desert State Park*

### BACK TO NATURE

Lagoons and marshes along the ocean beaches are good places to see egrets, herons and many species of waterfowl. With a license you can also go night-hunting for grunion (a type of whitebait) with a torch. Whale Point at La Jolla is obviously the best place to see migrating whales. Spring flowers are a colorful sight in Anza-Borrego Desert State Park, where you can also see various cacti, palms, century plants and strange elephant trees and perhaps glimpse animals like the desert bighorn sheep.

▶ *Continue east on county road S22 from Borrego Springs for 30 miles (48km) to Salton City and the Salton Sea.*

### **5** Salton City, California

East of Borrego Springs county road S22 offers fine views of the desert as it descends to Salton City and the shores of the Salton Sea, 234 feet (71m) below sea-level. This inland saltwater lake, more than 35 miles (56km) long and up to 15 miles (24km) wide, suddenly came into existence in 1905 when roaring flood-waters

Spring bursts into life at Anza-Borrego Desert State Park

of the Colorado River broke through a canal gate and drowned a desert depression. It is now a calm recreational lake used for swimming, boating, water-skiing and fishing. There are no natural outlets and over the years evaporation has concentrated the salinity of the water.

Salton City, halfway along the west shore, is the center for much of this activity. At the southern end of the lake, via Route 86, is the Salton Sea National Wildlife Refuge frequented by waterfowl.

▶ *Follow* **SR 86** *south from Salton City for 13 miles (21km), then turn west on* **SR 78** *for 57 miles (92km) through Ocotillo Wells and Julian to Santa Ysabel.*

### ❻ **Julian and Mission Santa Ysabel,** California

The flavor of the Old West lingers on at the picturesque little town of Julian, an old mining community that sprang to life following a gold strike back in 1870. You can recall those colorful days as you walk down Main Street, with its old false-fronted stores, and tour the now abandoned Eagle and Highpeak mines. These days Julian is the center of a lush orchard and farming area, and you can buy apples and other produce along the main road and taste the local wines on a tour of the Menghini Winery at weekends.

South of town via Route 79 you can enjoy a pleasant side trip to Cuyamaca Rancho State Park, on the forested slopes of the Laguna Mountains. Northwest of town, on Route 78, you can visit Mission Santa Ysabel, founded in 1818, where there is a small museum and an Indian burial ground.

ⓘ *Main and Washington streets, Julian*

▶ *From Santa Ysabel continue west on* **SR 78** *through Ramona to Escondido.*

### ❼ **Escondido,** California

Along the San Pasqual Valley Road (SR 78) beyond the poultry-raising town of Ramona, you will find one of Southern California's major visitor attractions. It is the 1,800-acre (728-hectare) San Diego Wild Animal Park, where more than 2,500 animals roam free in re-created natural habitat enclosures, although some are performers in animal shows. The park also features a giant aviary, small mammal exhibits, petting area, monorail ride, hiking trail and behind-the-scenes tours.

Escondido lies in rolling hill country surrounded by groves of lemons and avocados, golf courses and wineries that are open for tours and tastings. One of these is the Deer Park Winery on Champagne Boulevard, where there is also an interesting vintage car museum. Another area attraction is the little museum housing memorabilia of the band leader Lawrence Welk at the theater of the Lawrence Welk Resort. And for history buffs, there is Heritage Walk, featuring a collection of 19th-century buildings at Grape Day Park.

ⓘ *720 N Broadway*

▶ *From Escondido take* **I-15** *south for 25 miles (40km) to downtown San Diego.*

The Bernardo Winery, near Escondido, offers tours and tastings

---

**SCENIC ROUTES**

The coast road (county road S21) through the beach communities north of La Jolla offers constantly changing views of the windswept southern California shoreline. Inland, the most scenically rewarding stretches of road include the tree-lined 'Highway to the Stars' (S6) up to Palomar Observatory and the winding section of SR 78 between Ocotillo Wells and Julian, with its fine views of the desert and forested mountains.

---

**FOR HISTORY BUFFS**

Along Route 78 between Ramona and Escondido is San Pasqual Battlefield State Park, the site of a little-known clash on December 6, 1846, when an American army led by General Stephen Watts Kearny lost a bloody contest with Mexican forces under General Andrés Pico during the Mexican-American War (1846–48). You can see a short video and displays relating to the battle at the Visitor Center, and there is a self-guiding ½-mile (1km) loop nature trail.

---

**SPECIAL TO…**

On the drive back to San Diego, turn off I-15 at Mission Valley to visit Mission San Diego de Alcalá, known as the 'Mother of the Missions'. Founded in 1769, it was the first in the chain of 21 missions begun by the Franciscan Father Junipero Serra along the California coast during the period of Spanish colonization. During your tour you will see records in his handwriting and other historic relics.

## FACTS AND FIGURES (FOR VISITORS)

**Bordered by:** Mexico and Canada.

**IDD code:** 1. To call the UK dial 44.

**Currency:** Dollar ($) which is divided into 100 cents.

**Local time:** the US has four major time zones. Eastern Standard Time is three hours ahead of Pacific Standard Time, two hours ahead of Mountain Time and one hour ahead of Central Time. In April clocks are put forward one hour to take advance of extra daylight and they are put back again in late October. Eastern Standard Time is 5 hours behind Greenwich Mean Time (GMT).

**Emergency services:** there is no nationwide emergency system in the US. There are emergency numbers you can call, sometimes indicated on pay phones, but they vary from place to place. There is one all-America helpline: 1–800–336–HELP. The best thing to do is call the operator by dialing '0' to connect you.

**Business hours –**
**Banks:** Monday to Friday 9am–3pm. Closed weekends and public holidays (except at international airports). In some major towns and tourist areas, hours may be longer.
**Post offices:** some main post offices stay open 24 hours a day, but they usually open between 8am–6pm Monday to Friday, and 8am-noon on Saturdays. Stamps are available from drug stores, hotels, motels and transport terminals.

**Credit and charge cards:** these are widely accepted and one is essential when renting a car.

**Traveler's checks:** these are widely accepted. Note the numbers and keep the note separate from the cheques.

**Tourist information:**
The US does not operate a national tourist office in the UK, but a number of cities and states have their own tourism telephone enquiry lines. For US Visa information telephone 0891 200 290. US Embassy – 24 Grosvenor Square, London, W1A 1AE. Tel: 0171 499 9000.

**British Embassy:** this is based in Washington at 3100 Massachusetts Avenue NW. Tel: 202/462-1340. If you lose your passport or need information contact the consular section at 19 Observatory Circle NW. Tel: 202/986–0205.

## MOTORING IN THE USA

### ACCIDENTS
If you are involved in a traffic accident you must report it to the police immediately and describe the nature of assistance needed.

### BREAKDOWNS
The AAA (American Automobile Association) is a member of a worldwide association of motoring organisations (AIT) and can make available its motoring/travel services to visitors who produce a valid membership certificate of a member organisation.

In case of a breakdown try the AAA nationwide emergency road service number, 1–800–336–HELP, and you will be told how to obtain emergency information.

Help is also readily available from the efficient Highway Patrols. Just wait by the car. If it is a rented car, call the company and tell them.

### CARAVANS
Different states have different regulations. Check with the AAA for information on the area in which you are travelling.

### CAR HIRE AND FLY/DRIVE
Most car rental agencies require the driver to be aged at least 21, although some companies will rent to drivers of only 18 years. If a driving tour is planned, make sure that unlimited mileage is included (sometimes cars may only be driven in

certain states). Most of the national car rental companies will permit you to rent a car in one city and return it in another, but they may charge for this service.

Some operators feature fly/drive deals; sometimes the car is included in the cost of the holiday package. In some cases it is possible to hire a mobile phone with your car giving you added confidence in the event of emergencies.

## CHILDREN
Child restraints are required in all states. However the rules regarding age, height, weight etc vary from state to state. Note: under no circumstances should a rear-facing restraint be used in a seat with an airbag.

## CRASH (SAFETY) HELMETS
In many states it is compulsory for rider and passenger to wear crash helmets.

## DOCUMENTS
You need a valid driving license from your home country to rent a car although a International Drivers Permit is required for visitors from certain countries and is advisable for others.

Visitors wishing to enter Canada or Mexico should check on the documents needed, also passport and visa requirements.

## DRINKING AND DRIVING
A very dim view is taken of drinking and driving. As in most countries it is better not to drink and drive.

## DRIVING CONDITIONS
Driving is on the right. Motorways are called freeways, or interstate roads. Other roads are collectively known as highways. Toll roads (intercity turnpikes) are known as superhighways and charge 2–3 cents a mile. Distances are always given in miles and overtaking is permitted on the inside lanes of interstates, where there is a 55mph (88kph) speed limit. Two peculiarities of

American driving are that it is permitted in some areas for a motorist to turn right at a red traffic light after stopping, and that traffic in both directions must stop while a school bus is loading or unloading.

## FUEL
Petrol (gas) is very cheap. It is sold by the US gallon (3.8 litres), and rental cars generally run on unleaded gas, available in 3 grades. At many self-service gas stations it is necessary to pay first (or leave a credit card with the cashier) to release the pump.

## INSURANCE
Fully comprehensive insurance, which covers you for some of the expenses incurred after a breakdown or an accident, is advisable. This should be arranged with your hire car.

## MOTORING CLUB
The AA is affiliated to the American Automobile Association, 1000 AAA Drive, Heathrow, Florida, USA, 32746–5063.

## POLICE FINES
On-the-spot fines can be imposed for speeding.

## ROADS
As one would expect in such a vast country road conditions vary greatly. However, in general, from the superhighways to the minor roads, road standards are very good. But do bear in mind the type of terrain over which you are traveling; from desert to mountain or winter snow, all have their effect on how you should drive.

## ROUTE DIRECTIONS
Throughout the book the following abbreviations are used for US roads:
**I** – interstate highway
**US** – US highway
**SR** – state route

## SPEED LIMITS
The national speed limit in the US is 55mph (88kph) on dual carriageway highways and

expressways, although a few states have upped the level to 65mph (104kph) on rural Interstate highways only.

In cities and congested areas it is generally between 20 and 30mph (32–48kph).

Outside built-up areas the limit is usually 45mph (72kph).

Road signs indicate specific limits and these are strictly enforced.

The minimum speed limit posted on most interstate highways or expressways should be obeyed as rigidly as the maximum.

## CAMPING AND CARAVANNING SITES

Camping in the USA annually attracts millions who wish to get away from it all and enjoy the countryside. At least part of camping's appeal stems from its flexibility and modest cost. Recreational Vehicles (RV's) are very popular and come in all shapes and sizes. It is possible to hire those, along with all types of camping equipment.

The facilities available vary tremendously, from resort-style sites with many facilities, to primitive sites with few facilities but staggering views.

Many of the sites have special activities available, often for a fee, such as fishing, boating, skiing etc.

During the main holiday season it is always wise to book in advance as some sites are very busy.

### Off-site camping
Different regulations apply in different states. Check locally before camping.

### SITES
The following sites are located along the routes of the tours. Additional abbreviations used in the directions are listed below:

CR – County Road
FR – Forest Road
FM – Farm to Market
MM – MileMarker

**TOUR I**
**STURBRIDGE** Massachusetts
**Yogi Bear's Jellystone Park** 30
River Road, 01566, PO Box 600
(tel: 508/347 9570)
1½ miles south on 1–84 exit 2; at
Herbert Candies, ½ mile east on
River Road.
Open all year.

**PLYMOUTH** Massachusetts
**Ellis Haven** 531 Federal
Furnace Road, 02360 (tel:
508/746–0803)
From SR 3 exit 6, 1 mile west on
US 44, then 2½ miles southwest
on Seven Hills and Federal
Furnace roads.
Open 1 May to 1 October.

**TOUR 2**
**COLD SPRING** New York
State
**Clarence Fahnestock
Memorial State Park** 10512
RD 1, Carmel (tel: 914/225–
7207)
Off SR 301, 5 miles east of US 9.
Open 15 May to 25 October.

**RHINEBECK** New York State
**Interlake Farm Campground**
45 Lake Drive, 12572 (tel:
914/266–5387)
From junction US 9 and 9G
(north of village), 3½ miles south
on 9G to CR 19, 3½ miles east,
then ¼ mile south on Lake
Drive.
Open 15 April to 15 October.

**HUDSON** New York State
**Lake Taghkanic State Park**
12502 RD, Ancram (tel:
518/851–3631)
12 miles southeast via SR 82,
just east of Taconic State
Parkway.
Open 15 May to 25 October.

**SAUGERTIES** New York State
**Koa Saugerties-Woodstock**
882 Rt 212, 12477 (tel:
914/246–4089)
From I–87 thruway exit 20,
2¼ miles west on SR 212.
Open 1 April to 1 November.

**STONY POINT** New York
State
**Beaver Pond Campsite**
Harriman State Park, 10980

(tel: 914/947–2792)
Northbound on US 9W to Stony
Point, then 5 miles west on Gate
Hill Road.
Open 17 April to 11 October.

**TOUR 3**
**MONTAUK** New York State
**Hither Hills State Park** 11702
Belmont Lake State Park,
Babylon (tel: 516/668–2554)
3 miles west on SR 27.
Open 3 April to 24 October.

**GREENPORT** New York State
**Eastern Long Island
Kampgrounds** 11944 PO Box
89 (tel: 516/477–0022)
On CR 48, 1 mile west of SR 25.
Open 16 April to 11 October.

**TOUR 4**
**GAINESVILLE** Virginia
**Hillwood Camping Park**
14222 Lee Highway, 22065 (tel:
703/754–4611)
On US 29–211, 1¼ miles south-
west of I–66, exit 43A.
Open all year.

**LURAY** Virginia
**Yogi Bear's Jellystone Park**
22835 PO Box 191 (tel:
703/743–4002)
3 miles east on US 211; I–81,
exit 67 then 20 miles east.
Open 15 March to 15
November.

**TOUR 5**
**HARPER'S FERRY** West
Virginia
**Harper's Ferry Camp Resort**
25425 Rt 3, Box 1300 (tel:
304/535–6895)
1 mile southwest on US 340
from Shenandoah River Bridge,
¼ mile south via signs.
Open 1 April to 1 November.

**HAGERSTOWN** Maryland
**Greenbrier State Park** 21843
National Pike, Boonsboro (tel:
301/791–4767)
8 miles south via US 40.
Open 10 April to 25 October.

**GETTYSBURG** Pennsylvania
**Drummer Boy Campground**
1300 Hanover Road, 17325 (tel:
717/334–3277)
2 miles east on SR 116 at junc-

tion US 15 bypass, Hanover
Road exit, 1 block east on SR
116 from US 15 bypass.
Open 1 April to 31 October.

**FREDERICK** Maryland
**Gambrill State Park** 8602
Gambrill Park Road, 21701 Rt 8
(tel: 301/473–8360)
6 miles northwest on US 40 on
Catoctin Mountain.
Open 15 May to 25 October.

**TOUR 6**
**STRASBURG** Pennsylvania
**Mill Bridge Village
Campresort** PO Box 86 (tel:
717/687–8181)
From US 30 ½ mile south on
Ronks Road.
Open all year.

**LANCASTER** Pennsylvania
**Old Mill Stream Camping
Manor** 2249 Lincoln Highway
E, 17602 (tel: 717/299–2314)
5 miles east on US 30.
Open all year.

**HARRISBURG** Pennsylvania
**Gifford Pinchot State Park**
2200 Rosstown Road, 17339
Lewisberry (tel: 717/292–4112)
I–83 exit 15, ½ mile south of
Rossville off SR 74.
Open 8 April to 16 October.

**TOUR 7**
**WILLIAMSBURG** Virginia
**Anvil Campground** 5243
Mooretown Road, 23188 (tel:
804/565–2300)
I–64, exit 238 (Camp Peary),
west on Rochambeau Drive (Rt
F–137).
Open all year.

**Jamestown Beach Campsites**
23187 PO Box CB (tel:
804/229–7609)
I–64 exit 242A, 5¼ miles west on
SR 199; 4 miles south on SR 31.
Open all year.

**HAMPTON** Virginia
**Gosnold's Hope Park** 23669
(tel: 804/850–5116)
2¼ miles northeast of junction
US 258 via SR 278 and Little
Back River Road, 2 miles on
right off Little Back River Road.
Open all year.

**DOSWELL** Virginia
**Paramount's Kings Dominion
Campground** 23047 Rt 2, Box
57 (tel: 804/876–5355)
On SR 30, 1 mile east of I–95,
Doswell, exit 98; adjacent to
theme park.
Open 1 March to 16 October.

**TOUR 8**
**CHARLOTTE** North Carolina
**Paramount's Carowinds
Campground** 14523
Carowinds Boulevard, PO Box
410289 (tel: 704/588–3363)
From I–77 exit 90, 1 mile west
to Catawaba Trace.
Open 1 March to 30 November.

**CHIMNEY ROCK** North
Carolina
**Dogwood Travel Park** US 74
28720, PO Box 208 (tel:
704/625–2400)
1 mile west on US 64/74.
Open all year.

**ASHEVILLE** North Carolina
**Bear Creek RV Park and
Campground** 81 S Bear Creek
Road, 28806 (tel: 704/253–0798
Eastbound exit 47 off I–40, then
north ¼ mile on SR 191.
Open all year.

**CHEROKEE** North Carolina
**Adventure Trail Campground**
28719, PO Box 1673 (tel:
704/497–3651)
2¼ miles south on US 441 from
junction US 19E, 1½ miles east
on SR 1406 (Camp Creek
Road).
Open 1 May to 31 October.

**STATESVILLE** North Carolina
**Midway Campground Resort**
28677, Route 4, Box 199B (tel:
704/546–7615)
10 miles east of junction I–40
and I–77 on I–40 to Cool
Springs exit 162; west 1 block
on US 64, then south 2 blocks
on Campground Road.
Open all year.

**TOUR 9**
**STONE MOUNTAIN** Georgia
**Stone Mountain Park
Campground** 30086, PO Box
778 (tel:404/498–5710)
In Stone Mountain Memorial

Park on east side of Stone
Mountain.
Open all year; tent section
closed 30 October to 4 March

**MADISON** Georgia
**Talisman RV Resort** 2750
Eatonton Road 30650 (tel:
706/342–1799)
1½ miles south on US 441/129
from junction I–20 exit 51.
Open all year.

**EATONTON** Georgia
**Lake Sinclair** 31024 (tel:
404/468–2244)
10 miles south on US 129, 1
mile east on SR 212, 2 miles east
on CR 1062, follow signs to area.
Open 27 May to 3 September.

**FORSYTH** Georgia
**Middle Georgia Koa** 31029, Rt
3, Box 568 (tel: 912/994–2019)
From I–75 exit 61, ¼ mile east to
Johnstons Lane then ¼ mile
north.
Open all year.

**TOUR 10**
**MIAMI** Florida
**Miami South/Everglades Koa**
20675 SW 162nd Avenue, 33187
(tel: 305/233–5300)
23½ miles southwest; 4½ miles
west of US 1 via SW 216th
Street, then ½ mile north.
Open all year.

**HOMESTEAD** Florida
**Goldcoaster Mobile Home
and RV Park** 34850 SW 187th
Avenue, 33034 (tel:
305/248–5462)
On CR 9336 (old SR 27) Palm
Drive 1½ miles west of junction
US 1 and FL Tpk terminus.
Open all year.

**KEY LARGO** Florida
**America Outdoors** 97450
Overseas Highway, 33037 (tel:
305/852–8054)
On US 1 southbound at MM
97½.
Open all year.

**BIG PINE KEY** Florida
**Big Pine Key Fishing Lodge**
PO Box 513 (tel: 305/872–2351)
On US 1 at MM 33.
Open all year.

**SUGARLOAF KEY** Florida
**Sugarloaf Key Resort Koa**
33042, PO Box 469 (tel:
305/745–3549)
¼ mile south on CR 939 from
junction US 1, MM 20.
Open all year.

**KEY WEST** Florida
**Boyd's Key West
Campground** 6401 Maloney
Avenue, 33040 (tel:
305/294–1465)
On Stock Island, ¼ mile south of
junction US 1 MM 5 via
McDonald Avenue.
Open all year.

**TOUR 11**
**TAMPA** Florida
**Bay Bayou Traveler** 12622
West Memorial Highway, 33635
(tel: 813/855–1000)
I–75 exit 30, 11¼ miles west on
Hillsborough Avenue, just north
on Double Branch Road, ¼ mile
east on Memorial Highway.
Open all year.

**ST PETERSBURG** Florida
**St Petersburg Resort Koa
Kampground** 5400 95th Street
North, 33708 (tel:
813/392–2233)
I–275 exit 13, 5½ miles west via
38th Avenue North, veer onto
Tyrone (Bay Pines) and 1½ miles
west to 95th Street and right ½
mile.
Open all year.

**SARASOTA** Florida
**Sarasota Lakes RV Resort**
1674 University Parkway, 34243
(tel: 813/355–8585)
From I–75 exit 40, 5 miles west
on University Parkway.
Open all year.

**LAKELAND** Florida
**Sanlan Ranch Campground**
3929 US 98S, 33813 (tel:
813/665–1726)
5½ miles southeast on US 98, 1
mile south of Eaton Park.
Open all year.

**ORLANDO** Florida
**Yogi Bear's Jellystone Camp
Resort** 9200 Turkey Lake
Road, 32819 (tel: 407/351–4394)
¼ mile southwest off I–4 (exit

29) on SR 482, 1¼ miles southwest on Turkey Lake Road.
Open all year.

**TOUR 12**
**LOUISVILLE** Kentucky
**Louisville Metro Koa**
**Kampground** 900 Marchriott
Drive, 47129 (tel: 812/282–4474)
½ mile west of I–65,
Jeffersonville exit 1, then
Stansifer Avenue exit following
signs.
Open all year.

**BARDSTOWN** Kentucky
**Holt's Campground** 2351
Templin Avenue, 40004 (tel:
502/348–6717)
Just south on Highway 1430
from junction Highway 245.
Open all year.

**LEXINGTON** Kentucky
**Kentucky Horse Park**
**Campground** 4089 Iron Works
Pike, 40511 (tel: 606/233–4303)
On SR 1973, ½ mile east of I–75
exit 120.
Open all year.

**TOUR 13**
**ROCKFORD** Illinois
**Blackhawk Valley**
**Campground** 6540 Valley Trail
Road, 61109 (tel: 815/874–9767)
From I–39, exit 15, 2½ miles
west on Baxter Rd, 2 miles north
on SR 251, 1¼ miles east on
Blackhawk Rd, ½ mile south on
Valley Trail Rd, from I–90, exit
US 20, 6 miles west to SR 251S.
Open 15 April to 15 October.

**GALENA** Illinois
**Palace Campground** US 20,
61036 (tel: 815/777–2466)
1 mile west on US 20.
Open 1 April to 1 November.

**FULTON** Illinois
**Lock and Dam 13** 61252 (tel:
815/589–3229)
2 miles north on SR 84.
Open all year.

**DIXON** Illinois
**Dixon Springs State Park**
62938 RR 2, Golconda (tel:
618/949–3394)
Junction SR 145 and 146.
Open all year.

**TOUR 14**
**OTTAWA** Illinois
**Illini State Park** 61341 RR 1,
Box 60, Marseilles (tel:
815/795–2448)
6 miles east on US 6, then 2
miles south on county road, on
Illinois river.
Open all year.

**PEORIA** Illinois
**Jubilee College State Park**
61517 RR 2, Box 72, Brimfield
(tel: 309/243–7683)
15 miles west on US 150; from
I–74, Kickapoo exit.
Open all year.

**PETERSBURG** Illinois
**Lincoln's New Salem State**
**Park** 62675 RR 1, Box 244A
(tel: 217/632–7953)
2 miles south on SR 97.
Open all year.

**SPRINGFIELD** Illinois
**Holiday RV Center** 62629 RR
1, Box 195, Chatham (tel:
217/483–9998)
9 miles south on I–55, southbound exit 88, then 2 miles
south on West Frontage Road;
northbound exit 83, then 3 miles
north on West Frontage Road.
Open 1 April to 31 October.

**KANKAKEE** Illinois
**Kankakee River State Park**
60914 RR 1, Box 37,
Bourbonnais (tel: 815/933–1383)
7 miles northwest on SR 102.
Open all year.

**TOUR 15**
**MINNEAPOLIS** Minnesota
**Town and Country**
**Campground** 12630 Boone
Avenue South, 55378 (tel:
612/445–1756)
From I–35W, 4½ miles west on
SR 13, ¼ mile west on SR 101,
then ¼ mile south on Boone
Avenue.
Open 15 April to 1 November.

**ROCHESTER** Minnesota
**Rochester/Marchion Koa** 5232
65th Avenue SE, 55904 (tel:
507/288–0785)
½ mile southeast on US 52 from
junction I–90.
Open 1 April to 15 October.

**WINONA** Minnesota
**Winona Koa** 55987 Rt 6, Box
181 (tel: 507/454–2851)
6½ miles south on US 14/61 from
junction SR 43, between MM 19
and 20.
Open 15 April to 1 November.

**RED WING** Minnesota
**Frontenac State Park** 55041
(tel: 612/345–3401)
10 miles southeast on US 61.
Open 1 April to 31 October.

**HASTINGS** Minnesota
**Greenwood Campground**
13797 190th Street E, 55033 (tel:
612/437–5269)
3¼ miles south on US 61 from
junction SR 316, 1½ miles east
on 190th Street (CR 62).
Open 1 May to 15 October.

**TAYLORS FALLS** Minnesota
**Interstate State Park** 55084
Box 254 (tel: 612/465–5711)
1 mile south via US 8.
Open all year.

**TOUR 16**
**ST LOUIS** Missouri
**Dr Edmund A Babler**
**Memorial State Park** 63005
(tel: 314/458–3813)
20 miles west on SR 100, north
on 109.
Open all year.

**MURPHYSBORO** Illinois
**Lake Murphysboro State**
**Park** 62966 RR 4, Box 144 (tel:
618/684–2867)
4 miles west on SR 149.
Open all year.

**CAVE-IN-ROCK** Illinois
**Cave-in-Rock State Park** New
State Park Road, 62919, PO Box
338 (tel: 618/289–4325)
Just northeast off SR 1 on Ohio
river.
Open all year.

**CAPE GIRARDEAU** Missouri
**Trail of Tears State Park**
63701 (tel: 314/334–1711)
10 miles north on SR 177.
Open all year.

**TOUR 17**
**NEW ORLEANS** Louisiana
**Mardi Gras Campgrounds**

6050 Chef Menteur Highway,
70126 (tel: 504/243–0085
From I–10E, exit 239.
Open all year.

**HOUMA** Louisiana
**Capri Court Campground**
101 Capri Court 70364 (tel:
504/879–4288)
Junction US 90 and SR 316 3
miles north.
Open all year.

**BATON ROUGE** Louisiana
**Knight's RV Park** 14740
Florida Boulevard 70819 (tel:
04/275–0679)
I–12 exit 7, 1½ miles north on
O'Neal Lane, ¾ mile west on
US 190 (Florida Boulevard).
Open all year.

**TOUR 18**
**DALLAS** Texas
**Dallas Hi–ho Campground**
200 West Bear Creek Road,
75115 (tel: 214/223–4834)
18¼ miles south via I–35E, 2¼
miles west on Bear Creek Road,
exit 412.
Open all year.

**TYLER** Texas
**Tyler 554 Campground** 13805
CR 433 (tel: 903/882–6481)
Off I–20, Harvey Road exit 554.
Open all year.

**RUSK** Texas
**Rusk/Palestine State Park**
75785 Rt 4, Box 431 (tel:
903/683–5126)
Open all year.

**KARNACK** Texas
**Caddo Lake State Park** 75661
Rt 2, Box 15 (tel: 903/679–3351)
Open all year.

**JEFFERSON** Texas
**Brushy Creek** PO Drawer W
(tel: 903/665–2336)
8 miles west on highway 729, 5
miles southwest on highway
726, across dam, park right on
Lake O'the Pines.
Open all year.

**TOUR 19**
**HOUSTON** Texas
**Traders Village RV Park**
7979 N Eldridge 77041

(tel: 713/890–5500)
On US 290, exit Eldridge, south
¼ mile.
Open all year.

**GALVESTON** Texas
**Bayou Haven RV Park** 6310
Heards Lane, 77551 (tel:
409/744–2837)
I–45 exit 1A, ¾ mile south on
spur 342, ¼ mile west on Heards
Lane.
Open all year.

**SABINE PASS** Texas
**Sea Rim State Park** 77655, PO
Box 1066 (tel: 409/971–2559
10 miles south on SR 87.
Open all year.

**ZAVALLA** Texas
**Boykin Springs** 75980 (tel:
409/639–8620)
1 mile southeast on SR 63, ¼
mile southwest on FR 313.
Open all year.

**LUFKIN** Texas
**Berry Farm RV Park** 1107 N
John Redditt 75901, PO Box
151835, 75915 (tel:
409/634–8184)
From south junction US 59 and
Loop 287, 3½ miles northwest on
Loop 287.
Open all year.

**COLDSPRING** Texas
**Double Lake** 77331 (tel:
713/592–6462)
1½ miles west on SR 150, 1 mile
south on SR 2025, 2 miles southeast on FR 210.
Open all year.

**TOUR 20**
**SAN ANTONIO** Texas
**Admiralty Park** 1485 N Ellison
Drive, 78251 (tel: 210/647–7878)
At junction Military Avenue
West and North Ellison Drive, 1
mile west of junction Highway
151 and Military Avenue West.
Open all year.

**NEW BRAUNFELS** Texas
**Hill Country RV Resort** 131
Ruekle Road 78130 (tel:
210/625–1919)
I–35 exit 184, just east on
Ruekle Road.
Open all year.

**AUSTIN** Texas
**Austin Capitol Koa** 7009 I–35S,
78744 (tel: 512/444–6322),
6 miles south off I–35; southbound exit S Congress Avenue,
exit 226B, northbound, William
Cannon Drive, exit 228.
Open all year.

**BURNET** Texas
**Inks Lake State Park** Rt 2, Box
31 (tel: 512/793–2223)
9 miles west on SR 29, 3 miles
south on Park Road 4.
Open all year.

**JOHNSON CITY** Texas
**Pedernales Falls State Park**
78636 Rt 1, Box 450 (tel:
512/868–7304)
14 miles east on Ranch Road
2766.
Open all year.

**FREDERICKSBURG** Texas
**Fredericksburg Koa** 78624 Rt
1, Box 238 (tel: 210/997–4796)
5 miles east on US 290 at county
road 1376.
Open all year.

**KERRVILLE** Texas
**Americamp Leisure Resort**
400 Benson Drive, 78028 (tel:
210/896–6052)
5 miles west of junction I–10
and SR 16 on Benson Drive.
Open all year.

**BANDERA** Texas
**Yogi Bear's Jellystone Park
Camp Resort** Maple Street and
Highway 173, 78003, PO Box
1687 (tel: 512/796–3751)
On Highway 173, ⅛ mile west
junction Highway 16.
Open all year.

**TOUR 21**
**DENVER** Colorado
**Cherry Creek State Park** (tel:
303/699–3860)
1 mile south of I–225, on Parker
Road.
Open all year.

**BOULDER** Colorado
**Boulder Mountain Lodge
Campground** 91 Four Mile
Canyon Road 80302 (tel:
303/444–0882)
From US 36, 4 miles west on SR

119, 1 block northwest on Four Mile Canyon Road.
Open all year.

**ESTES PARK** Colorado
**Estes Park Campground** 3420 Tunnel Road, 80517, PO Box 3517 (tel: 303/586–4188)
2 miles west on US 36, then 3½ miles southwest on SR 66 to end of road.
Open 27 May to 11 September.

**GRAND LAKE** Colorado
**Elk Creek Campground** 143 CR 48, 80447, PO Box 549 (tel: 303/627–8502)
¼ mile north on US 34, 2 blocks west on CR 48.
Open all year.

**WINTER PARK** Colorado
**Idlewild** 80482 (tel: 303/887–3331)
1 mile south on US 40.
Open 15 July to 10 September.

**EMPIRE** Colorado
**Mountain Meadow Campground** 80438, PO Box 2 (tel: 303/569–2424)
3½ miles west of I–70, exit 232 on US 40.
Open 1 June to 1 October.

**BLACK HAWK** Colorado
**Central City/Blackhawk Koa** 661 Highway 46, 80403, 661 Highway 46, Golden (tel: 303/582–9979)
5¼ miles north on SR 119, ½ miles east on SR 46.
Open all year.

**TOUR 22**
**SALT LAKE CITY** Utah
**Camp VIP** 1350 W N Temple Street, 84116 (tel: 801/328–0224)
North of I–80 west exit 118/Redwood Road east 1 mile.
Open all year.

**MIDWAY** Utah
**Deer Creek Lake State Park** 84049, PO Box 257 (tel: 801/654–0171)
7 miles southwest of Heber City on US 189.
Open 15 April to 1 November.

**PARK CITY** Utah
**Hidden Haven Campground** 2200 Rasmussen Road, 84060 (tel: 801/649–8935)
18 miles east of Salt Lake City off I–80; 1 mile west via Frontage Road from Park City exit.
Open all year.

**FARMINGTON** Utah
**Lagoon's-Pioneer Village Campground** 375 N Lagoon Lane, 84025 (tel: 801/451–8100)
US 89 and I–15, Lagoon exit 325 pr 327.
Open 17 April to 31 October.

**TOUR 23**
**LAS VEGAS** Nevada
**Boulder Lake RV Resort** 6201 Boulder Highway, 89122 (tel: 702/435–1157)
East of SR 93/95; exit Russell Road, ¼ north at Desert Horizons Road.
Open all year.

**DEATH VALLEY NATIONAL MONUMENT** California
**Furnace Creek** 92328 (tel: 619/786–2331)
In Furnace Creek.
Open all year.

**Mesquite Spring** 92328 (tel: 619/786–2331)
5 miles south of Scotty's Castle on Grapevine Road.
Open all year.

**TOUR 24**
**PHOENIX** Arizona
**Desert's Edge RV Park** 22623 N Black Canyon Highway, 85027 (tel: 602/869–7021)
17 miles north; adjacent to I–17, Deer Valley E exit, ½ mile north on Frontage Road.
Open all year.

**APACHE JUNCTION** Arizona
**Koa Apache Trail** 1540 S Tomahawk Road, 85219 (tel: 602/982–4015)
1 mile north of US 60, exit Tomahawk Road.
Open all year.

**TUCSON** Arizona
**Cactus Country RV Resort** 10195 S Houghton Road, 85747

(tel: 602/574–3000)
16 miles southeast on I–10, ¼ mile north on Houghton Road, exit 275.
Open all year.

**PICACHO** Arizona
**Picacho Koa** PO Box 368 (tel: 602/466–7401
1 block west of I–10; northbound exit 212, southbound exit 211A, then 1¼ miles south.
Open all year.

**TOUR 25**
**ALBUQUERQUE** New Mexico
**Albuquerque-West RV Park** 5739 Ouray Road NW 87120 (tel: 505/831–1912)
I–40 exit 155, ¼ mile north on Coors Road, then west on Quail.
Open all year.

**BERNALILLO** New Mexico
**Albuquerque Bernalillo North Koa** 87004, PO Box 758 (tel: 505/867–5227)
From I–25 exit 240.
Open all year.

**SANTA FE** New Mexico
**Rancheros de Santa Fe Camping Park** 87505, Rt 3, Box 94 (tel: 505/983–3482)
10½ miles east of Plaza on Frontage Road; off I–25 exit 290.
Open 15 March to 1 November.

**TAOS** New Mexico
**Taos Valley RV Park** 87557 PO Box 200 Ranchos de Taos (tel: 505/758–4469)
2½ miles southwest on SR 68.
Open 1 March to 1 November.

**CIMARRON** New Mexico
**Cimarron Canyon State Park** 87749, PO Box 147, Ute Park (tel: 505/377–6271)
11 miles west on Highway 64.
Open all year.

**LAS VEGAS** New Mexico
**Las Vegas Koa** 87701 Anton Chico Rt, Box 16 (tel: 505/454–0180
¼ miles south of I–25, exit 339 on E Access Road.
Open 1 March to 30 November.

**TOUR 26**
**SEATTLE** Washington
**NE Seattle Lake Pleasant RV Park** 24025 Bothell-Highway
SE 98021, 24025 Bothell (tel:
206/487–1785)
From I–405 exit 26, 1½ miles
southwest.
Open all year.

**PORT TOWNSEND**
Washington
**Fort Warden State Park**
98368 (tel: 206/385–4730)
1 mile north.
Open all year.

**PORT ANGELES** Washington
**Al's RV Park** 521 N Lee's
Creek Road, 98362 (tel:
206/457–9844)
3½ miles east on US 101, ¼ mile
north on Lee's Creek Road, off
US 101.
Open all year.

**HUMPTULIPS** Washington
**Campbell Tree Grove** 98552
(tel: 206/288–2525)
5 miles north on US 101, 6 miles
on FR 22, 14 miles on FR 2204.
Open 15 May to 15 September.

**OLYMPIA** Washington
**American Heritage
Campground** 9610 Kimmie
Street SW, 98512 (tel:
206/943–8778)
At exit 99 from I–5, ¼ mile east
on 93rd Avenue, then ¼ mile
south on Kimmie Street SW.
Open 20 May to 5 September.

**TOUR 27**
**BIG SUR** California
**Big Sur Campground** 93920,
SR 1 (tel: 408/667–2322)
Off and adjacent to SR 1; 2
miles north of Pfeiffer Big Sur
State Park.
Open all year.

**SAN LUIS OBISPO**
California
**El Chorro Regional Park**
93401 (tel: 805/781–5219)
5 miles north on Highway 1.
Open all year.

**SALINAS** California
**Cabana Holiday** 8710
Prunedale North Road, 93907

(tel: 408/663–2886)
8 miles north; on northwest
corner of junction SR 156 and
US 101.
Open all year.

**TOUR 28**
**OAKLAND** California
**Anthony Chabot Regional
Park** 94619, 9999 Redwood
Road (tel: 510/562–2267)
580 Castro Valley exit, turn left
on Castro Valley Boulevard,
right on Redwood Road.
Open all year.

**GROVELAND** California
**Yosemite Pines RV Park**
20350 Old Highway 120, 95321
(tel: 209/962–5042)
SR 120 1 mile east of Groveland
exit old Highway 120.
Open all year.

**MIDPINES** California
**Yosemite/Mariposa Koa** 6323
Highway 140, 95345, PO Box
545 (tel: 209/966–2201)
7 miles northeast of Mariposa on
SR 140; 23 miles west of
Yosemite National Park.
Open all year.

**TOUR 29**
**RIVERSIDE**
**Rancho Jurupa Park** 4800
Crestmore Road, 92509 (tel:
909/684–7032)
Highway 60 to Rubidioux
Boulevard, left on Mission to
Crestmore Road.
Open all year.

**PERRIS** California
**Palm View RV Park** 22200
River Road, 92570 (tel:
909/657–7791)
5½ miles west on SR 74, 1 mile
south on River Road.
Open all year.

**HEMET** California
**Mountain Valley RV Park** 235
S Lyon Avenue, 92543 (tel:
714/925–5812).
1 block south of SR 74 and 79.
Open all year.

**PALM SPRINGS** California
**Golden Sands RV Park** 1900
San Rafael Road, 92262 (tel:
619/327–4737)

Northeast area, 3 miles east of
SR 111, entrance to Aerial
Tramway at end of San Rafael
Road.
Open all year.

**TWENTYNINE PALMS**
California
**Twentynine Palms RV Resort**
4949 Desert Knoll Avenue,
92777 (tel: 619/367–3320)
From SR 62, 2 miles north via
Adobe Road, then right on
Amboy Road, ½ mile east.
Open all year.

**SAN BERNARDINO**
California
**San Bernardino Koa** 1707
Cable Canyon Road, 92407 (tel:
909/887–4098)
15 miles northwest on I–215,
Devore exit, then 1 mile south-
east.
Open all year.

**TOUR 30**
**SAN DIEGO** California
**Campland on the Bay** 2211
Pacific Beach Drive, 92109 (tel:
619/581–4260)
From I–5 northbound exit
Grand Avenue, 1 mile west to
Olney then south ¼ mile, south-
bound exit Balboa/Garnet, south
on Mission Bay Drive to Grand
Avenue.
Open all year.

**OCEANSIDE** California
**Casitas Poquitos RV Park**
1510 S Hill Street 92054
(619/722–4404)
From I–5, exit Oceanside
Boulevard, ¾ mile west, then 1
block south.
Open all year.

**PAUMA VALLEY** California
**Rancho Corrido
Campground** 14715 Highway
76, 92061, PO Box 180 (tel:
619/742–3755)
On SR 76, 7 miles east of I–15.
Open all year.

**JULIAN** California
**Cuyamaca Rancho State
Park** 92036 Star Rt (tel:
619/765–0755)
9 miles north of I–8 on SR 79.
Open 1 May to 30 September.

# INDEX

# Index

## Index & Acknowledgments

### The Automobile Association
wishes to thank the following libraries and photographers for their assistance in the preparation of this book.

FRANK S BALTHIS/HILLSTROM STOCK PHOTO INC 5, 82, 83, 105, 107, 149; GERRY BROOME PHOTOGRAPHY/HILLSTROM STOCK PHOTO INC 44, 45; HEATHER R DAVIDSON /HILLSTROM STOCK PHOTO INC 34; WILLIAM B FOLSOM/HILLSTROM STOCK PHOTO INC 40; DAVID F GLOBES/HILLSTROM STOCK PHOTO INC 80; ROBERT HARDING PICTURE LIBRARY 104; RAY F HILLSTROM/HILLSTROM STOCK PHOTO INC 71, 76; KENNEDY SPACE CENTER 62; CURTIS MARTIN/HILLSTROM STOCK PHOTO INC 133, 142; NATURE PHOTOGRAPHERS LTD 86 (R Tidman), 99 (K Carlson), 137 (P R Sterry); BUD NIELSEN/HILLSTROM STOCK PHOTO INC 46/7, 102, 103, 126; JACK OLSON/ HILLSTROM STOCK PHOTO INC 33, 35, 40/1, 50, 73, 75, 77l; JAMES P ROWAN/HILLSTROM STOCK PHOTO INC 74, 77b, 88; KAY SHAW/HILLSTROM STOCK PHOTO INC 81; SPECTRUM COLOUR LIBRARY 24, 28, 37, 48, 66, 68, 69, 109, 136; THE STOCK MARKET 32 (Lance Nelson), 36 (Kunio Owaki 1995), 72/3 (James Blank), 78 (Audrey Gibson 1987), 91 (Kunio Owaki 1990), 92 (Dave Wilhelm 1993), 101a (Bill & Jan Moeller 1986), 101b (Mark E Gibson 1987), 106 (Mark E Gibson 1986), 110 (Chris Rogers), 113 (James Blamk), 120/1 (Michele Burgess 1994), 128 (Mark E Gibson 1986), 139 (Thomas Ives), 140 (Pete Saloutos 1992); TONY STONE IMAGES front cover – inset; CAROLYN THORNTON/HILLSTROM STOCK PHOTO INC 51, 97; WORLD PICTURES back cover – a; ZEFA PICTURES LTD front cover – main picture, inside flap, 19, 22, 23, 25, 26, 29, 30, 30/1, 38, 39a, 39b, 43, 49, 52, 53, 64, 65, 67, 70, 84, 85, 87, 90, 93, 94, 95, 96, 98, 108, 111, 114, 115, 116/7, 123, 124, 125, 131, 134, 138/9, back cover – b, c;
All remaining pictures are held in the Association's own library (AA PHOTO LIBRARY) with contributions from: P BENNET 59, 61; E DAVIES 27, 42; R G ELLIOTT 7, 14, 15, 16, 18, 20/1; R HOLMES 6, 8, 120/1, 122, 143a, 144, 145, 146, 147b, 148, 151a, 151b, 152, 153, 154, 155, 156, 157; J LYNCH 9; M LYNCH 10, 11, 12; D LYONS 55, 60; K PATERSON 135, 141, 147a; L PROVO 54, 56, 57, 58; E ROONEY 2, 17; A SOUTER 63; P WOOD 150.

### Contributors
**Copy editor:** Janet Tabinski    **Indexer:** Marie Lorimer